"Get your kicks, on Route 66..."

Weird Highway

Missouri & Kansas

Route 66
History &
Hauntings
Legends & Lore

© *Copyright 2016 by Troy Taylor*
& American Hauntings Ink
All Rights Reserved, including the right to copy or reproduce this book, or portions thereof, in any form, without express permission from the author and publisher.

Original Cover Artwork Designed by
© Copyright 2015 by April Slaughter & Troy Taylor

This Book is Published By:
Whitechapel Press
American Hauntings Ink
Jacksonville, Illinois | 217.791.7859
Visit us on the Internet at http://www.whitechapelpress.com

First Edition – June 2016
ISBN: 978-1-892523-27-3

Printed in the United States of America

Introduction

There is no greater highway in American history than Route 66 – the legendary "Mother Road" – which began in downtown Chicago and stretched all of the way to the Pacific Ocean. For millions of people, it represents a treasure trove of memories and a link to the days of two-lane highways, family vacations, lunches at roadside tables, and greasy-spoon diners that ceased to exist decades ago. For many, it conjures up images of souvenir shops, tourist traps, cozy motor courts, and cheesy roadside attractions that have since crumbled into dust. To others, Route 66 makes them think of rusty steel bridges, flickering neon signs, classic cars, and drive-in theaters. To others, the highway holds stories of ghosts, haunted hotels, roadside spirits, mysterious vanishings, and bewildering anomalies, too.

It's America's most famous highway – even though officially it no longer exists.

Route 66 began simply to meet the needs of a growing nation. It gained both fame and infamy during the Dust Bowl days of the Great Depression, as the highway became an escape route for the thousands of families who moved westward from Oklahoma, Texas, and Arkansas. It was the migrants and travelers, seeking salvation from the drought, whose plight was immortalized in John Steinbeck's Grapes of Wrath. In the book, he called Route 66 "the mother road, the road of flight." The nickname stuck and for many years, Route 66 was seen as a passage to hope for struggling "Okies" and those who were down on their luck. During World War II, Route 66 became a military conduit, providing a fast-moving passage for men, munitions, and equipment to move about the country. The continuous convoys kept the highway busy and the pockets of roadside merchants filled. In spite of this, however, Route 66, a road designed for civilian travel, paid the price in wear and tear caused by the military vehicles. It eventually weakened and began to decline, a development that did not go unnoticed in Washington. By this time, officials were already considering a wider and faster highway system that could handle the toughest traffic demands. By the time the war ended, the demise of Route 66, although still years away, had become inevitable.

For a few years, though, a return to peace time brought new prosperity and a tourism boom to America. Spurred on by Bobby Troup's musical hit "Get Your Kicks on Route 66," people were anxious to travel the country and the merchants of the highway cashed in. As traffic on the road increased, new businesses sprang up and an explosion of tourist traps, curio shops, and neon signs began to appear in just about every town on Route 66's path. Motor courts became "motels," diners became "restaurants," and general stores changed into "trading posts." Hundreds of new billboards helped to spread the word about these booming businesses.

It was an era of good times that we now look back on with nostalgia, but it was never meant to last. By the middle 1950s, the interstates were making their way west and over the next 15 years, Route 66 began to vanish. It was ripped up, downgraded, and re-aligned and the hundreds of towns that were dependent on the highway's traffic were slowly strangled in the process. Many of them became literal ghost towns, fading reminders of the days that once were. By the end of the 1960s, with the damage done, "America's Main Street" had ceased to be a through route to California. It was not officially decommissioned, though, until the stubborn citizens of Williams, Arizona, the last town to be bypassed, lost a legal battle to stop it in 1984.

Although long stretches of Route 66 still remain today, most of it is a hard to define mix of original roadbed, access roads, abandoned fragments, and lost highways. It has been re-configured in so many ways that even diehard travelers can sometimes become lost and turned around as they try and follow the road's often lonely miles.

Almost everyone who dreams of the glory days of Route 66 has ventured out onto at least one section of the Mother Road, looking for old alignments and often finding broken pavement and dead ends. In other places, we can often find true gems of the road, offering little-known places and sites to adventurers, sometimes found by tracing the rows of rickety telephone poles and reliable railroad tracks that Route 66 usually shadowed. For those who become lost and wonder if they are still on the old road, we watch for abandoned stores, broken and dead neon signs for businesses that have long since vanished, and even creaky motor courts that sometimes still eke out a living from travelers that are now few and far between. The past still manages to be present – however elusively – along the remains of Route 66.

I can honestly say that I'm one of those who has ventured out in search of Route 66, following it all of the way from my home state of Illinois to the West Coast. It was a trip that helped to cement my love for the road, for weird places, ghostly highway tales, unusual people, and eccentric sites, all of which eventually led to this series of books. It began merely as a collection of ghost stories from the path of the highway, but it turned into much more than that. With all of the books that I have written over the years, I have yet to pen a title that is not filled with history, strange facts, and curious wonders. My volumes about Route 66 are no exception. Soon after I started the series, I began to realize that it was a weird road trip of all of the oddness that the highway had – and still manages -- to offer. This is truly a chronicle of the weird – ghost stories, monsters, haunted places, quirky hotels, abandoned places, favorite diners, forgotten spots, classic roadside attractions, and just about anything that left me chucking, a little unnerved, or just scratching my head in confusion. It's the nostalgia of Route 66, mixed with the dark side of the highway's legends and lore. The series has a little of everything: abandoned drive-ins, oddball trading posts, UFO landing sites, spook lights, giant spacemen, and just about everything else about Route 66 that we still find fascinating today.

I had a great time writing these books and I hope you have a great time reading them. I have to confess, though, that the series will end with a little sadness. Once completed, it's like closing the door on something that really doesn't exist anymore. Or does it?

It was once said that the whole world traveled down Route 66, but it's not that way anymore. It's a lost part of American history, but while gone, it is certainly not forgotten. Any other American highway would have become ancient history a long time ago, but there is something about this road that has remained within our collective imagination. What is it about this particular highway that conjures up so many ghosts of days gone by? No one can say for sure, but few can deny that Route 66 is more than just some old roadway. Route 66 is a trip back in time to a weird, lonely, and magical place in American history, and if you plan it just right, it's one you can still recapture. Doing so is as easy as turning your steering wheel, taking a little time, and leaving the mind-numbing miles of the interstate behind. Just follow the road signs back to an era when you could still "get your kicks on Route 66."

I can promise you that you won't be sorry that you did.

Troy Taylor
Summer 2016

Highway to the West
The History of Route 66

The Automobile Club of America has set out to secure a macadamized road from New York to San Francisco. As yet, it is too soon to figure out how many millions it would cost to build 3,500 miles of good macadam road across mountains and prairies, but it is not too early to remark that the automobile promises to be a strong and valuable ally of the bicycle in the great missionary work of securing better country roads throughout the United States.

"Automobiles and Good Roads,"
Chicago Tribune, March 26, 1900

The cross-country highway that eventually became Route 66 was years in the making. It began with the rise in popularity of the American automobile and with the demand they created for new roads. As automobiles slowly grabbed hold of the American imagination, enthusiasts quickly realized how limited they were when it came to decent roads on which to drive them. By 1902, an outcry was raised in Chicago when representatives from the nine largest automobile clubs in the country met to combine forces and to start making plans for a national network of highways that would cross the entire country. They met at the Chicago Coliseum during the much-ballyhooed run of the Chicago Auto Show with the idea of launching a new organization through which they could lobby for their goal.

The new organization became the American Automobile Association (AAA), and loyal to its members, AAA made its first order of business the promotion of a transcontinental road that would stretch from New York to California. This was the beginning of all of the "highways" to come and the start of a long journey toward a system that was designed to connect all of America's towns and cities by road, from east to west, north to south, and all points in between.

By the time of the Chicago meeting in 1902, there were about 11,000 automobiles in America. All of them were rambling about to the best of their ability on muddy tracks and dirt trails, their drivers desperate for good roads to drive on. Within five years, the number of drivers looking for decent roads had increased to an amazing 300,000. They clamored for new roads, and the more autos that were purchased, the louder the hue and cry became. Harry Radford, president of the Cartercar Motorcar Company of Pontiac, Michigan, wrote, "It is my notion, and facts bear me out, that the motor driven vehicle has done more than any other agency toward improved highways."

Throughout the early 1900s, the new-fangled motor cars puttered their way into the hearts of those who longed to be free from the days of horses and bicycles. Of course, the main obstacle in the early days was money. With price tags of anywhere from $650 to $5,000, automobiles of the era were still considered a luxury. In those days, a good horse and wagon cost only about $200, which made many wonder why they should waste the money on a machine that had to be restricted to recreational use. There just weren't enough decent roads to drive them on. Common sense suggested that people should invest their hard-earned dollars in a reliable horse and wagon instead.

But common sense had little to do with the demand for the new motor cars. Much to the surprise of automobile manufacturers, people went crazy for cars. None of the fledgling auto makers could keep up with demand and often ran six months behind in filling orders. Once America's business sector realized the potential of the automobile, demand increased even more. Automobiles were bringing prosperity to the country and the need for bigger, better roads became paramount. Transportation was providing Americans with the means to obtain better goods and, at the same time, was making it possible for farmers and small companies to make their goods available to a wider range of customers. In addition, Americans would soon be able to travel farther than most had ever dreamed, allowing them to see and experience their country firsthand. It was truly the beginning of a new era.

America now had the vehicles with which to travel and now they only needed the roads to take them where they wanted to go. As it had been with the railroads in the nineteenth century, there were a handful of visionaries who saw what America needed for her future. There was no question about it – America's first transcontinental highway had to be built.

Cyrus Avery – Father of Route 66

Thanks to the American Automobile Association, the idea of the coast-to-coast highway soon came to the attention of the general public. Slowly, average Americans began to realize what it would mean to travel freely from one end of the country to the other if, of course, there was ever a practical method to do so. People began to hunger for such a method and soon it seemed to be on the minds of everyone.

Well, almost everyone... Because, as it is with every new idea, there were the naysayers who claimed that such an endeavor was impossible. A highway of that sort, they claimed, could hardly be profitable. It would bankrupt the government! It was a shortsighted opinion, but it did have some validity. No one had ever attempted a building project of such grand design. In those days, it seemed as impossible as sending a man to the moon. Who would build it? How would it work? Where would the money come from to build so many miles of road? No one knew it at the time, but a mountain of commerce was already forming to support the transcontinental highway.

But it would take someone like Oklahoma visionary Cyrus Avery to turn the dream into a reality. Long before he conceived of Route 66, Avery had a passion for roads. He longed for an America with good, state-to-state motorways that travelers could use with ease and would not have to constantly worry about getting lost.

No one knows where his passion for highways began. Avery had been born in Stevensville, Pennsylvania, in 1871, and when he was a teenager, his family moved west to what was then the Indian Territory of Oklahoma. After graduation from William Jewell College in Liberty, Missouri, Avery married Essie McClelland and moved back to Oklahoma, where they lived for the rest of their lives.

Avery's interest in roads began with the Ozark Trails: an unorganized system of roads that connected to St. Louis, Missouri, to Amarillo, Texas. He was impressed with work being done by some of the local highways advocacy groups, especially the Good Roads movement in Missouri, and in 1907, he moved from Vinita, Oklahoma, to Tulsa, where he began his climb to national prominence.

Living in Tulsa, he invested in the oil industry and became very aware of how roads affected his and other businesses. Five years later, he sought out and secured the post of county commissioner. He wanted the job for one reason – it gave him the opportunity to observe the need for an improved system of highways. And it also gave him a platform from which to promote the idea of improving roads throughout the state of Oklahoma.

One of his first acts was to devise an effective method for maintaining the current roads. His solution was the "split-log-drag" method, where horses were used to drag large split logs up and down the road, usually after a good rain. This smoothed out the roadway, tamped down the dirt path, prevented potholes, and kept the road fairly smooth – unless it was driven over after it rained, of course. When that happened, the road turned into a muddy, rutted mess. Even so, the public appreciated his efforts and he was dubbed the "Father of Good Roads" in Tulsa County.

In 1913, William Hope Harvey, the businessman, author, politician, and social thinker who established a famous Arkansas health resort called Monte Ne, sent out an invitation to "organize a delegation of commercial clubs, good roads and automobile associations" with the goal of forming a new Ozark Trails organization. Avery was one of the first on the invitation list and he gladly accepted the responsibility.

Cyrus Avery

Thanks to Avery's presence, the group quickly gained notoriety and became an effective force for change. In 1914, an article appeared in the *Oklahoman* that stated, "The Ozark Trails Association, embracing the states of Missouri, Kansas, Arkansas and Oklahoma, is one of the strongest and most active good roads organizations west of the Mississippi River." In just a short time, the group had the enthusiastic support of both road boosters and Oklahoma state leaders.

The association planned its second annual convention in May 1914, and soon began looking for locations for the host city. Aware of the influence that the group might bring to whatever city hosted the event, various road associations along the trails competed vigorously to try and get the meeting held in their town. But there was no contest – Avery's hometown of Tulsa received the honor.

William Hope Harvey, who was now the president of the Ozark Trails Association, wanted to create a spectacle and get as much publicity as possible, so he traveled to the meeting in an unusual way – on foot! He traveled from his home in Arkansas and brought with him a supply of paint and brushes, giving all of the Ozark Trail markers along his route a fresh coat of paint. When necessary, he even installed new signs on the existing telegraph poles found along the route.

On May 15, Harvey walked into Vinita, Oklahoma, on what would soon be Route 66. After a foot soak, he joined Avery and a growing number of Ozark

Trail enthusiasts who were already in town. Together, they walked to Tulsa, repairing and replacing road markers all of the way into the city.

A few weeks later, the newly marked Ozark Trail saw a revitalized campaign of roadwork and improvements and the method most commonly used was Avery's split-log-drag system.

Bolstered by his success with the Ozark Trails, Avery began to be appointed to various offices and positions. First, he joined the board of directors of the Northeast Oklahoma Chamber of Commerce. Then, he became the founder and president of the Albert Pike Highway Association. Next, the Associated Highways of America elected him as its president in 1921. Finally, in February 1924, he was named as the Oklahoma Highway Commissioner, a position that would make him nationally known – and lead to the creation of Route 66.

Toward the end of 1924, Avery was recruited by the U.S. Bureau of Public Roads to help develop a new system of interstate highways. Avery accepted the Bureau's offer and throughout 1925 worked with a committee to connect hundreds of existing roads into a nationwide network. It was the dawn of the American automobile. Cars had finally become available to the average person and families were taking to the road like never before. They wanted to travel and Cyrus Avery was one of the people who helped them to do it.

Avery was given broad authority and made sure that one of the chosen routes, designed with the backing of officials in Illinois and Missouri, cut directly across his home state of Oklahoma as part of a Chicago to Los Angeles thoroughfare. When first presented, this unconventional route was not well received. Avery dug up every bit of supporting evidence that he could find, including the opinion of Thomas Wilby, who had pushed for the same route as early as 1911. It took months for Avery to overcome the committee's reluctance and even when they finally accepted it, there was more disagreement, this time over the proposed numbering assignments.

While U.S. Route 60 was Avery's first choice, he was immediately challenged by the governor of Kentucky, who demanded the more prestigious zero-ending number for a highway across his state, which had been tentatively listed as U.S. 62. As the argument escalated, the governor went a step further and stated that the Kentucky highway, which started in Newport News, Virginia, should connect with Avery's route in Springfield, Missouri, to create a true east-west highway called Route 60. This would break up Avery's route and leave the stretch between Springfield and Chicago demoted to "branch" status. This was an idea that Avery refused to consider. The debate raged into 1926 when Avery realized that he needed to reach a settlement over the issue before upcoming elections at home jeopardized his political appointment. In a hasty resolution, he deferred to Kentucky and opted for number 66, a number his chief engineer, John Page, inadvertently discovered had not been assigned to anything. Avery liked the sound of the double sixes and found that it was an acceptable alternative. At last, with everyone satisfied, Washington finally granted approval and Route 66 was designated on November 11, 1926.

To help promote the new highway, Avery organized the U.S. 66 Highway Association shortly after leaving office, and through its efforts, Route 66 was soon entrenched as America's premiere highway. Avery passed away in 1963 at the age of 90 and will always be remembered as the man who created the legendary "America's Main Street."

Building the Mother Road

Despite an ongoing debate about the constitutionality of the federal government intervening in the road-building efforts of individual states, the Federal Aid Road Act was passed in 1916. At a White House ceremony that was attended by representatives from farm organizations, the American Automobile Association, the American Association of State Highway Officials, and members of Congress, President Wilson signed the bill into law.

George Diehl, president of AAA, was determined to see that American roads were paved. He told reporters, "The majority of states have provided for definite systems of state highways, which they are constructing as rapidly as available means permit. Every effort should be directed now toward having federal funds apply on these state systems and not frittered away on countless little disconnected local roads."

There was a lot at stake with the new program. It allotted $150 million to be spent over a five-year period, and how the money was spread out was to be decided by the secretary of agriculture. The states were all required to match the federal funds they were given. The money was distributed quickly and, almost as if by magic, turned into roads. Progress was swift and by October 20, there were 17,369 miles of road under some form of construction. As the new roads came together, the dream of a national highway was becoming a reality.

By 1926, roads across the state lines were about two-thirds improved. By that time, more than 25 states boasted continuously improved roads over their entire length. In fact, the 1920s are still seen today as the "golden era" of American road-building. Work was being carried out in every state in the union and new, paved roads were rapidly appearing.

As the national highway, which would soon be Route 66, came into being, the days of a motorist finding his way by luck were coming to a close. The open road was out there, calling to the American traveler, and tourists gladly accepted the invitation to drive. The first choice for motorists before Route 66 was the Old Trails Highway, which had been established in 1912 as a coast-to-coast series of roads that extended from New York to Los Angeles. It was made up of roads that followed many of America's most historic trails including

Braddock's Road, Cumberland Road (or National Pike), Boone's Lick Road, the old Santa Fe Trail, and the Grand Canyon Route. Signs were few and far between, but many enterprising organizations and publishers put out maps and guidebooks to help motorists find their way. The New York Times extolled the virtues of the Old Trails Road, "It traverses mountains, plain and forest, and is rich in varied scenery, while offering splendid road conditions and very little desert country."

Tourist routes, like the National Old Trails Road, were far more "civilized" than during the earliest days of automobiles. By 1924, motorists were assured that it was no longer necessary to carry a large supply of gasoline with them since "gasoline stations are found along the road." Furthermore, hotel accommodations and automobile campgrounds could be found in just about every city and small town. Where the dusty trails were once slow and treacherous, the new paved roads allowed for a speed of at least 18 miles per hour. At one time, a coast-to-coast trip took months. By the 1920s, it could be enjoyed in only 20 to 30 days.

Motoring could still be an adventure, though. Experts still had many recommendations for long distance trips, including no less than one set of skid chains, a good horn for use on mountain curves, one set of tools, a jack, good cutting pliers, four extra tire tubes, three spark plugs, a water jug or canteen, one flashlight, an axe, a small shovel, radiator hose connections, lamp bulbs, and a tow rope or cable.

By later in the 1920s, however, much of the earlier sense of danger had vanished. Adventurous drivers had been replaced by a more subdued motoring class, which was exemplified by families who took vacations by car. These new tourists sought both adventure and the open road, but were not looking for the same sort of thrills as their highway predecessors. Even so, while tamer than ever before, the highways still had a sense of mystery about them. With no exit signs to guide them, nor billboards or signs that promised food, gas and lodging, scores of motorists truly embraced the unknown. Touring by car could still be seen as an exploration into new and uncharted territory.

But change was coming, as was Route 66.

On New Year's Day, 1927, the U.S. Bureau of Public Roads announced a new road-marking system that would forever change the way that the American public navigated the nation's roads. Uniform marking for U.S. highways had arrived, announced the New York Times, and now 80,000 miles of highway would be marked in a manner resembling a giant checkerboard to link section to section and connect each section to the other.

The days of remembering trail names, color marks, insignias, and other various designations were over. Instead, a simple black-and-white shield with bold, black numbers would provide all of the information that a motorist would need. At the time, there were 22 states with identification shields already in place and 20 additional states were preparing the roadways for the 1927 automobile touring system.

For the first time, motorists could determine – simply by looking at a highway number – which road they were traveling on and which direction they were going. The beauty of this new system was in its simple numbering scheme: Main transcontinental received even numbers from 10 to 90, in multiples of 10. North-to-south routes were designated with odd numbers such as 1, 21 and 31.

The single exception to the multiple of 10 numbering rule was U.S. Highway 66. This glaring anomaly did not escape the attention of a New York Times journalist who correctly predicted that "No. 66 is a highway that is expected to prove of great importance."

The numbering system was an instant success and it created a brand new market for road maps, guidebooks, and every conceivable kind of tourist literature and advertising. Familiar names were still used to describe the best routes in all of these publications, but the new official highway numbers were added for clarity. For example, one guidebook stated, "The recommended route is the National Old Trails Road, as it has been known for years. This is now a combination of United States Routes 40, 50, 350, 85 and 66."

As the new guidebooks and maps flooded the market, it spurred a renewed wanderlust in Americans who promptly demanded – and began taking – longer vacations. No longer satisfied with just two weeks a year, the emerging tourists began taking as much as four-week reprieves from their hectic lives. As people began snatching up automobiles, they wanted leisure time, and plenty of it.

The newspapers of the day agreed that the notion of touring required a great deal of time and planning. There was a lot to see in the way of scenic wonders across America. There was no television in those days and average people only saw the Rocky Mountains, the Grand Canyon, and Yellowstone Park in books and in photographs. They wanted to see those things in person and were desperate to take the highway in order to see them.

As people became more aware of the emerging highways, the Old Trails Road remained the most popular route for traveling from east to west. The reasons were obvious, since this cross-continent path included much of the country's most picturesque scenery, especially in the Southwest. It traveled near the Grand Canyon and along the Colorado River, as well as the Petrified Forest, the Painted Desert, cliff dwellings and Indian pueblos, the Mojave Desert, Raton Pass, Walnut Canyon National Monument, and scores of other points of interest.

The 1930 summer tourist season, in spite of the tumbling stock market and slumping economy, broke all previous records with more than 45 million

Americans taking to the highways. In July, a national parks record was established with over 1 million visitors driving into parks during a single week. In fact, traffic at the national parks and monuments was so high that 12 of the 21 operating at the time opted to remain open all year around. This decision paid off for the parks in the Southwest, which began seeing their heaviest traffic in the winter months.

At the same time, roadside entrepreneurs soon discovered that these newly arriving tourists had brought their wallets along on their vacations. Vacationers were spending money, and lots of it. Anyone who thought they had some sort of gimmick discovered they could quickly turn it into cash. Soon, a new racket called the "tourist trap" began to appear across the landscape of America. It was designed for the sole purpose of convincing the tourists to part with their money.

The tourist traps needed a way to get people into their locations as they passed by on the highway, which created work for the advertising men. They unveiled an entirely new twist in advertising and it was simple and very attention-getting – they helped the roadside showmen to employ the services of larger-than-life statues, dinosaur sculptures, bright colors, huge billboards, wild claims, far-fetched slogans, bumper stickers, and oddly-shaped buildings that were guaranteed to catch the eye of the tourist.

With all of the automobiles and all of the advertising hoopla, competition began heating up in all facets of roadside service. Hotels, motels, diners, auto camps, drive-ins, hot dog stands, filling stations, repair garages, and every sort of related business literally battled it out in the streets. All of them competed for – and most received – their slice of the pie.

William Bryant, chairman of the Detroit AAA, was right on target when he announced that roadside vacations were financially profiting the entire country, from the gas stations to the restaurants to the motor lodges. "Competition for the dollar of the traveler has to be one of the keenest struggled on the national arena... perhaps as keen as anything business or industry has witnessed in the history of the world."

And he was right. The new marker shields that sprang up on the highway now known as Route 66 meant freedom and adventure for the tourist and prosperity for the merchants of the road. Suddenly, while the new highway was still being paved, life had become good for those who traveled, lived, and worked along Route 66.

Dust Bowl Days

But the good times couldn't last forever. The Great Depression soon began settling in on the entire country, making it difficult to feed the family, let alone take an automobile vacation across America. There was nowhere in

Dust storms swept across the Great Plains, wreaking havoc on an American economy already ravaged by the Depression.

the country, though, that was hit by the hard times as badly as the American Great Plains.

By 1933, the final 12 miles of Route 66 between El Reno, Oklahoma, and the east end of the new Canadian River bridge near Bridgeport was paved and open to traffic. The highway was almost entirely surfaced with only a three-mile stretch between the west end of the bridge and Bridgeport still to be completed. Under different circumstances, this would have been a reason for the people of Oklahoma to celebrate. Yet, the festivities were dampened by the winds that were beginning to blow across the farms and fields of the state. The eerie howling was a predecessor of the dark times that were coming to the Heartland. Within a few short years, the central west would experience the most severe drought of the twentieth century.

It all began with a few rain-starved years that dried up the land, destroying grass, crops, and spawning choking clouds of dust. By 1935, dry regions stretched from New York and Pennsylvania, across the Great Plains, and as far west as California. What came to be called the "Dust Bowl" covered about 50 million acres in the south-central plains.

In Oklahoma, tumbleweeds became a familiar sight as wind whipped across the Panhandle, wearing down the crops, trees, and even houses. The land was literally sandblasted with relentless wind storms that stripped the fields bare, churned up the soil, and sent tons of dust into the air. As far as the eye could see, the only thing visible was barren earth, divested of every living thing and coated with thick, cloying dust. There was no point in trying to work the land with the plow for nothing would grow. Entire crops of grain failed, or were lost to the winds. Thousands of jackrabbits, which were doomed to starvation, swarmed like locusts, hoping to find whatever scraps of food remained. They devoured anything that was left growing, devouring the desperate attempts that farmers made to coax anything from the ground.

At the same time that farmers were battling the rabbits, a deadly new disease called "dust pneumonia" was born as a result of the unending winds. The disease struck the very old and very young, and doctors were at a loss to stop it. There were no known remedies for the condition except to advise people to remain indoors as much as possible and to wear masks over their noses and mouths.

One by one, farmers saw their hope of a future decimated. Many of them held on as long as they could, their farms turning into deserts by the dust and wind. On Wednesday, April 11, 1935, the worst dust storm on record blew unabated for two days and dumped tons of dirt over the land. Visibility throughout Oklahoma was cut to one-fifth of a mile and dust blew into homes through every crack, door frame, and window sill. Dismayed housewives were unable to see from the living room to the kitchen and saw footprints left behind on their dust-covered floors. Farmers could only look wistfully at the once fertile lands that were transformed into desert wastelands. What could they do? Where could they go? With nothing left but hope, they gathered together, loaded their furniture into trucks, and formed a ragged caravan of cars. A grim headline appeared in the *Oklahoman*: "Record Barrage of Dirt Sends Families out of Panhandle in Search of Homes Elsewhere."

There was only one chance left to them now – the road.

Many of the Oklahomans heard stories of California, a lush, green place that was rich with crops and where jobs were plentiful. California farmers needed field hands to help pick all of the ripe vegetables, luscious fruits, and white cotton. California became the "promised land." The refugees of the Dust Bowl were willing to work hard and wanted to regain their lives in a place where the dust wasn't blowing and where crops would grow again.

Rusty, broken-down Model T's, overloaded with household belongings and crowded with family members, began moving westward. The vehicles coughed and bounced along the rural roads until they joined up with the new transcontinental highway – the newly dubbed "Mother Road."

Route 66 embraced the "Okies," as they came to be called, and carried them toward California. The highway became more than just a thoroughfare that took tourists on vacations to see America's natural wonders. It became an escape route that guided the dispossessed safely to a new place of hope – a place where dreams could come true. A fresh and better life was just waiting for them around the next bend in the road.

It would be thanks to the Dust Bowl that Route 66 would gain its greatest fame – and earn a place in the American imagination. The saga of the Okies was told by author John Steinbeck in what is perhaps his finest book, *The Grapes of Wrath*. It quickly became an American classic after it was published in 1939. That year, it sold more than a half-million copies and garnered the praise of readers and critics alike. Route 66 literally became a major character in the book. Steinbeck wrote:

> *Highway 66 is the main migrant road. 66 – the long concrete path across the country, waving gently up and down the map, from Mississippi to Bakersfield – over the red lands and the gray lands, twisting up into the mountains, crossing the Divide and down into the bright and terrible desert, and across the desert to the mountains again, and into the rich California valleys.*
>
> *66 is the path of the people in flight, refuges from dust and shrinking land, from the thunder of tractors and shrinking ownership, from the desert's slow northward invasion, from the twisting winds that howl up out of Texas, from the floods that bring no richness to the land and steal what richness is there. From all of these, the people are in flight, and they come into 66 from the tributary side roads, from the wagon tracks and the rutted country roads.*
>
> *66 is the mother road, the road of flight.*

War Comes to Route 66

The Great Depression came to an end just before the United States entered into World War II, ushering in another legendary era in American history. During the war, Route 66 was used to transport vehicles and supplies from one end of the country to the other. And the military traffic often had the highway all to itself. The rationing of rubber tires and gasoline, imposed by the government in 1942 as part of the war effort, greatly reduced travel on U.S. 66.

Most activity centered on the training bases in the desert, where the warm temperatures and clear air permitted year-round exercises, but the Army, Navy, and Marine facilities stretched along Route 66, from Missouri to Los Angeles. Many were built as secret facilities omitted from road maps until the appearance of *A Guide Book to Highway 66*, which was written by Jack Rittenhouse in 1946. Rittenhouse, a Los Angeles advertising copywriter, drove the highway from L.A. to Chicago in a tiny Bantam coupe in March 1946, enduring winter ice storms and twisting roads. He eventually printed 3,000 copies of the book.

The *Guide* located most of the military bases constructed along Highway 66. In the Ozarks, near Waynesville, Missouri, was Fort Leonard Wood, and in Oklahoma there were the Army Air Field in North Miami and Tinker Air Field in Oklahoma City. Further west at El Reno was a German prisoner-of-war camp at an old Army fort, and there was a second German camp at McLean, just over the line into Texas. Air fields were built in the Oklahoma Panhandle at Foss, and in Amarillo, Texas, to protect the U.S. Helium Plant, a vital supply for Navy surveillance blimps.

In New Mexico, a large tourist complex for military personnel developed on Route 66 along Central Avenue, near the Albuquerque Army Air Field. The highway motels and cafes here also served scientists from Los Alamos, who were hard at work on the "Manhattan Project," making the first atom bomb. West of Albuquerque, in the mountains around Fort Wingate near Gallup, valuable uranium ore was mined for the project.

Near Kingman, Arizona, a major Army Air Base was built for training night bomber pilots, many of which used motels on Route 66 as barracks. Across the Colorado River was the Desert Training Center. During the spring and summer of 1942, General George Patton trained more than 60,000 troops there for Operation Torch, preparing for the British-American invasion of North Africa. Between Needles and the Daggett Air Field in California, tank maneuvers and night bivouacs appeared along Route 66 until October, when the troops shipped overseas.

It was an active and patriotic time along Route 66, when the highway was largely abandoned by the droves of travelers and tourists that had once crossed the country in waves. In spite of this, the military kept the cafes and motels hopping as trucks and supplies used the road that vacationers had temporarily left behind.

Getting Your Musical Kicks on Route 66

With the end of the war, a new period of prosperity brought even more people to America's greatest highway. Tourists flocked to Route 66. Among them were Bobby Troup, a Pennsylvania songwriter who was freshly discharged from the Marines, and his wife, Cynthia. They left their hometown in Lancaster in February 1946 to seek their fortune in Los Angeles. Like everyone else at the time, they drove most of the way on Route 66. In their case, though, they wrote a jazz verse about their trip that became a post-war anthem that captured the imagination of the nation.

Bobby Troup was born to a musical family in Lancaster, Pennsylvania, in 1918. His father ran a successful music store and when he passed away in 1937, Troup enrolled at the University of Pennsylvania's Wharton School of Business to prepare himself to take over the family enterprise. But when he got to school, Troup found himself lured by the theater department, where he penned production songs and musicals. He joined the Embassy Club, a fertile ground for musical talent. It was with the Club that Troup met a young singer, Cynthia Harte, a society girl who had dreams of a theatrical career, who encouraged his writing.

In 1941, the Sammy Kaye Band recorded a song that Troup wrote for a production called "Daddy," and it spent nine weeks at #2 on the national Sunday Serenade radio hour. The record's success took Troup to New York to write for the Tommy Dorsey Band and Harry James. Royalties bought him a new car, a green convertible, which was mentioned in the song, and he bought a matching sedan for his mother.

Bobby Troup

But any show business plans that Troup had at that time were temporarily altered by the attack on Pearl Harbor on December 7, 1941. He joined the Marines in March 1942, and married Cynthia in May, before he was sent to South Carolina and then on to Saipan Island in the Pacific. While serving overseas, he met a number of black servicemen with blues and jazz backgrounds that meshed with his own. They formed a jazz band, which included a soldier named Johnny Johnson, from St. Louis, who would become a pianist for Chuck Berry a few years later. In 1945, Troup was given shore leave in Long Beach, and he went to see the hot jazz clubs on the Sunset Strip in Hollywood. He began making plans to return to L.A. after the war was finally over.

Troup was released from service in December 1945, and he returned to his mother's home in Lancaster, where Cynthia had been living, raising their two daughters, during the war. While waiting for his discharge papers to arrive, Troup began talking about returning to California to try his skills as a songwriter in Hollywood. Although his mother urged him to stay in Pennsylvania, or at least on the East Coast, the lure of Hollywood called to him. They would go to California, he decided, and try to make it there.

The Troups began planning their route with AAA highway maps. They would take U.S. 40 to St. Louis, where they would pick up U.S. 66 for the drive to the coast. They planned 10 days of driving to make it to California. After

Troup's discharge arrived on February 1, they packed up the Buick and, leaving the girls with Bobby's mother, they drove to Harrisburg and on to the new Pennsylvania Turnpike. The high-speed toll road had opened in 1940 as the first modern expressway in the country, cutting through the Allegheny Mountains for 160 miles to Irwin, east of Pittsburgh.

On the turnpike, Bobby and Cynthia enjoyed the peacetime thrill of unrationed gasoline and the thrill of nearly unlimited speed. As they looked over the road map during a lunch stop at a Howard Johnson's, Cynthia suggested that they write a song about Route 40, but Bobby thought it was silly since they'd soon be on Route 66, the real road to the west. Still, the seed of a highway song had been planted in both their minds – and it would soon take root.

The Troups left the turnpike and picked up U.S. 40, the old National Road, through West Virginia and Ohio, where they stayed the night with friends. They continued on across Indiana and Illinois, trying to make it to St. Louis by the weekend, so that they could see Louis Armstrong perform at the Club Plantation, a nightclub at Grand and Delmar. In East St. Louis, the National Turnpike joined U.S. 66 and took them over the Mississippi River. Keeping herself occupied during the drive, Cynthia began rhyming new numbers into quick riffs, "Six, nix, picks, kicks," finally whispering to Bobby, "Get your kicks on Route 66." Bobby let out a laugh, knowing that the alliteration of suggestive sexuality was a surefire hit. He told Cynthia, "That's a darling title! God damn! That's a great title!"

With the rhyme in mind, the Troups took U.S. 66 out from St. Louis and then southwest across Missouri, stopping at Meramec Caverns, near Stanton. When they made it to cowboy county in Oklahoma, they began collecting snapshots of cattle ranches and small-town cafes and visited the recent memorial to Will Rogers that had been dedicated in Claremore. By Monday, they had made it to Oklahoma City and began crossing the open vistas of the Great Plains, which had finally recovered from the Dust Bowl years. Driving west across the Texas Panhandle, they hit a midnight snowstorm near Amarillo and took refuge in a highway motel. Once it cleared, they kept motoring west on U.S. 66, now a narrow, two-lane road through the drylands of eastern New Mexico. In Albuquerque, they stopped for rest and haircuts. They followed the highway into the Indian lands at Gallup, then crossed the Painted Desert of Arizona. At Kingman, they detoured north to see the Boulder Dam and the first casinos of Las Vegas.

For the Troups, the trip over the California line and then later, down into the Los Angeles Valley, was a welcome change. The fruit orchards and the warm weather was a reward for their long drive from wintry Pennsylvania. Route 66 ran along the foothills into Pasadena and down the new Arroyo Seco Freeway into downtown L.A. They took the last leg of U.S. 66 to Hollywood and a motel on Ventura Boulevard. It was now Friday, February 15, just seven days since they had started their journey. It was a remarkable time for the narrow, two-lane road that was Route 66 in the post-war winter of 1945.

Once settled, Troup was eager to see the musical sights, especially the Hollywood nightclubs that he had visited while on wartime shore leave. More than anything, he wanted to see the Nat King Cole Trio at the Trocadero on Sunset Boulevard. Cole was well-known in the jazz circles of L.A. and was fresh from his wartime hit, "Straighten Up and Fly Right," which had been inspired by his minister father's sermons when he was growing up. As a child, Cole's family had migrated north to Chicago, where the boy showed early talent on the piano. By high school, he had formed a small band with his brother. In 1937, Cole joined a musical road show that folded, broke, in Los Angeles. Stranded in the city, he decided to try and make his way in the local jazz scene, working with several small groups. He developed an elegant keyboard technique, traveled east to New York, and studied the be-bop style that was then emerging in Harlem. He returned to Los Angeles to form his own trio, with Oscar Moore on the electric guitar and Johnny Miller on the standup bass. During the war, the trio became the premiere jazz group in L.A., breaking the color barrier at the Trocadero.

Within days of arriving in the city, Troup arranged to meet Cole through Bullets Durgom, the trio's new manager whom Bobby knew through contacts with Tommy Dorsey. Troup was introduced as the composer of the pre-war hit, "Daddy." When Cole asked about new songs, Troup played him a recently penned ballad, "Baby, Baby All the Time." Cole then asked if Troup had anything more appropriate for his upbeat piano style – and the rest was history.

Troup told him that, while driving to L.A. with his wife, he had written half a song about Route 66, with lyrics set to a twelve-bar blues beat:

> *If you ever plan to motor west, travel my way,*
> *Take the highway that's the best,*
> *Get your kicks on Route 66!*
> *It winds from Chicago to L.A.,*
> *More than two thousand miles all the way,*
> *Get your kicks on Route 66!*

Nat King Cole was no stranger to highway travel and perhaps that's what made him love the song so much. But whatever the reason, he urged Troup to finish the song for a Capitol recording session in March, and Durgom arranged for Bobby to use a CBS studio on Sunset Boulevard. Amid the distraction of rehearsing bands, Troup unfolded his AAA highway map and began working on a second verse, trying to rhyme the names of towns

Nat King Cole

between St. Louis and Los Angeles to give the song a sense of rapid motion. Some names, like Albuquerque, seemed impossible, but Troup finally worked out a lyric-bound itinerary, with names about every 250 miles, including St. Louis, Missouri; Joplin, Missouri; Oklahoma City, Oklahoma; Amarillo, Texas; Gallup, New Mexico; Flagstaff, Arizona; Winona, Arizona; Kingman, Arizona; Barstow, California; and San Bernardino, California. Winona is the only town out of sequence -- it was a very small settlement east of Flagstaff, and might indeed have been forgotten if not for the lyric "Don't forget Winona," written to rhyme with "Flagstaff, Arizona."

One of the peculiarities of the song – for many people – was in the pronunciation of "Route." Instinctively, Troup assumed his eastern Pennsylvania accent, saying "rewte" instead of the Midwestern "rout." This dialect boundary ran just west of Pittsburgh along the Ohio line, which marked the song's "route" as Eastern speech. More glaringly, Troup called the road *Route 66*, instead of the *Highway 66* of John Steinbeck and Woody Guthrie. Who, among others, had always referred to the road by its Western name. Calling a highway a "route" was common in the East and, like the pronunciation, revealed the song as an outsider's description of 66 as a tourist road to California. The now iconic song changed the face of the highway from the Dust Bowl "road of flight" to a highway for dreamers in post-war America.

Cole was happy with the lyrics and immediately logged the song for the Capitol recording session. The Trio recorded three versions of it during March and April 1946. "Route 66" was released on April 22, and by mid-May, the national music weeklies were calling it a hit. It was immediately covered by Georgie Auld and his Orchestra on April 30, and by Bing Crosby and the Andrews Sisters on May 10.

Within two weeks, the royalties from the Capitol release allowed the Troups to make a down payment on a house in North Hollywood, their California dream realized beyond their wildest dreams. On May 2, their fourth wedding anniversary, they moved into a bungalow on Alcove Avenue, less than three months after leaving Pennsylvania. In celebration, Cynthia took the AAA highway map and pasted her U.S. 66 snapshots on it, together with sections of the song sheet, drawings, and colored lines to map the route and the towns where they had stayed overnight. Framed over the mantle, the Route 66 song map was a visual record of their journey and Hollywood success.

Once projected into the national culture, "(Get Your Kicks on) Route 66" became a musical map of the highway for post-war travelers. Years later, Bobby Troup was told that his song was used in just such a manner in the roadside diners along Route 66: "They'd drop a nickel into the jukebox and plan the next day's drive through 'Saint Loo-ey and Joplin, Missouri.'"

Since those days, the song has been subsequently covered by many artists, including Chuck Berry, The Rolling Stones, Depeche Mode, Brian Setzer, Tom Petty, and dozens of others. Depending on the version of the tune that you hear, it's a great song and it probably went further in cementing the idea in people's minds of taking a trip on Route 66 than anything else that had been written about the famous highway. It became the essential booster for getting people out onto the open road during the late 1940s and into the 1950s.

Route 66 wasn't just a highway anymore – it was a state of mind.

The Golden Era Begins to Dim

U.S. 66 – sometimes called the Main Street of America – not only is one of the most important highways between Chicago and the West Coast, but it is also one of the nation's most rewarding vacation routes.
Chicago Tribune, November 24, 1957

Route 66 – the highway memorialized in poetry, gasoline, song and memories of millions of persons who traveled it or watched the television show – will be no more. Beginning January 1, Illinois is dropping the U.S. Highway 66 designation from its maps and road signs on the 290-mile highway between Chicago and St. Louis. It will be known as Interstate 55.
Chicago Tribune, November 28, 1976

By the 1950s, the highway had become a genuine celebrity. Families could leave their homes in the East and Midwest and drive out to the Grand Canyon or the Painted Desert. They could go all of the way to the Pacific on a highway that passed through towns where Abraham Lincoln once lived, Jesse James robbed banks, and Will Rogers learned to twirl his famous rope. They could cross over Mark Twain's famous river, visit caves where outlaws hid from the law, and pass through small towns where real-life cowboys still punched cattle. They could stop and buy chunks of petrified wood in Arizona, or shot glasses and spoons from the Ozarks. There were snake pits, prairie dog villages, wild critters, and genuine Indians, sitting like wooden statues and selling rings and bracelets made from silver and turquoise. The lure of Route 66 grew even greater in the late 1950s when Walt Disney created Disneyland among the orange groves of Southern California.

But it was also in the 1950s that the bright lights of fame that had shone on Route 66 for so many years began to grow dim. In 1954, President Dwight D. Eisenhower established a President's Advisory Committee on a National Highway Program. The Committee marked the start of the decline of the legendary highway. Eisenhower had been intrigued by the efficient German autobahn during his tenure as supreme commander of the Allied Forces during World War II and envisioned such a system in America.

The final report by the Committee led to the enactment of the Federal Aid Highway Act in 1956, which spelled out the guidelines for a 42,500-mile national interstate highway system. Despite the fact that the old highway was being maintained, and had been turned into a four-lane road in many locations, it was clear that Route 66 could no longer handle the increasing volume of traffic.

The coming of the interstates was long and laborious. Construction cost tens of billions of dollars, yet the federal government not only persisted, it footed the bill. A piece of Route 66 was replaced here and there, bypasses were constructed around towns and cities, and little by little the old highway was turned into a service road as it was replaced.

By the start of the 1960s, travelers were no longer motoring from one location to the next. They were intent on seeing how quickly they could get to their destination. As interstates replaced the blue ribbons of highways, auto vacations and road trips began to change. With their smooth surfaces, gradual curves, and occasional exits, the new expressways were allowing a scenery-killing speed of 70 and 75 miles per hour.

In Missouri, Route 66 was swallowed by the new Interstate 44, a full-speed expressway where cars could cruise from St. Louis to Joplin in a matter of hours. At the kind of speed the interstate allowed, stopping to get a bite to eat or use the restroom was a major inconvenience. So, instead of forcing motorists to exit the interstate, states built "rest areas" that provided motorists with easy on and off access. Built in pairs, the rest areas were situated on each side of the expressway to meet the needs of travelers moving in both directions and were situated about 50 miles apart.

The new roads were in great demand, and thanks to the flow of money from the government, they were constantly in the works. At the time, most travelers embraced the new roads, although many were frustrated over construction delays and confusing road signs that often carried several names for a single route. It was impossible to ignore the fact, though, that change was coming. It was essential to embrace it, or be left behind by progress. The inevitable end was coming for Route 66.

Originally, the national interstate plan was supposed to take 12 years to complete. It ended up taking twice that long. Finally, the last stretch of U.S. Highway 66 was bypassed in 1984, near Williams, Arizona, when a final stretch of the Mother Road was replaced by a section of Interstate 40.

Bypassing Route 66 had actually taken five different interstates – Interstate 55 from Chicago to St. Louis; Interstate 44 from St. Louis to Oklahoma City; Interstate 40 from Oklahoma City to Barstow, California; Interstate 15 from Barstow to San Bernardino; and Interstate 10 from San Bernardino to Santa Monica. The opening of the interstates made it possible to drive all the way from Chicago to the Pacific Ocean without stopping, someone commented. The government called this progress, but thankfully, not everyone agreed.

Even as the Route 66 road signs were being auctioned off and the road maps changed, history buffs and activists came forward and began trying to protect the legacy of the legendary road. They remain today and are a wide array of people from all walks of life who believe that the spirit of the Mother Road will never be forgotten. They are people (like me, and probably like you, if you're reading this book) who want to see the highway's history survive. We are the people who get a thrill when we hear about someone reading or watching *The Grapes of Wrath* for the first time, or listening to a cool version of the classic song, or actually getting off the mind-numbing interstate and driving a stretch of the lost highway that remains.

Route 66 lives on in the hearts and minds of thousands of people, and remnants of the road remain in every one of the eight states that Route 66 crosses. In many of those places, the old signs are returning, the name never really surrendered. There are still motor courts, filling stations, curio shops, and tourist attractions that thrive on the nostalgia that is still felt by those of us who refuse to give up on America's past.

Come along now, get behind the wheel, and let's recapture a little of the lost people, places, and ghosts that linger from the America of yesterday.

Missouri
Motoring West Through the "Show Me State"

As U.S. 66 left the prairie state of Illinois and crossed the Mississippi River into Missouri, the route changed a number of times over the years, including across the now-defunct Chain of Rocks Bridge, through the urban decay that was once the great city of East St. Louis, and across the McKinley or McArthur Bridges. The river crossings that were used by Route 66 over the years have now become a tangled mess of inner-city and semi-rural roads that have become dead ends, truncated roads, and lost bridges. Scattered along these routes out of Illinois are ghostly reminders – like the Luna Café in our previous volume – of a time when the road from east to west (and west to east) flowed in a continuous stream.

Route 66 cut diagonally across Missouri from the city of St. Louis to the open plains west of Springfield. As it sliced through the Ozarks, it followed the same route as a stage line that was established by the United States government two decades before the Civil War. During the war, the trail was an important military route that was traveled by both Union and Confederate soldiers. It was during that time that the federal government installed a telegraph line along the road with stations in St. Louis, Rolla, Lebanon, Marshfield, and Springfield. The old stage line, previously known as the Kickapoo Trail, the Osage Trace, the Springfield Road, and the Military Road, then became known as the Old Wire Road.

Near Springfield, the road connected with what would become the Ozark Trail. It headed west and eventually ended in Santa Rosa, New Mexico. The Ozark Trails Association established that road in 1915, and in August 1922, the newly formed Missouri Highway Commission designated seven roads throughout the state, including the Old Wire Road, as the new Highway U.S. 66. The next job was to cobble them all together, and work on that progressed at a rapid pace until January 1931, when the last section of hardtop was completed in Pulaski County. This made Missouri the third of eight Route 66 states to complete its paving for the entire state.

The new U.S. 66 helped Missouri to grow and prosper and become one of the most popular vacation destinations in America. Rivers, lakes, and a wealth of forest locations attracted sportsmen from around the country. Travelers and vacationers found a wealth of motels, tourist courts, resorts, and lodges to choose from, and there were scores of diners, cafes, curio shops, and gas stations to serve them.

Among the most visited tourist attractions in the state were the caves. Signs painted on barns to advertise the caves became common sights throughout the Midwest, especially along Route 66. By the time that travelers arrived in Missouri, they were almost brainwashed into stopping. As an incentive, one cave owner, Lester Dills, offered to paint farmers' barns for free if they allowed him to advertise on them. Very few of the farmers refused his offer.

As with the other states through which Route 66 passed, the highway underwent many alignment changes in Missouri. Roads were straightened to make them safer, towns were bypassed to make things faster, and two-lane highway was eventually upgraded to four lanes. With the passage of the Federal Highway Aid Act in 1956, Missouri almost immediately began work on its new interstate. Lebanon holds the dubious honor of being the first town in Missouri to be bypassed by the new interstate. By the start of the 1980s, Interstate 44 had replaced most of U.S. 66 across the Show Me State and a section of highway at Devil's Elbow was the last to be bypassed in 1981.

But regardless of such "progress," many stretches of Route 66 still survive today and are just waiting for the adventurous traveler to explore them. Many of the small towns on the classic route still have the same vintage feel as they did when they were places to stop along the Mother Road. You may have to look a little harder to find some of these gems today, but it's definitely worth the trouble.

Chain of Rocks Amusement Park

When U.S. 66 crossed the Mississippi River over the old Chain of Rocks Bridge, one of the first attractions to greet motorists was the **Chain of Rocks Amusement Park**, which flourished for nearly a half century on the banks of the river. Oddly, the amusement park came about because of the city of St. Louis's search for clean water.

By the 1840s, St. Louis was suffering from serious drinking water problems – old Choteau Pond, the city's original water source, was polluted by nearby homes, slaughterhouses, and waste from the nearby Collier Lead Company. The Mississippi River itself was much too tainted to be taken home for drinking or any other household purpose. In 1872, the city opened Bissell's Point Waterworks, four miles north of downtown. But by 1886, the growing city had overwhelmed it and so construction was authorized for a northern waterworks extension at Chain of Rocks.

Chain of Rocks Waterworks ended St. Louis's water problems, but it did nothing to improve the horrendous appearance of the water itself. Drawn water was settled in basins before it was pulled by pipes into town. This process removed the actual mud and grit from the water, but left the color of it a weak shade of brown. By end of the decade there were other problems. In 1888, the *St. Louis Globe-Democrat* urged citizens not to drink in the dark after an eel appeared in a downtown sink. In 1895, the city's Health Commissioner investigated other forms of life found in the drinking water and pronounced them a "breed of miniature crabs." The locals endured the issues with the water, but everyone cringed when Mayor David R. Francis succeeded in bringing the 1904 World's Fair to St. Louis. The city would truly be in the limelight and visitors had to be able to safely drink the water.

In 1901, the Municipal Assembly ordered the appointment of three hydraulic engineers to clear the water at Chain of Rocks. The three men traveled along the Mississippi River, visiting large and small towns to see how they managed to clean up their own water supplies. They discovered that workers in Quincy, Illinois, were purifying their water with iron and milk of lime. Two weeks before the World's Fair, the taps of St. Louis began offering clear, fresh water. The Chain of Rocks Waterworks became a place of wonder.

In 1918, a park was created at Chain of Rocks, on a bluff that overlooked the waterworks. The 40-acre park offered fountains and goldfish ponds, walking paths, seven varieties of roses, and a flower garden that spelled out the words "Chain of Rocks" in multi-colored blooms. By the latter 1920s, the festive atmosphere around the waterworks began to attract developers, and soon, on property adjacent to the grounds, a small amusement park appeared.

Little is known about the early years of the amusement park. One of the only certainties is that it was started by Christian Hoffman, who moved the

Whip, a Dodgem pavilion (bumper cars), and a hand-carved carousel onto the grounds in 1927. In 1929, he added the Swooper, a metal contraption that swung riders around and around, lengthwise, like an elongated Ferris Wheel (it's hard to describe!). The ride was built by the Eli Bridge Company in Jacksonville, Illinois, which had invented the portable Ferris Wheel for carnivals and midway attractions. Only 19 Swooper rides were ever built.

What is known about Hoffman was that he was difficult to get along with. He was a German immigrant with a thick accent and a stubborn, rude nature, which did not endear him to the staff or suppliers. It would take the next owner of the park, Carl Trippe, to make the place famous on Route 66.

Trippe was a former clerk for the Railway Express Company who started the Ideal Novelty Company in 1935. Ideal specialized in jukeboxes and vending machines and supplied them to venues all over St. Louis. In the early 1940s, he contracted with Chain of Rocks Amusement Park to supply the machines for its penny arcade. A dispute started between Trippe and Hoffman, which ended in Hoffman throwing him and his machines out of the park. Trippe turned the tables on him, though, by buying up all of the stock in the park that he could find, taking it over, and kicking Hoffman out.

He immediately began renovating and remodeling the park. He shamed Hoffman's meager food stands by building the Sky Garden Bar and Restaurant. The elegant dining room offered breathtaking views of the Mississippi, as well as an observation deck with coin-operated binoculars. Trippe moved his office into the building's second floor and kept an adjoining apartment for his family during the busiest times of the year.

During his time at Chain of Rocks Amusement Park, Trippe received praise for his involvement with the community. In 1944, he staged a fair at Emerson Electric Company, offering attendees a Ferris Wheel, carousel, and horse show. Trippe also sponsored the Ozark AAU Junior Swimming Meet at the Chain of Rocks Amusement Park swimming pool every year. The year before his death, he established an Easter Egg Hunt at the park, an annual event that continued on for years after he passed away.

Trippe suffered a fatal heart attack in January 1955. By 1958, his widow, Margaret, started trying to sell the park. She approached William Zimmerman and Ken Thone, a pair of brothers-in-law who operated Holiday Hill Amusement Park at Natural Bridge and Brown Roads in St. Louis. Zimmerman owned Holiday Hill and before that had operated a golf range. Thone was a former auto repairman and Navy captain, who managed Holiday Hill for Zimmerman. Both men liked Margaret Trippe's offer and Zimmerman bought the park and Thone began to run it. The Trippe family gave the men a 99-year lease on the property itself.

After getting some advice from a veteran roller coaster man, Thone and Zimmerman tore down the Comet, an aging wooden coaster. They took down

The Fun Fair at Chain of Rocks Park

an old sky ride that had frayed cables and old decking, tore down the bandstands, and built a new bath house for the swimming pool. Although they kept the Haunted Cave, the Mad House, the Dodgem pavilion, the Rocket, the Whip, the carousel and the Swooper, they turned Trippe's indoor roller rink into a miniature golf course. Then, as a final step in making a fresh start, they renamed the amusement complex, now calling it **Fun Fair** at Chain of Rocks Park.

At their Holiday Hill park, the two men had previously made a lot of money at the start of the season by contracting for school outings and picnics. They aggressively marketed the same idea at Fun Fair. In the early 1960s, they even enlarged the park and hired a carnival operator from Florida to provide additional rides for the school outing season in May and early June. The portable, trailer-mounted rides could be set up and taken down in a day's time and almost doubled the number of rides offered by the amusement park. During the early part of the season, Thone hired between 150 and 200 employees and then whittled it down to just the essential crew for the rest of the summer.

Like Carl Trippe, Thone had a taste for the unusual. He employed all sorts of oddball people, from sideshow refugees to long-time carnival folks, who had been on the circuit for years. Trippe had once displayed a petrified mummy on his midway, so Thone decided to hire his own sideshow attraction – a rather strange performer named Digger O'Dell. He was known for his feats of endurance, such as the time when Fun Fair buried him in a concrete-block coffin for a month. The coffin was 36-inches tall, eight feet long and three feet wide. It had an air conditioner and a toilet but had a glass top so that people could look down on Digger inside of his tomb. It was also equipped with a microphone so that customers could ask him questions. Many thought that he came out at night, but former employees insisted that he didn't. He stayed in there, 24-hours-a-day, seven-days-a-week for 30 days with only a hole through which he could receive food and water.

Over time, the huge swimming pool became a financial drain so Thone teamed up with local radio stations to host "Splash Parties," and the wild, wet concerts became regular events. The local station would send a disc jockey and local rock bands would play. A few times, they even had some big name guest acts like Paul Revere and the Raiders and Ike and Tina Turner. The parties became so big that they were able to financially carry the park through the second half of the summer season.

Business at Fun Fair grew through the 1960s, peaking in the summer of 1970. The next year, Six Flags Over Mid-America opened in Eureka, west of St. Louis, and this marked the beginning of the end for Chain of Rocks. They began to see the teenagers trickling away, enticed by the new park's single admission price, larger venue, and wider variety of rides and attractions.

In 1973, a fire destroyed the Sky Garden Bar and Restaurant. Then, two years later, Holiday Hill closed when its site was acquired for an expansion of the parking at Lambert International Airport. Fun Fair absorbed the other park's attractions, including the Octopus, a Skydiver, electric cars, a Ferris Wheel, and an army of toy tanks.

By the fall of 1976, Fun Fair was reeling under a new set of taxes that had been imposed on them by the city, including an amusement tax and a higher sales tax, and Zimmerman and Thone realized that they had endured as much as they could – the show was over. Hoping to attract buyers, they left all of the rides assembled that winter, looking sad and forlorn in the gray under the gray, Midwestern skies.

They managed a meager re-opening in the spring, but worse luck followed bad luck in June 1977, when a fire swept through Fun Fair, destroying the old Dodgem car pavilion and the hand-carved wooden carousel. Disheartened, Zimmerman and Thone closed Fun Fair for good after Labor Day that summer. St. Louis became the first major city in America without its own amusement park and the longest-lived amusement spot on Route 66 was gone for good.

Meet Me in St. Louis!

Located in the center of the country, many people forget just how old the city of St. Louis actually is. Founded in 1763, before the United States was officially a country, it was discovered by a man named Pierre Laclede, who believed it was the perfect place for a Mississippi River trading post. After establishing a small village, he named it St. Louis, in honor of King Louis IX of France.

The settlement thrived and within a few years was home to more than 300 people, most who lived in homes that had been quarried from along the river.

Over the next four decades or so, the city was the property of France, Spain (although most residents never knew it since the treaty had been written in Europe), France again, and finally, the United States. There were few Americans there in the early 1800s. The population was mostly French, Indians, slaves and free Blacks. The Louisiana Territory, which included St. Louis, was transferred to the United States in 1804 and, at the time, the town included a bakery, two taverns, three blacksmiths, two mills, and a doctor. From St. Louis, President Thomas Jefferson sent Lewis and Clark to explore the new territory in May 1804. When they returned two years later, the city became the "Gateway to the West" for the mountain men, settlers, and adventurers who set out into the new frontier.

The first steamboat arrived in St. Louis in 1817, which began an era when the city would become one of the most important ports on the Mississippi. Before long, it became common to see more than 100 riverboats lining the stone levee on any day. By 1850, river traffic had increased so much that St. Louis was the second largest port in the entire country, second only to New York City. On some days, as many as 170 steamboats fought for space along the levee, many of them the "floating palaces" of legend. Such ships came with fine furnishings, imported carpets, glistening chandeliers, elegant staterooms – and a contingent of gamblers willing to part any fool from his money.

It was also during this time that travel to the western states truly began in earnest after the discovery of gold in California. St. Louis saw additional prosperity as the last "civilized" city before the west began, outfitting scores of wagon trains, trappers, traders, and miners. By 1890, when the frontier had been deemed as "closed," St. Louis boasted more than a half-million residents.

"The World Came to St. Louis"

One of the greatest events in the history of St. Louis was undoubtedly the Louisiana Purchase Exposition – the 1904 World's Fair – which opened on April 20, 1904. It was a time of great celebration and the chance for the city to finally come into its own. It was no longer the frontier outpost that provided the gateway to the Wild West – it was now a glittering, modern place, ready to take its place on the world stage.

The Louisiana Exposition was proclaimed as the "greatest World's Fair to ever be held." St. Louis had campaigned hard for an earlier fair in 1893, but the Columbian Exposition had gone to Chicago. The loss of this event instilled a great desire on the part of the eminent citizens of St. Louis, especially David R. Francis, who would soon be elected governor of Missouri, to snag the next gala event to come along. A few years later, people began to talk of a fair to celebrate the centennial anniversary of the Louisiana Purchase. What better place to have it than in St. Louis, the Gateway to the West? Civil leaders pledged to raise $15 million to the event, the same amount Jefferson paid for the Louisiana Purchase, and the site of the 1904 World's Fair was awarded to St. Louis.

After lengthy debate, the western side of Forest Park was chosen as the physical site for the fair. Businessmen on the south side of the city, especially the powerful brewers like William Lemp and Adolphus Busch, were very unhappy with the decision, stating their part of the city was a more attractive and viable location, mostly thanks to the proximity of the Mississippi River, but their lobby was unsuccessful. In fact, they would not raise much enthusiasm for the fair on the west side until the Jefferson Hotel was constructed and streetcars and other city services were improved. After that, every businessman in the city rallied around the effort, and by 1903, there had been 94 hotels built to meet the needs of fair attendees. There were 15 more completed by the time the fair opened in April 1904.

The section of the park that was chosen for the fair covered a little more than 650 acres, but it was soon obvious that more land would be needed. Additional tracts were leased from the new, but unoccupied, Washington University campus and this nearly doubled the size of the fairgrounds. Preparations ran at a feverish pitch for several years and as the actual centennial date of April 1903 approached, it was obvious that the fair was not going to open on time. A dedication was held anyway on April 30, 1903, with thousands of troops parading through the grounds and President Theodore Roosevelt on hand to deliver the opening address. Right after that, everything was shut down again and Congress granted the request for a postponement of one year to 1904. This gave the organizers more time to obtain foreign exhibits and to get more companies to plan displays.

By the cold spring of 1904, the Exposition was ready to open. Organizers began to panic, though, on April 20, when a late snowstorm slowed all of the operations. Luckily, the snow was cleared away and on April 30, the fair opened. The (second) Opening Day ceremony was held in the Plaza of St. Louis and included prayer, music, and an assortment of speeches. John Phillip Sousa led his band and a choir of 400 performed a song called "Hymn of the West," which had been written for the occasion. William Howard Taft, the United States Secretary of War, made the principal address and Mayor David Francis touched a gold telegraph key that alerted President Roosevelt to officially start the fair. At that same moment, 10,000 flags unfurled, fountains began to spray geysers into the air, and the fairgrounds opened to almost 20 million visitors from around the world over the course of the next seven months.

The architecture and design that went into the fair was breathtaking. A few years before, Peninsular Lake in the park had been re-shaped and re-designed. The lake acquired a new name, the Grand Basin, and it was

The Grand Basin at the St. Louis Fair of 1904

connected throughout the park with lagoons to provide waterways for boating during the festivities. Above the lake, on the natural semi-circular hill now known as Art Hill, was the Festival Hall, the centerpiece of the fair and one of its foremost attractions. It had a gold-leaf dome that was larger than the one atop St. Peter's Basilica in Rome. On each side were smaller pavilions from which three cascades of water descended 400 feet from the top of the hill to the lake. Along the cascades were large staircases that were adorned with statues, benches, and landscaped gardens.

    The Colonnade of States, linking Festival Hall and the many fair pavilions, was flanked by giant seated figures, seven on each side, each representing a state that had been created from the Louisiana Purchase. Eight ornate exhibition palaces surrounded the Great Basin. These included Mines and Metallurgy, Liberal Arts, Education and Social Economy, Manufacturing, Electricity, Varied Industries, Transportation, and Machinery. The building that housed the Palace of Machinery had parking space for the 140 automobiles that had been driven to the fair from as far away as Boston. That fact alone was almost as much a marvel as the other wonders of the fair. Long-distance driving was still in its infancy and it was only the year before, in 1903, that an automobile had been driven from coast to coast for the first time. Each of the exhibition palaces was different in design and all were massive in size, each covering several acres.

Although the buildings were detailed, highly decorated, and looked as though they had been built to stand forever, they were actually made from temporary, insubstantial materials. They had been constructed from what was called "staff," a mixture of fibers such as burlap and manila fibers soaked in gypsum plaster, commonly known as plaster of Paris. The hardened material was very adaptable and could be used just like wood. By pouring staff into molds, many ornamental pieces that appeared to be carved by hand in marble could be achieved in a short time. The structure under the staff was always steel or wood so that the buildings didn't simply collapse.

A few of the fair structures were meant to be permanent. One of these was the Palace of Art, constructed of limestone. The building that would be used by more than 20 nations to house priceless works of art during the exposition. Two temporary buildings flanked the center one and a smaller sculpture building was located on the south, creating a beautiful courtyard between them.

The Palace of Art

The temporary buildings were removed after the fair and the Palace of Art was donated to the city and today houses the St. Louis Art Museum.

The area of the park now occupied by the St. Louis Zoo was called the Plateau of States, where many states erected houses to greet visitors and to show off their individual attractions. Some of the buildings were replicas of important historic sites like the Cabildo of New Orleans where the Louisiana Purchase had been signed, Tennessee's Hermitage, and Virginia's Monticello. Missouri, the host state, constructed a lavishly decorated building made entirely of native materials. It was designed to be permanent, with a large dome and a heating and cooling system, something that no other building on the fairgrounds could boast at the time. Unfortunately, on November 19, just two weeks before the end of the fair, the building and all of its contents were destroyed by fire. The fire was caused by faulty electric wiring. Electric lighting, still in its infancy in 1904, was a requirement in all the buildings for its decorative effect. Some of the furnishings were saved from the blaze and are on display today in the Governor's Mansion in Jefferson City. No attempt was made to replace the structure.

The U.S. Fisheries building was one of the fair's most popular attractions. It had 40 glass-fronted fish tanks that surrounded a center pool for seals. Nearby was the Bird Cage, the largest of its kind ever built. It was created by the Smithsonian Institution to allow sightseers to walk through the cage and interact with the numerous species of birds inside. After the fair, the cage was donated to the city and it became a part of the St. Louis Zoo. Visitors can still experience it today.

The Grand Basin was the focal point of the fair's activities. Boat parades were held daily along the lagoons and waterways that led away from the Basin and flowed between the exhibition buildings. North of the Basin was the Plaza of St. Louis, where the official proceedings were held. The Plaza was graced with a tall monument for the Louisiana Purchase and the statue of St. Louis. Stretching away from the Plaza was Louisiana Way, the main thoroughfare of the grounds. On one side of it was the United States building and on the other was the French Palace, honoring the two countries involved in the Louisiana Purchase.

The hill to the west of Forest Park provided a space large enough for the agricultural exhibits and the largest building on the fairgrounds, the Agriculture Palace. It was here that brewers and distillers from around the country showcased their wares. The Agriculture Palace had an eastern facade that was one-third of a mile long. The area was covered with displays showing various types of grasses, pools containing water plants, and windmills. Livestock shows took place there every day. Near the north entrance to the Agriculture Palace was a giant floral clock that was 112-feet in diameter. It was made from flowers and foliage and had giant hands that were operated by compressed air. The hands were controlled by a master clock in a small pavilion at the top of the clock at the number 12. The gardens were illuminated at night with thousands of lights hidden in the foliage, a breathtaking sight when artificial lighting was still a novelty. Thomas Edison himself was brought to the fair to oversee the proper installation of the electrical exhibits.

Washington University's new campus not only provided much of the space needed for the fair, but it also served as the model for the ideal university. The Administrations Building (Brookings Hall) was the site of all the official meetings and the receptions for important guests. Other buildings furnished space for exhibits, offices, and meeting rooms. At the western end of the campus, the athletic fields and gymnasium were used for an elaborate physical culture program and also for the Olympics of 1904, when the United States became the first English-speaking nation to host the games.

At the eastern end of the campus were halls representing foreign countries, including China, Sweden, Brazil, and others. The British Building was a copy of Queen Anne's Orangery at Kensington Gardens. After the fair, it was purchased by the university and for years it housed the School of Fine Arts.

The college abandoned the building in 1926, when the school was moved into the new Bixby Hall.

Perhaps the most fascinating of the exhibits at the fair to turn-of-the-century visitors was the Philippines Reservation. This was the largest and most expensive of the foreign displays, and it brought 1,100 Filipinos to live in St. Louis for almost seven months. One of the goals of the fair's Anthropological Division was to show Americans how people of "exotic" cultures lived. The U.S. had taken control over the Philippines from Spain in 1898, and people were curious to see the various communities of "primitive" people set up on 47 acres around Arrowhead Lake. Each tribe constructed its own village of thatched huts and houses on stilts along the water. The tribe's customs and homes fascinated visitors, and in turn, the Filipinos were enthralled by the trappings of modern society. One tribal chief created a problem when he refused to let his tribe be viewed until a telephone was installed in his hut. Another tribe caused a scandal with their demand for dogs, the main staple of their diet.

A scene from the Philippines Reservation at the Fair.

What most people remembered when they later recalled the 1904 Fair was the Pike, an inviting one-mile section along the northern edge of the fairgrounds. This area was like a giant amusement park with concessions and attractions that had not yet become standard at fairs everywhere. It was here that hotdogs and ice cream cones were first sampled. Fairgoers were introduced to "fairy floss," a new treat that was to become known as cotton candy. The fair popularized peanut butter and Dr. Pepper, billed as a "health drink." The forerunner of the ice pop also made its first appearance at the Pike. Known as the "fruit icicle," it was made of fruit juice frozen in a narrow tin tube. Another welcome "first' from the Pike was iced tea. It was first served almost as a fluke. A tea house was having a hard time selling hot tea on summer days and one of the employees suggested that they try serving it over crushed ice.

The attractions of the Pike undoubtedly influenced the design of future fairs and amusement parks, just as the White City at the Columbian Exposition in 1893 had influenced the St. Louis event. At the eastern end of the Pike was

The Pike – one of the most popular and exciting attractions of the Fair

the spectacular Tyrolean Alps concession, which had been created by the beer brewers of St. Louis. A castle had been built, along with other structures, to create the illusion of life in the Alps. There were yodelers, musical shows, and a storybook Alpine village. The massive manmade mountain range was crowned with real snow. Visitors could take a train ride into the mountains and dine in the Great Hall, where many official gatherings were held. President Roosevelt was honored there at a banquet given by the brewers. An elevator took guests to the peaks of the Ortler, where a waterfall tumbled into the lake. The whole exhibit was a stunning display created from humble paint, canvas, rock and plaster. It left quite an impression on fairgoers, most of whom would never have the opportunity to visit the real Alps. It also sold enormous quantities of cold beer, which was what it had been designed to do.

Next to the Alps was an Irish village with reproductions of medieval buildings. It featured a restaurant, a facsimile of Blarney Castle, and a theater where visitors could enjoy a show. Also on the Pike was Hagenbeck's Animal Paradise, which attracted large crowds in those days before modern zoos, and visitors were able to see bears, elk, mountain lions, and an assortment of exotic animals.

All types of foreign cultures were represented, as were displays about topics as diverse as the deadly Galveston flood, the North Pole, and the Siberian wastelands. When visitors had enough of education, they could enjoy entertainment. Fairgoers could catch a performance by a little-known comedian named Will Rogers or hear the new ragtime music, which originated in St. Louis. Scott Joplin, one of the most famous ragtime composers, wrote "Cascade Rag" in honor of the fair. Other rags at the time were "On the Pike" and "Strolling Down the Pike." In addition to hearing the strains of "Meet Me in St. Louie," visitors might experience the Magic Whirlpool, the Water Chutes, or the Scenic Railway.

There was no greater ride at the fair than the immense Observation Wheel. The 250-foot-high wheel was created by George Ferris, an engineer who debuted his creation at the 1893 Columbian Exposition in Chicago. The "Ferris Wheel" was so successful that it was brought to St. Louis. Sadly, the wheel never left the city at the end of the fair. It was scheduled to be taken to Coney Island, but the demolition contractor for the fair found it to be too much trouble to disassemble.

The giant Ferris Wheel that had first appeared at the 1893 Columbian Exposition in Chicago proved very popular in St. Louis, too.

So, he dynamited it and sold the scrap for $1,800. The original wheel became the model for all such attractions to follow, but there has never been another of such gigantic proportions.

The visitors came throughout the summer and into the fall of 1904. But as December approached, a sense of sadness filled the air. The Exposition closed down at midnight on December 1. From early morning right up until the time the clock struck midnight, thousands gathered to stroll the Pike one last time and to pay homage to David Francis, the man responsible for bringing the fair to the city. Schools and businesses closed for the day. It was like a carnival that was tinged with grief. The fair's closing night became one of the wildest nights ever witnessed in St. Louis with the authorities on high alert, should the celebration turn overly buoyant.

As the midnight hour approached, Mayor Francis made a final speech from the Plaza of St. Louis and then he threw a switch that plunged the entire fairgrounds into darkness. A band played "Auld Lang Syne" and then suddenly the air was filled with blinding fireworks as "Farewell" was spelled out, followed by "Good Night."

The Louisiana Purchase Exposition of 1904 had come to an end.

The destruction of the fairgrounds began on December 2. Demolition was started by the Chicago Housewrecking Company, which had been awarded the $450,000 contract to remove the fair buildings. Even though the fair was officially closed, visitors were able to view the demolition for a 25-cent admission. The demolition process produced mountains of staff, the fiber and plaster of Paris material from which nearly all of the pavilions had been constructed. Useful only for landfill, it was hauled away over miles of railroad tracks that had been laid down before the fair for the construction and removal of the buildings on the grounds. The tracks were covered with asphalt during the fair and then opened again to remove the debris when the fair ended.

The exhibition buildings were removed quickly, as the contract specified that the demolition be completed within six months, but many of the concessions on the Pike remained in place for months. Some of the buildings were so unusual that it was believed that buyers could be found for them. One of them, a cabin that once belonged to General Ulysses S. Grant, had been moved to the fairgrounds to be used by the Blanke Coffee Company. No one knew what to do with it at the end of the fair but it was finally purchased by Adolphus Busch and moved to Gravois Road. It is now a part of the Anheuser-Busch company attraction, Grant's Farm.

The buildings representing the various states and countries were the easiest to get rid of. Many of the ones made from permanent materials were purchased and hauled to nearby sites for use as homes. The New Jersey building was moved to Kirkwood, where it served as an apartment building for a time. The New Hampshire house, after undergoing alterations, became a home on Litzinger Road. The Oklahoma structure was taken to El Reno, Oklahoma, where it became an Elks Lodge. The Michigan and Minnesota structures became permanent fair buildings in their home states. The New Mexico building became a public library in Santa Fe. The Iowa building become an asylum for alcoholics. Belgium's building was purchased by Anheuser-Busch and was used for many years as the company's glass works. The Swedish building was taken to Lindsborg, Kansas, where it became the Art Department for Bethany College. The 50-foot statue of Vulcan, a donation from the city of Birmingham, Alabama, was removed to its home city on seven freight cars and while it rusted in storage for years, it was later restored on Red Mountain overlooking the city. Many other statues from the fair were given to the city of St. Louis and were assigned to parks and public places.

An attempt was made to preserve the Pike as a permanent attraction in St. Louis, with the reproduction of the Alps being the major benefit of the plan. However, officials at Washington University viewed an amusement center of this sort as being too big a distraction for the students and lobbied against the idea. Adolphus Busch finally purchased the Alps, planning to install them as an attraction in Forest Park, along with a summer theater. This plan never came about and eventually the mountain range was destroyed.

Although little remains from the fair in the city today, the Louisiana Exposition has never been forgotten. Never again would a World's Fair be held that had the magnitude of the St. Louis Fair, and while others would follow, the magnificence of that brief season in 1904 would leave a lasting mark on the country, and perhaps the world.

"Eat-Rite, or Don't Eat at All!"

When Highway 66 made it to St. Louis, the city was already more than 150 years old, with well-established streets and neighborhoods. Thanks to this, and because of the city's growth, the route through St. Louis was altered many times. Today, this makes following the twisting and confusing path of what was once Route 66 through the city a daunting task.

After marveling at the towering Gateway Arch (which no motorist during Route 66's heyday ever saw!) and a stop at historic Union Station, it's worth your time to stop in at the **Eat-Rite Diner** at 622 Choteau Avenue, a tiny little dive that's a few blocks south of the Cardinal's Busch Stadium. During the daytime, you have to elbow up to the counter – which only seats 13 customers at a time – and you might share the space with cops, postal workers, and even local celebrities like Chuck Berry, Mayor Francis Slay, and others. At night, though, it's a true classic diner of Route 66, where you find yourself eating next to people you don't know, that you'll never see again, who didn't attend your high school, and don't care what you do for a living. They just want a good burger and the Eat-Rite is where you'll find it. It's a place that earned the motto "Eat-Rite, or don't eat at all." The menu hasn't changed much in 45 years, because it doesn't have to.

City records aren't clear, but the brick walls of 622 Chouteau Avenue were likely laid in the 1930s. The nearby St. Raymond's Maronite Church was a hub for Lebanese immigrants back then, and two of them, Elias and Elizabeth Mahanna, began grilling burgers there in 1935. They called it White Kitchen. Eventually, the location was purchased by the Powers family, who really put the place on the map.

During this period, the heyday of Route 66, the concept of the diner took off across America. By the 1940's, when the post-war economy started to boom, blue-collar families found themselves with extra cash to eat out. In St. Louis, L.B. Powers' family rode that wave. L.B.'s uncle ran the Courtesy Diner at Olive and 18th Streets. Employed there at age 16, L.B. fell in love with a customer – a receptionist named Dorcas, whom he quickly married. Before long, the couple had five children and had taken over six diners on the south side of the city, including the old White Kitchen. They started calling the chain Eat-Rite in 1963.

By that time, America's middle class was the city for the suburbs, and diners followed them. Restaurant owners tried to spruce up their eateries by adding booths and waitresses and hiding the kitchens, but the Eat-Rite on Chouteau Avenue stayed like it was: just a kitchen, counter, and stools. The neighborhood had turned into a slum, but the Powers' stuck it out. Their gamble paid off in the 1980s, when Ralston-Purina starting cleaning up the area. They eventually sold off the other Eat-Rites to employees and friends, but they held onto the place on Choteau Avenue.

Today, L.B. and Dorcas no longer work the counter, but the restaurant is part of the family. They have relegated Eat-Rite's bookkeeping to their daughter, Tina. Two of their sons married Eat-Rite waitresses; one of them, David, works the morning shift, sometimes with his son, Josh. Many Eat-Rite employees have stuck with the family for decades, some of them speaking of L.B. and Dorcas as adoptive parents.

In recent times, St. Louis has had it tough. The policeman's shot that killed a young man in Ferguson, Missouri, in 2014 seized the attention of the entire country. The fallout from the incident made local residents realize that they don't enjoy protection, power, or money in equal measure – and that no one agrees on who is to blame for that, let alone how it can be fixed. Eat-Rite itself had a rough time that fall. Twice, its exterior was hit by vehicles. The first time was so bad the owners had to shutter the place for a month to replace a wall. Inside the eatery, the atmosphere was tense as unrest gripped the city.

But the staff kept pouring the coffee and flipping the burgers. Regulars kept coming back to sip from the cups and munch on the sandwiches. Curious travelers kept dropping in, going away with a smile.

The Eat-Rite will endure, just like the city that surrounds it.

Beer So Good Some Will Die for It... Legends & Lore of the Lemp Mansion

Not far off one of Route 66's southern routes through the city is a place that has become known throughout the country for its many legends and tales of ghosts. It is a house that is linked closely to perhaps the greatest industry in St. Louis's history. In 1929, Gerald Holland wrote in the *American Mercury* magazine that "whatever odium may be attached to beer in other parts of the Republic, its status in St. Louis is as firmly grounded as James Eads' span across the Mississippi... beer made St. Louis."

And he was right. Beer was the lifeblood of St. Louis for decades, especially after the arrival of thousands of German settlers in the 1830s. They wanted

The Lemp Mansion in St. Louis, regarded as one of the most haunted houses in America.

beer and were determined to have it, creating brewing empires whose memories still linger today.

The Lemp family came to prominence in the middle 1800s as one of the premier brewing families of St. Louis. For years, they were the fiercest rival of Anheuser-Busch and the first makers of lager beer in middle America, but today, they are largely forgotten and remembered more for the house they once built than for the beer they once brewed. That house stands now as a fitting memorial to decadence, wealth, tragedy, and suicide. Perhaps for this reason, there is a sadness that hangs over the place and an eerie feeling that has remained from its days of disrepair and abandonment. It has since been restored into a restaurant and inn, but yet the sorrow seems to remain. By day, the mansion is a bustling restaurant, filled with people and activity, but at night, after everyone is gone and the doors have been locked tight...

Someone – or something -- still walks the halls of the Lemp Mansion.

The story of the Lemp brewing empire began in 1836 when Johann Adam Lemp came to America. He lived for a time in Cincinnati and then came west to St. Louis. In 1838, he opened a small mercantile store at what is now

Delmar and Sixth Streets. In addition to common household items, he sold vinegar and beer that he made himself. Both items were soon in great demand, so he opened a small plant and offered beer from a small pub that was attached to the factory. During this time, Adam introduced to St. Louis to one of the first lager beers in America. This new beer was a great change from the English-type ales that had previously been popular, and the lighter beer soon became a regional favorite. Business prospered and by 1845, the popularity of the beer was enough to allow him to discontinue vinegar production and concentrate on beer alone.

The company expanded rapidly, thanks to a demand for the beer. Needing a larger operation, plus a cool location to lager the beer, which meant it had to be stored for a time in a cool place, he purchased land above a limestone cave south of the city. The cave, which was located at the present-day corner of Cherokee and De Menil Place, could be kept cool by chopping ice from the nearby Mississippi River and depositing it inside. Adam excavated and expanded the cave to make room for the wooden beer casks and soon, the new company was in operation. The Lemp Western Brewing Company grew throughout the 1840s and within a few years, was one of the largest in the city.

William Lemp

Adam Lemp went from a poor immigrant to one of the most respected men in the city. He died in August 1862 and left his thriving business in the hands of his son, William. Under his leadership, the brewery began to grow in ways that Adam could have never conceived of.

William Lemp had been born in Germany in 1836, just before his parents came to America. He spent his childhood there and was brought to St. Louis by his father at age 12. He was educated at St. Louis University, and after graduation, he joined his father at Western Brewery. At the outbreak of the Civil War, he enlisted in the military and served with the St. Louis Home Guard, which was pro-Union. He was mustered out after taking part in the defense of the St. Louis Arsenal. Soon after, he married Julia Feickert and the couple would have nine children together.

After his father's death, William began to expand the brewery. He purchased a five-block area around the storage house on Cherokee Street, which was located above the lagering caves, and began the construction of a new brewery complex. By the 1870s, the Lemp factory was regarded as the largest in the entire city. A bottling plant was added in 1877, and artificial refrigeration was installed one year later. Lemp had a fascination with progress and new inventions and constantly updated the operation.

By the middle 1890s, the Lemp brewery was becoming known all over America. The company's most popular line, Falstaff, became a favorite across the country, something that had never been accomplished by a regional brewery before. Lemp was the first brewery to establish coast-to-coast distribution of its beer, shipping it out in refrigerated railroad cars. After expanding across America, Lemp also spread to overseas markets, and by the late 1890s, the beer could be found in Canada, Mexico, Britain, Germany, Central and South America, the West Indies, the Hawaiian Islands, Australia, Japan, and beyond. The brewery, ranked as the eighth largest in the country, had grown to the point that it employed over 700 men and as many as 100 horses were needed to pull the delivery wagons in St. Louis alone. Construction of new buildings, and renovations of the current ones, continued on a daily basis at the Lemp brewery.

The Lemp's brewery made beer that became popular all over the country. Their most famous brand was "Falstaff," which was advertised using the Lemp's shield logo.

In addition to William Lemp's financial success, he was also well-liked and popular among the citizens of St. Louis. He was on the board of several organizations, including the planning committee for the 1904 World's Fair, and many others. His family life was happy and his sons were very involved in the business. In November 1892, when the Western Brewery was incorporated as the William J. Lemp Brewing Co., his son, William Jr., was named as vice-president and his brother, Louis, was made superintendent. William Jr., or Billy as he was commonly known, was born in St. Louis on August 13, 1867. He attended Washington University and the United States Brewer's Academy in New York. He was well-known in St. Louis for his flamboyant lifestyle, and in 1899 married Lillian Handlan, the daughter of a wealthy St. Louis manufacturer.

Louis was born on January 11, 1870. He learned the brewer's trade from some of the best master brewers in Germany and assisted his brother in the management of the company. He became involved with several political and civic organizations in St. Louis and as a young man explored his passion for

The Lemp Brewery was one of the largest in the city, employing hundreds of men and shipping beer all across the country, and around the world.

sports. He would turn this passion into horses and became a successful breeder. In 1906, he sold his interest in the brewery and moved to New York to work with horses permanently. He and his wife, Agnes, had one daughter, Louise, and Louis died in New York in October 1931.

William's other sons were Frederick, Charles, and Edwin and he had three daughters, Anna, Elsa, and Hilda. In 1897, Hilda married the son of one of William's best friends, Milwaukee brewer Frederick Pabst. William and Julia also had one other child, an infant that died that was not carried to term.

During the time of the Lemp Brewery's greatest success, William Lemp also purchased a home for his family a short distance away from the brewery complex. The house was built by Jacob Feickert, Julia Lemp's father, in 1868, and was likely financed by William. In 1876, Lemp purchased it outright for use as a residence and as an auxiliary brewery office. Although already an impressive house before, Lemp immediately began renovating and expanding it and turning it into a showplace of the period. The mansion boasted elegant artwork, handcrafted wood decor, ornately painted ceilings, large beautiful bathrooms, and even an elevator that replaced the main staircase in 1904. It was a unique and wondrous place and one fitting of the first family of St. Louis brewing.

Ironically, in the midst of all of this happiness and success, the Lemp family's troubles truly began.

The first death in the family was that of Frederick Lemp, William Sr.'s favorite son and the heir apparent to the Lemp empire. He had been groomed for years to take over the family business and was known as the most ambitious and hardworking of the Lemp children. Frederick had been born on November 20, 1873, and attended both Washington University, where he received a degree in mechanical engineering, and the United States Brewers Academy. In 1898, Frederick married Irene Verdin and the couple was reportedly very happy. Frederick was well-known in social circles and was regarded as a friendly and popular fellow. He also spent countless hours at the brewery, working hard to improve the company's future. Some would later say that he worked himself to death.

In 1901, Frederick's health began to fail and he temporarily moved to Pasadena, California, for health reasons. By December, he was greatly improved and after his parents visited with him after Thanksgiving, William returned to St. Louis

Frederick Lemp

with hopes that his son would be returned to him soon. Unfortunately, that never happened. On December 12, Frederick suffered a sudden relapse and he died at the age of only 28. His death was brought about by heart failure, due to a complication of other diseases.

Frederick's death was devastating to his parents, especially to his father. Brewery secretary Henry Vahlkamp later wrote that when news came of the young man's death, William Lemp "broke down utterly and cried like a child... He took it so seriously that we feared it would completely shatter his health and looked for the worst to happen."

Lemp's friends and co-workers said that he was never the same again after Frederick's death. It was obvious to all of them that he was not coping well and he began to slowly withdraw from the world. He was soon rarely seen in public. Before his son's death, Lemp had taken pleasure in paying the men each week. He also would join the workers in any department and work alongside them in their daily activities or go personally among them and discuss any problems or any questions they had. After Frederick died, though, these practices ceased almost completely.

William slowly recovered from his terrible loss, but then on January 1, 1904, he received the crushing news that his closest friend, Frederick Pabst, had died. William fell apart after this and by February 13, 1904, his suffering became unbearable.

When William awoke that morning, he ate breakfast and mentioned to one of the servants that he was not feeling well. He finished eating, excused himself, and went back upstairs to his bedroom. Around 9:30, he took a .38 caliber Smith & Wesson revolver and shot himself in the head with it. There was no one else in the house at the time of the shooting except for the servants. A servant girl, upon hearing the sound of the gunshot, ran to the door but she found it locked. She immediately ran to the brewery office, about a half-block away, and summoned Billy and Edwin. They hurried back to the house and broke down the bedroom door. Inside, they found their father lying on the bed in a pool of blood. The revolver was still gripped in his right hand and there was a gaping and bloody wound at his right temple. At that point, Lemp was still breathing but unconscious.

They called the family physician, Dr. Henry J. Harnisch, by telephone and he came at once. He and three other doctors examined William, but there was nothing they could do. William died just as his wife returned home from a shopping trip downtown. No suicide note was ever found.

Billy Lemp

The Lemp Brewery was very involved in the 1904 World's Fair and Billy took his father's place on the various boards that he was supposed to sit on. Later that year, he became the new president of the company. Billy was a volatile individual but had a good head for business. He spent a fortune on his lavish lifestyle, but the company was in its heyday and was making more money than can be imagined. In 1899, he had married Lillian Handlan, the daughter of a wealthy manufacturer, who had been nicknamed the "Lavender Lady" because of her fondness for dressing in that color. They had a stormy marriage and in 1906, became embroiled in a messy, scandalous divorce trial that had the whole city talking. When it was over, Lillian left St. Louis and Billy went into seclusion at his country estate. In 1915, he married Ellie Limberg, the widow of St. Louis brewer Rudolph Limberg and daughter of Caspar Koehler, president of the Columbia Brewery.

In 1911, the last major improvements were made to the Lemp brewery when giant grain elevators were erected on the south side of the complex. With the shadow of Prohibition beginning to fall across the land, Lemp, like many other breweries, began producing a near-beer malt beverage called Cerva. While Cerva did sell moderately well at first, revenues were nowhere near enough to cover the operating expenses used to make it. Eventually, it would be abandoned. It was also in 1911 that the Lemp mansion was converted and remodeled into the new offices of the brewing company with private offices and rooms for the clerks.

Business was slow for all German-American brewers through World War I, but the Lemp Brewery fared worse than some of the others. Billy had allowed the company's equipment to deteriorate and by not keeping abreast of industry innovations, much of the brewing facilities had become outdated.

And to make matters worse, Prohibition had arrived and it had a devastating effect on all American brewers, including the Lemps. Brewers were stunned by the passing of the amendment and by the Volstead Act, which made Prohibition enforceable by law. The more resourceful companies had attempted to market their near-beers, but as alcohol actually became illegal, sales for these inferior brews began to dwindle and then disappear.

This seemed to signal the death of the company. As the individual family members were quite wealthy aside from the profits from the company, there was little incentive to keep the brewery afloat. Billy gave up on the idea that Congress would suddenly repeal Prohibition and he closed the Lemp plant down without notice. The workers learned of the closing when they came to work one day and found the doors shut and the gates locked.

Will decided to simply liquidate the assets of the plant and auction off the buildings. He sold the famous Lemp "Falstaff" logo to brewer Joseph Griesedieck for the sum of $25,000. He purchased the recognizable Falstaff name and shield with the idea that eventually the government would see Prohibition for the folly that it was and that beer would be back. Billy Lemp no longer shared the other man's enthusiasm, though, and in 1922, he saw the brewery sold off to the International Shoe Co. for just $588,000, a small fraction of its estimated worth of $7 million in the years before Prohibition.

It was the end of an era for the Lemp family.

Prohibition was only a part of what turned out to be a dismal decade for the Lemp family. It began with the death of Elsa Lemp, who was born in 1883 and was the youngest child in the family. After the death of her mother in 1906, she became the wealthiest unmarried woman in the city after inheriting a portion of her father's estate. In 1910, she became even richer when she married Thomas Wright, the president of the More-Jones Brass and Metal Co. They moved into a home in Hortense Place in St. Louis' Central West End. During the years between 1910 and 1918, their marriage was reportedly an unhappy and turbulent one. They separated in December 1918, and in February 1919, Elsa filed for divorce. Unlike the sensational divorce of her brother, Elsa's legal battle was kept quiet and the details of the divorce were not revealed. It was granted, however, in less than an hour and the reasons were cited as "general indignities."

Elsa Lemp

By March 8, 1920, though, Elsa and Wright had reconciled and the two were remarried in New York City. They returned home to St. Louis and found their house filled with flowers and cards from friends and well-wishers, but all was not happy with the newly re-married couple. Whether she was plagued by regret or bothered by something else, Elsa slept little that night, claiming that her stomach was bothering her. When her husband awoke the next morning, Elsa told him that she was feeling better but wanted to remain in bed. Wright agreed that this was the best thing for her and he went into the bathroom and turned on the water in the tub.

He later stated that he heard a loud noise and when he went to see what it was, he found his wife in bed. A pistol lay next to her and she had been shot. No suicide note was ever found and Wright claimed that he had no idea she owned a gun. The only other persons present that morning were members of the household staff. None of them heard the shot, nor did they see any sign that Elsa intended to end her life. They quickly summoned Dr. M.B. Clopton and Samuel Fordyce, a family friend. Strangely, the police were not notified of Elsa's death for more than two hours and even then, the news came indirectly through Samuel Fordyce. Wright became "highly agitated" under the scrutiny of the police investigation that followed and his only excuse for not contacting the authorities was that he was bewildered and did not know what to do.

The mysterious circumstances of Elsa's death left many unanswered questions. To this day, there are many who believe she did not commit suicide, but was murdered. That mystery, however, will likely never be solved.

Tragically, Billy was the next family member to die and his death was also mysterious. It was clear that he committed suicide, although no clear cause was ever cited. He took his own life on December 19, 1922. On that morning, Lemp secretary Henry Vahlkamp arrived at the Lemp brewery office to find Billy already at his desk. The two of them were joined shortly after by Olivia Bercheck, a stenographer for the brewery and Billy's personal secretary. Billy had not been feeling well lately and Vahlkamp commented that he looked better.

"You may think so," Billy replied, "but I am feeling worse."

A short time later, while she was downstairs, Oliva Bercheck heard a loud noise. When she came upstairs, she found Billy lying on the floor of his office. He had shot himself in the heart with a .38 caliber revolver. When discovered, Lemp was still breathing, but he expired by the time a doctor could arrive. Captain William Doyle, the lead police investigator on the scene, searched Lemp's pockets and desk for a suicide note, but as with his father and his sister before him, Billy left no indication as to why he believed suicide was the answer to his problems.

Oddly, Lemp seemed to have no intention of suicide, even a short time before. Apparently, the final turn in his downward spiral had come on quite suddenly. After the sale of the brewery, he had discussed selling off the rest of the assets, like land parcels and saloon locations, and planned to then just "take it easy." Not long after that announcement, he had even put his country estate up for sale, stating that he planned to travel to Europe for a while. Even a week before his death, he had dined with his friend August A. Busch, who said that Lemp seemed "cheerful" at the time and that he gave no indication that he was worrying about business or anything else. "He was a fine fellow," Busch added, "and it is hard to believe that he has taken his own life."

With Billy gone and his surviving brothers involved with their own endeavors, it seemed that the days of the Lemp empire had come to an end at last. The two brothers still in St. Louis had left the family enterprise long before it had closed down. Charles worked in banking and finance and Edwin had entered a life in seclusion at his estate in Kirkwood, Missouri, in 1911. The great fortune they had amassed was more than enough to keep the surviving members of the family comfortable through the Great Depression and beyond.

But the days of Lemp tragedy were not yet over.

Disaster continued for the Lemp family. William Lemp III seemed to have inherited his father's troubles with women and went through a nasty divorce in 1936. Three years later, though, he attempted to revive the Lemp name and entered into an agreement with Central Breweries of East St. Louis, Illinois, and licensed them to use the Lemp name in connection with their beer. In return, the brewery would pay him royalties on all beer sold with the name of Lemp. In October 1939, Central changed its name to the William J. Lemp Brewing Company and launched a massive advertising campaign to announce the rebirth of the famous Lemp name. Lemp beer began to officially be brewed again on November 1, and initial sales exceeded all expectations. The new endeavor seemed destined for success.

In the end, it barely lasted a year. By September 1940, the William J. Lemp Brewing Company was in serious trouble. They had accumulated a mountain of liabilities and owed back taxes, payrolls, accounts, and interest on second mortgage bonds. Trading on the company's common stock was suspended on December 19, because the company was deemed insolvent and wiped out. Early the following year, it was officially bankrupt.

The once strong name of Lemp was now unable to dominate the market as it once had. Ems Brewing Co. took over the brewery in December and they immediately terminated the contract with William Lemp III. Starting on March 1, 1945, they discontinued the name "Lemp" in connection with beer. The plan to bring the Lemp label back to life had failed miserably and the Lemp empire had now breathed its last.

William never lived to see it all fall apart. He suffered a massive brain hemorrhage in December 1943, and died where he was standing.

By the late 1920s, only Charles and Edwin Lemp remained from the immediate family. Throughout his life, Charles was never much involved with the Lemp Brewery, although he was named as treasurer around 1900 and was second vice-president in 1911. His interests had been elsewhere, and when the family home was renovated into offices, he made his residence at the Racquet Club in St. Louis.

He ended his connections with the family business that same year and took the first of what would be many positions in the banking and financial industries. In 1917, he became vice-president of the German Savings Institution and then on to Liberty Central Trust in 1921. He stayed on here for several years and eventually got into the automobile casualty business as president of the Indemnity Company of America. In 1929, Charles moved back to the Lemp mansion and the house became a private residence once more.

He continued to look after his real estate holdings and investments, and among them was the East St. Louis, Columbia and Waterloo electric railroad line, which went out of business in 1932. Lemp also enjoyed traveling, which he did extensively until World War II interfered. He was also involved with politics and was a powerful member of the Democratic Party in St. Louis.

Despite his very visible business and political life, Charles remained a mysterious figure who became even odder and more reclusive with age. He remained a bachelor his entire life and lived alone in his old rambling house with only his two servants, Albert and Lena Bittner, for company. By the age of 77, he was arthritic, quite ill and in constant pain. Legend has it that he was deathly afraid of germs and wore gloves to avoid any contact with bacteria. When he could stand his ailments no more, he ended his life.

On May 10, 1949, Alfred Bittner went to the kitchen and prepared breakfast for Charles as he normally did. He then placed the breakfast tray on the desk in the office next to his bedroom. Bittner later recalled that the door to the bedroom was closed and he did not look inside. At about 8:00, Bittner returned to the office to remove the tray and found it to be untouched. Concerned, he opened the bedroom door to see if Charles was awake and discovered that he was dead from a bullet wound to the head. Bittner hurried to inform his wife of what had happened and she contacted Richard Hawes, Lemp's nephew, who then summoned the police to the mansion.

When the police arrived, they found Charles still in bed and lightly holding a .38 caliber Army Colt revolver in his right hand. He was the only one of the family who had left a suicide note behind. He had dated the letter May 9, and had written "In case I am found dead blame it on no one but me" and had signed it at the bottom.

The Lemp family, which had once been so large and prosperous, had now been almost utterly destroyed in a span of less than a century. Only Edwin Lemp remained and he had long avoided the life that had turned so tragic for the rest of his family. He was known as a quiet, reclusive man who had walked away from the Lemp Brewery in 1913 to live a peaceful life on his secluded estate in Kirkwood. Here, he communed with nature and became an excellent gourmet cook, animal lover, and conservationist. He collected fine art and entertained his intimate friends.

Edwin managed to escape from the family "curse" but as he grew older, he did become more eccentric and developed a terrible fear of being alone. He never spoke about his family or their tragic lives, but it must have preyed on him all the same. His fears caused him to simply entertain more and to keep a companion with him at his estate almost all the time. Edwin passed away quietly of natural causes at age 90 in 1970.

After the death of Charles Lemp, the family mansion was sold and turned into a boarding house. Shortly after that, it fell on hard times and began to deteriorate, along with the nearby neighborhood. In later years, stories began to emerge that residents of the boarding house often complained of ghostly knocks and phantom footsteps in the house. As these tales spread, it became increasingly hard to find tenants to occupy the rooms, and because of this, the old Lemp Mansion was rarely filled.

The house's decline continued until 1975, when Richard Pointer and his family purchased it. The Pointers began remodeling and renovating the place, working for many years to turn it into a combination restaurant and inn. But they were soon to find out that they were not alone in the house. The bulk of the remodeling was done in the 1970s and during this time, construction workers reported that ghostly events were occurring in the house. Almost all of them confessed that they believed the place was haunted and told of feeling as though they were being watched. They spoke of hearing unexplained sounds and complained of tools that vanished and then returned in different places from where they had been left.

At one point in the renovations, a painter was brought in to work on the ceilings. He stayed in the house overnight while he completed the job. One day, he ran downstairs to tell one of the Pointers that he had heard the sound of horses' hooves on the cobblestones outside his window. Pointer convinced the painter that he was mistaken; there were no horses and no cobblestones outside the house. In time, the man finished the ceilings and left, but the story stayed on Pointer's mind. Later that year, he noticed that some of the grass in the yard had turned brown. He dug it up and found that beneath the top level of soil was a layer of cobblestones. During the Lemps' residency in the house, that portion of the yard had been a drive leading to the carriage house.

Later in the restoration, another artist was brought in to restore the painted ceiling in one of the front dining rooms. It had been covered over with paper years before. While he was lying on his back on the scaffolding, the artist felt a sensation of what he believed was a "spirit" moving past him. It frightened him so badly that he left the house without his brushes and tools and refused to return and get them. A few months after this event, an elderly man came into the restaurant and told one of the staff members that he had once been a driver for the Lemp family. He explained that the ceiling in the dining room had been papered over because William Lemp hated the design that had been painted on it. The staff members, upon hearing this story, recalled the artist saying that he had gotten the distinct impression that the "spirit" he encountered had been angry. Was it perhaps because he was restoring the unwanted ceiling painting?

During the restorations, Pointer's son, Dick, lived alone in the house and became quite an expert on the ghostly manifestations. One night, he was lying in bed reading when he heard a door slam loudly in another part of the house. No one else was supposed to be there and he was sure that he had locked all of the doors. Fearing that someone might have broken in, he and his dog, a Doberman pinscher named Shadow, decided to take a look around. The dog was spooked by this time, and having also heard the sound, she had her ears turned up, listening for anything else. They searched the entire house and found no one there. Every door was locked, just as Pointer had left them. He reported that the same thing happened again about a month later; again, nothing was found.

After the restaurant opened, staff members began to report their own odd experiences. Glasses were seen to lift off the bar and fly through the air, sounds were often heard that had no explanation and some people even glimpsed apparitions that appeared and vanished at will. In addition, many customers and visitors to the house reported some pretty weird incidents. It was said that doors locked and unlocked on their own, the piano in the bar played by itself, voices and sounds came from nowhere and the ghost of a woman was seen occasionally. Some claimed that it was Lillian Handlan, Billy's ex-wife and the famed "Lavender Lady," even though she never actually lived in the house. Perhaps the indignities that she suffered at the hands of her former husband managed to draw her to his family's home after death.

And while the ghostly atmosphere of the place has admittedly attracted a number of curious patrons, it has also caused the Pointers to lose a number of valuable employees. One of them was a former waitress named Bonnie Strayhorn, who encountered an unusual customer while working one day. The restaurant had not yet opened for business when she saw a dark-haired man seated at one of the tables in the rear dining room. She was surprised that someone had come in so early, but she went over to ask if he would like a cup of coffee. He simply sat unmoving and did not answer. Bonnie frowned and glanced away for a moment. When she looked back moments later, the man was gone. She has continued to maintain that he could not have left the room in the brief seconds when she was not looking at him. After that incident, she left the Lemp Mansion and went to work in a non-haunted location.

The house has attracted ghost hunters from around the country. Many of them are lured by the publicity the house has received as a haunted location. The mansion has appeared in scores of magazines, newspaper articles, books, and television shows over the years, first gaining national attention in November 1980, when *Life* magazine included it in an article entitled "Terrifying Tales of Nine Haunted Houses."

As the years have passed, the Lemp Mansion has continued to lure visitors who are looking for strange and ghostly happenings and I have stayed the night here many times myself. As Paul Pointer once said, those who come to this house are rarely disappointed and I would have to agree. While not all of my stays at this old house have been eventful ones, at least when it comes to ghosts, I have to admit that the vivid sense of history that I have experienced when I'm here more than makes up for the lack of anything supernatural. If you're a ghost hunter, or a history buff, then I encourage you to visit the mansion of the once-mighty Lemp family. Their empire may have crumbled long ago but there is much to see here among the ruins of yesteryear.

Route 66's Best Frozen Custard

Another alignment of U.S. 66 through St. Louis took travelers through another maze, which eventually deposited them on Chippewa Street. As a reward for navigating the twists and turns, travelers should always stop at **Ted Drewes Frozen Custard**, where locals and tourists alike have beaten the summer heat with frozen deliciousness since 1941.

It all started with Ted Drewes, Sr., who was a St. Louis celebrity after winning the Muny Tennis Championships each year from 1925 to 1936. He

also won the National Public Parks Singles title four years in a row. During the late 1920s and 1930s, he traveled with his family to Florida every winter to continue playing tennis. While in Florida, Ted Sr. opened his first frozen custard stand in 1929. In 1930, he opened another stand on Natural Bridge Road in St. Louis and then a second on South Grand in 1931. In 1941, the family opened the Chippewa Street location on what was then Route 66.

The place was a runaway success, not only for locals, but for almost anyone traveling U.S. 66 when they came through St. Louis. As business got bigger, so did the stand. Ted Drewes, Jr. decided to expand the number of serving windows several times, eventually reaching 12 windows by 1985. The stand became famous for its custard, delicious hot fudge sundae, and for the most popular item, the "concrete," which was created in 1959. The concrete is a malt or shake that is so thick it has to be served upside down.

And it's not just frozen custard, Ted Drewes Christmas trees have become an annual tradition that dates back more than 50 years. Each fall, family members travel to their farm in Nova Scotia, where they personally select which Canadian Balsam firs they are bringing back home to St. Louis. Ted, Jr. once joked that the same people buy Christmas trees from them every year, "and they don't even know we sell frozen custard!"

Across the street from this Route 66 icon is another longtime highway fixture, the **Donut Drive-In**. Opened in 1953, little has changed about the place since then. In fact, in all of those years, the shop has only had three different owners. If you're passing through St. Louis, it's a place you don't want to miss.

When Ted Drewes and the Donut Drive-In opened, Chippewa Street was a quiet little road that had become one of the many alternates for Highway 66 through the city. Only occasional hotels and restaurants could be found as Route 66 prepared to leave the urban sprawl of St. Louis behind. As Chippewa Street became Watson Road, business and traffic began to thin a little. After sunset, some distance from the bright lights of St. Louis, things were a little darker on the edge of town. This was a place where people with secrets came so that those secrets could be kept.

It was the home of Route 66's most famous "no-tell motel."

Mystery & Mayhem at the Coral Court Motel

Few motels on Route 66 -- or just about anywhere, for that matter -- had the kind of questionable reputation that was enjoyed by the infamous Coral Court Motel, located just outside the city limits of St. Louis. When it came to mystery, intrigue, and the sheer tawdriness of the "no-tell motel," you couldn't beat the Coral Court.

The brick motor court, located at 7755 Watson Road, was designed in the 1940s and was a classic example of an Art Deco-style motel. The Coral Court first became famous because of its prime location on Route 66. Heading west on the Mother Road, it was the perfect place to stop after a day-long drive from Chicago. Later, it would earn its seamy reputation as a perfect hiding spot for philanderers and for its grim connection to a St. Louis kidnapping and murder case.

The Coral Court was first imagined by John Carr in 1941. It was painstakingly designed by architect Adolph L. Struebig, who was hired by Carr to give him a little something special. There were a lot of "mom and pop" motels in those days, with eight or so units, but Carr didn't want that. He told Struebig that he wanted something outstanding. Construction was started that summer and by early 1942, the Coral Court was greetings its first guest. The first 10 bungalows were built in a grand style with honey-colored, glazed bricks and large glass block windows. Each unit had two rooms and two garages and this helped the Coral Court to become an immediate success.

After World War II, 23 additional units (or 46 rooms) were designed by architect Harold T. Tyre. They used the same materials and varied only slightly from the original units. The new units featured triangular glass block windows, but the overall look of the place remained. Another expansion took place in 1953, with the addition of three more (ordinary-looking) two-story units, also designed by Tyre, at the back of the property. A swimming pool was added in the early 1960s.

A postcard from the Coral Court Motel

For many locals, the Coral Court was sort of a rite of passage. Attending a late night, post-prom party or swiping a Coral Court towel or matchbook was the thing to do for St. Louis teenagers. For those who wanted to remain anonymous, the motel was the place to go for an illicit rendezvous. It soon began to be known as St. Louis' best "no-tell motel." The reasons why were simple: the rooms could be rented for a rest period of 4 or 8 hours, which was originally created as a courtesy for truck drivers, but had obvious benefits for lovers. Each room had its own garage, so cars were hidden from prying eyes. And the management of the Coral Court was absolutely discreet. Thanks to this, the legend of the motel spread up and down Route 66, from Chicago to Los Angeles.

The most publicly notorious moment in the motel's history, though, came from its connection to the Bobby Greenlease kidnapping case in 1953. The incident received national attention and became known as one of the most tragic crimes of the 1950s. It also brought lasting infamy to the Coral Court, largely due to the fact that the Coral Court was used as a hideout by the kidnappers – and the fact that half of the $600,000 ransom vanished at the motel.

Bobby Greenlease, Jr. was the son of Robert and Virginia Greenlease, residents of Mission Hills, Kansas, a prominent suburb of Kansas City. Robert Greenlease was one of the largest Cadillac dealers in the nation. In comparison to the wealth of the Greenlease family, Bobby's kidnappers, Carl Austin Hall and Bonnie Heady, were dead broke. However, both had known privilege earlier in their lives. It had been at military school that Hall had met Paul Greenlease, Bobby's older, adopted brother. Hall later inherited a large sum of money from his father, but lost it all in bad business ventures. After that, he turned to crime. He was arrested for robbing cab drivers -- his total take from his "crime spree" was only $38 -- and he was sent to the Missouri State Penitentiary. In prison, he dreamed of the "big score" and began planning the kidnapping that would help him to retire.

Bobby Greenlease

After getting out of prison, Hall moved to St. Joseph, Missouri, and he started dating Bonnie Heady. She was no catch, having a reputation not only for being "easy," but also for occasionally dabbling in prostitution. The good news was that she owned her own home and she and Hall often drank themselves into a stupor there, never being bothered by anyone. They had a violent relationship, and in fact, when Heady was later arrested for kidnapping, she still bore the bruises of her latest beating. Her willingness to put up with Hall's abuse is probably a clue as to why she agreed to go along with his kidnapping scheme.

During the summer months of 1953, Hall and Heady made repeated trips to Kansas City to follow the Greenlease family. After some debate, they decided that Bobby would be the easiest prey. At that time, the boy was enrolled at Notre Dame de Sion, a fashionable Catholic school. In the late morning of September 28, Heady entered the school and told a nun that she was Bobby's aunt. She and Virginia Greenlease had been shopping at the Country Club Plaza, she told the nun, when Virginia had suffered a heart attack. Heady said that she had come to take Bobby to the hospital. When Bobby was brought out of his class, he immediately took Heady's hand in his, as if he knew her. Heady would later say, "he was so trusting."

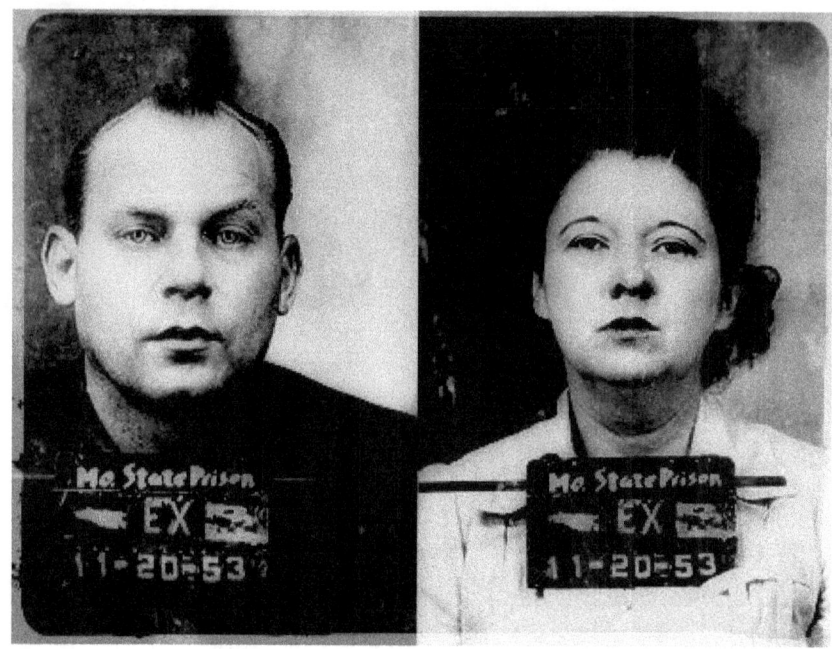

Murderous kidnappers Carl Austin Hall and Bonnie Heady

Heady met Hall a few minutes later at the Katz Drugstore and they drove across town, and across the state line into Kansas. When Bobby was taken across the state line, the Lindbergh Law (named for the famous kidnapping case) went into effect and the taking of Bobby Greenlease became a federal crime. And it was just about to get worse.

In a vacant field in Overland Park, Heady got out of the car and walked a short distance away while Hall killed Bobby. First, he tried to strangle the little boy, but the rope he used was too short. Then, he punched him in the face, knocking out one tooth. Finally, he pushed Bobby down and shot him in the head with a .38 caliber pistol. The boy was dead less than 30 minutes after he had been abducted. After that, they drove back to St. Joseph and buried the body in the backyard of Heady's home. Hall had dug the grave the night before. After the body was covered, he planted flowers in the freshly churned soil, hoping to cover all evidence of the horrific crime.

The Greenlease family got their first inkling of trouble when the nun who had released Bobby from school called to inquire about Virginia's health. Soon after, they received ransom demands from Hall. He also mailed them a pin that Bobby had been wearing when he was taken. The killer demanded a ransom of $600,000 in $10 and $20 bills.

Robert Greenlease called several of his closest friends and they began putting together the money. He also called the head of the local bank, Arthur Eisenhower (brother of Dwight D. Eisenhower) and the two men put together a plan to record the serial numbers of all of the ransom bills. While the money was being accumulated, Hall called the Greenlease residence repeatedly. He continually reassured them that Bobby was alive. Finally, a week after the kidnapping, the money was delivered.

Actually, it was delivered two times because Hall couldn't find it the first time.

Finally, after almost bungling a second money drop on a dark country road, Hall was able to retrieve the ransom. It was just after midnight on October 5, when Hall made one last phone call to a friend of Robert Greenlease, Robert Ledterman, who had been assisting with the ransom payment. He promised Ledterman that the family would have Bobby back within 24 hours.

While Robert and Virginia waited for word of where to find their son, Hall and Heady drove to St. Louis with a money bag that weighed more than 85 pounds. As they traveled, word of the kidnapping leaked to the media and it became a nationwide sensation. When they arrived in St. Louis, Hall and Heady were stunned to find themselves at the center of the story. They ditched their car and started using taxicabs. They rented a small apartment on Arsenal Street on the south side of St. Louis and decided to lay low. Hall soon grew restless and tired of Heady. One afternoon, he left the drunken woman passed out in the apartment and vanished. He left behind a few thousand dollars, but kept the rest for himself. He was off to live "the good life."

A short time later, Hall hooked up with an ex-con cab driver and a prostitute. The three of them ended up at the Coral Court Motel on Route 66. It was renowned as a place where a fellow could stay for a while with no questions asked. Rumor had it that the motel's owner, John Carr, was mob-connected and had operated a posh brothel in St. Louis for many years.

Hiding out at the Coral Court, Hall began to lavish money on his seedy new companions. The prostitute would later say that Hall stayed so drunk, and was so nervous, that he couldn't perform sexually. As for the cab driver, Hall had turned the man into his own personal valet. He gave the man fistfuls of money and told him to buy new clothes and whatever else he thought he might need. What the cab driver brought him was trouble. The owner of the cab company was a man named Joe Costello, a well-known local gangster. When Costello heard about the big-spending customer, he contacted a corrupt St. Louis police lieutenant named Louis Shoulders. Since Costello and Shoulders always denied stealing the ransom money, it is unknown whether Costello figured out that Hall was the Greenlease kidnapper and gave Shoulders a tip for the arrest of a lifetime -- or whether they simply conspired to rip Hall off.

What is known is that Hall, guided by the cab driver, rented an apartment on the edge of St. Louis. A short time after moving in, he was arrested by Shoulders and a patrolman named Elmer Dolan. Hall was picked up for questioning about the large amount of money that he was flashing around. He was taken to the police station on Newstead Avenue and allegedly, the remaining ransom money was stuffed into a suitcase and a footlocker. The footlocker, which contained about $300,000, was recovered, but the elusive suitcase was never seen again.

Once he was arrested, Hall almost immediately broke down. Heady was quickly arrested at the small apartment where Hall had abandoned her. On October 7, police officers and reporters raced for Heady's house in St. Joseph, where they dug up Bobby's body from the backyard.

And once Hall and Heady confessed to the crime, they resigned themselves to being executed for the murder. When a federal jury in Kansas City returned the verdict, it has been said that Heady actually smiled. On December 18, only 81 days after the kidnapping, Hall and Heady were executed side-by-side at the Missouri State Penitentiary. The pair had declined to seek mercy at the trial and did not appeal the verdict. Missouri authorities had a second chair installed in the gas chamber so that Heady and Hall could be executed at the same time. Heady was the only woman to ever be put to death in the Missouri gas chamber and it's said that she talked cheerfully to the guards and the officials while she was being strapped in. She did not fall silent until Hall finally told her to shut up.

Amidst the widespread anger about the murder of Bobby Greenlease, there was also an immediate investigation into the money that went missing. The glory that should have led to promotions for Shoulders and Dolan became a dirty scandal that highlighted the widespread corruption of the St. Louis police department in the 1950s.

The two officers were later convicted in a federal court on perjury charges, for lying about the sequence of events from the time they arrested Hall until the time the money was brought to the police station and counted. Various police clerks and officers testified that they never saw the men carrying anything when they entered the station with Hall, and they certainly did not see the suitcase or the foot locker. Shoulders stated that the money was outside in the car and that he brought it into the station after bringing Hall inside.

The theory was that Shoulders and Dolan, who both left the station on personal errands after booking Hall, returned to Hall's apartment and stole half the money. They brought the remaining half to the station through the rear door. Hall's statement, not surprisingly, directly contradicted that of Shoulders and Dolan. Hall maintained that the money had been left in the apartment when he was arrested.

Over time, numerous theories have been floated as to who actually took the money. Most pointed fingers at Shoulders and his connection with mobster Joe Costello, while others blamed the corruption in the police department itself. Costello was accused of taking the money by the FBI, who followed him for years, tapping his phones, and questioning his associates. They could never make the theft charges stick, but Costello was eventually arrested on weapons charges and sent to prison.

If the cops and Costello didn't take it, where did the money go? Some have suggested that Coral Court owner John Carr may have been involved. If Carr knew about the money (and it's possible that he did), he could have entered Hall's room using a pass key and walked out with half the money, believing that Hall would never miss it. And even if he did miss it, what would he be able to do about it? When John Carr died, he was a multi-millionaire. Could any of that remaining fortune have been part of the Greenlease kidnapping money? Obviously, we will never know.

Whoever took the money, though, it was gone. For many years after, it was news whenever any of the bills linked to the missing Greenlease money turned up. But where was it coming from? No one knew and now, with so many principals in the case long dead, it can only be realized that the vanished money will always remain a mystery – a lingering stain on the history of the Coral Court Motel.

John Carr died in 1984 and left the Coral Court to his wife, Jessie, and head housekeeper, Martha Shutt. Jessie and her second husband, Robert Williams, operated the place until August 1993, but by then, a lack of regular maintenance had taken its toll. Even though many Coral Court fans tried to protect the place from destruction, there was nothing they could do to protect it from the wishes of the owners. They didn't want to bother with the Coral Court anymore and their attorney advised them to sell the property.

As the fate of the place became clear, the concern of its supporters shifted to trying to prevent any further damage to the place while it was on the market. Although the motel was roped off and patrolled regularly by the police, it did not prevent "souvenirs-seekers" and vandals from breaking into the rooms. Some even loaded the bricks into their cars, hoping they would become valuable later on. Tragically, this only brought about the definite destruction of the motel.

The Coral Court was closed in 1993 and razed two years later. The motel was on the market for almost three years but no one could afford the steep price tag and the money that would be needed for renovation. Finally, in June 1995, the motel (except for one unit) was demolished. Luckily for Coral Court supporters, the Missouri Museum of Transportation, with help from scores of volunteers, worked for weeks to disassemble a complete Coral Court unit and move it, piece by piece, to the museum. The exhibit opened in May 2000 and remains on display for anyone who wants to catch a glimpse of the motel's history as it played out on Route 66.

Unfortunately, there is little trace remaining at the site of the Coral Court today. It is now a subdivision called Oak Knoll Manor, although the original, distinctive stone gates are still in place. It's hard to imagine the drama, passion, and excitement that once played out at one of America's original "no-tell motels" but it's a story that could have only taken place on Route 66.

Leaving St. Louis

Not far from the Coral Court were other reminders of Route 66, like the **Wayside Motel** and **La Casa Grande Motel** with flashing neon signs that were sure to get the attention of highway travelers. Both of them remain open today, still seeing a trickle of Highway 66 enthusiasts who are passing through the area.

One lost location is the **66 Auto Court**. In contrast to the Coral Court, it was more typical of the motor courts of the era. The motor court was a series of two-unit stucco bungalows that were placed in a semicircle around a driveway. Each unit had a front and rear entrance. The front opened onto the driveway, the rear onto a grassy courtyard. Each unit offered hot water, heat, insulated rooms, and free radio.

Further along the alignment was the **"66" Park In Theatre**, which was built in suburban Crestwood in 1948. The "66" drive-in provided patrons with free pony rides, sliding boards, a merry-go-round, and, of course, movies under the stars. A pair of frisky bear cubs even entertained the customers in the early days. Before the days of commonplace air conditioning, the drive-in advertised "cool breezes." The concession stand was a busy place and even had baby bottle warmers on hand. During the 1950s and 1960s, weekend crowds, including parents with pajama-clad kids, jammed into the "66" Park In. Teenagers, more interested in the backseat of the car than the movies, used the "66" as a "passion pit." Sometimes on summer nights, cars, trucks, campers, and even school buses, stood bumper to bumper for blocks, all waiting to get in. Located on a prime piece of real estate, the "66" managed to stay open for more than 40 years, an era during which more than half of America's drive-in theaters closed down.

The "66" Park In finally closed for good in 1993 and a year later, was demolished to make room for a shopping center. It's now long gone, but not quite forgotten for those who still dream about the old days of Route 66.

The 66 Park In Theatre lasted for more than 40 years on one of St. Louis's Route 66 alignments.

A few miles to the west, Watson Road (Route 66) merges with the original highway's replacement. It is soon apparent that Interstate 44 has erased short sections of Route 66 in Missouri – but even so, most of it was not destroyed. Beyond the city, long segments of the highway still exist, running parallel to the interstate, serving as frontage roads or as a business loop through a country town. Sometimes it wanders off into the woods or turns into a country or state road. Driving out of St. Louis, past the chain hotels and fast food franchises, a few of the old places – vintage motels, gaudy fireworks stands, and genuine filling stations – still cling to what remains of the old highway.

Along one of the alignments out of St. Louis, at Pond (now part of Wildwood), was the **Big Chief Hotel**, a Spanish Mission Revival building with white stucco walls, terra-cotta tile roof, exposed rafter ends, and a prominent bell tower. It was an unusual look for St. Louis in the 1920s, when it was built. The Big Chief was the brainchild of William Clay Pierce of the Pierce-Pennant Oil Company in St. Louis. His plan was to build a chain of motor courts on Highway 66 between Springfield, Illinois, and Tulsa, Oklahoma, with the intention of bringing first-class hotels to the roadside. It was a brilliant plan that would put the oil and gas company into the hotel business, since it was already making a fortune because of Highway 66. People were traveling like never before. They bought cars and the cars needed gas, which Pierce provided. In the early days of Route 66, motorists tended to camp by the road, or to stay in tourist camps. There were few hotels, except in major cities.

The Big Chief Hotel as it looks today on old U.S. 66

Pierce envisioned something better and the stretch of Highway 66 through Ponds seemed to be the best place for it. The road stood out because, in 1928, it was already paved. It would be years before the rest of Route 66 was fully paved.

Pierce's first experiment was a motor court in Rolla, followed by the Spanish Mission court on the old ridge road at Pond. The Big Chief was unusual in that it was not only one of the first motor courts in Missouri, but it also offered full service dining, an oddity at the time. It was also one of the largest courts in the state. In 1935, a guide to Missouri listed only nine courts with more than 30 cabins. The Big Chief had 62, each with its own garage.

Advertisements boasted that the Big Chief offered cabins with "hot and cold running shower baths," a playground, Conoco gas station, and a grocery store. A one-night stay was $1.50. The dining room offered a 75-cent steak dinner, a 40-cent plate lunch, or a 5-cent sandwich. In the evenings, dining room tables were pushed aside to allow for dancing. Bar service was added when Prohibition ended in 1933.

William Pierce's ambitious plan to tie his chain of motor courts to his service stations was abandoned in 1930. He sold the chain to Henry Sinclair of the Sinclair Refining Company, who planned to extend it to Mexico – but it didn't quite work out that way. In 1933, Highway 66 had been realigned away from the hotel and to the flat lands of the Meramec River Valley. The Big Chief remained popular as a local destination, though, sponsoring a series of fall dances and attracting conferences and meetings.

The Big Chief survived the lean years of World War II by furnishing housing for employees of the nearby Weldon Spring Ordinance Works. That change to longer term housing continued after the war, when the cabins were rented to workers at a Weldon Spring uranium processing plant. By 1949, the restaurant had closed. Over the years the rented cabins fell into disrepair and were demolished. The restaurant building, however, survived, and in the early 1990s was restored and returned to its original function as a restaurant. Listed in the National Register of Historic Places in 2003, the Big Chief is one of the few surviving full-service restaurants left on Missouri Route 66 and provides a feel for roadside stops during the 1930s.

For the first 30 miles or so west of St. Louis, the highway is bordered by the **Henry Shaw Gardenway**, a section that was planted in native trees and shrubs before World War II to honor the man who founded the Missouri Botanical Gardens in St. Louis in 1858. Saplings, which matured into thick stands of hickory, oak, and dogwood, cover the rolling hills on either side of the road. The highway was carved through limestone formations and the trees, native grass, and rugged hills give the traveler a glimpse of the Ozark terrain that will be found further along the road.

Forgotten Summer Resorts

As a traveler motors along U.S. 66, the spectacular Meramec River finally comes into view. Rising in south central Missouri and winding northward to the Mississippi, the Meramec has always been one of the state's most popular recreational streams. The interstate rushes by the Meramec with little regard to the history that once played out here.

During the later years of the nineteenth century, a number of popular summer reposts were developed along the Meramec River, southwest of St. Louis, including Meramec Highlands, Valley Park, and Castle Park. As the Frisco Railroad trains started running on a regular basis to the Meramec Highlands and Valley Park stations, the Meramec River became a popular attraction for wealthy St. Louis families. The high cost of the train fare managed to prohibit frequent visits by the common folk, so the city's elite mostly had the region to themselves.

In 1893, the Frisco Hotel was built in Valley Park. Originally constructed for the track crews who were pushing the railroad west across Missouri, it soon began to appeal to wealthy St. Louis customers who wanted to enjoy the amenities offered on Valley Park's section of the river. The town began to boom with restaurants, grocery stores, and clothing and dry goods stores.

By 1894, the wealthy were well-acquainted with the area when the Meramec Highlands Inn was opened. Providing access to the river on a grand scale, the inn had its own train depot, swimming beach, boathouse, rental cottages, a Chinese pagoda-style dance pavilion, tennis courts, stables, croquet courts, and a mineral water bath house. Offering a sweeping view of the Meramec River Valley, the inn offered 125 state rooms with "sanitary plumbing" and electric lights. It became the premiere resort of the region with a bowling alley, billiards, barbershop, bakery, wine cellar, restaurants, banquet rooms, performance stage, and large verandas, where guests could gather for fresh air and to take in the scenery.

For a few years, the inn attracted not only wealthy St. Louis citizens who wanted to escape the summer heat, but affluent travelers on the railroad, as well. But this success would not last. In 1896, streetcars began operating that deposited guests right on the resort's doorstep, providing one-way passage for just five-cents. This allowed the common folk to afford the trip to the resort areas, too. Soon after, the wealthy clientele began staying away. The patronage of the inn dropped every year from 1900 to 1903, so a concerted bid was made to increase the number of guests during the 1904 World's Fair. The fairgrounds were only an hour from the resort by train. Brochures were printed and heavy advertising appeared, but few came to the Highlands Inn until room rates were dropped to just $1 per night. But this bargain surge in business was not enough to save the place. The inn closed after the following season.

During the next few decades, more attempts to continue the inn's operations were unsuccessful. In 1925, the hotel and its cottages were sold to private individuals. The main building was destroyed by fire in 1926, although 12 of the 15 cottages remain in the hands of private residents today.

Although the wealthy began seeking more secluded resorts, the masses began flocking to the Meramec Highlands in the early twentieth century. Traveling on two electric streetcar lines, they came to the new hotels, lodges, and gambling clubs that sprang up on the banks of the river. The beaches attracted numerous visitors who wanted to escape from the city heat during the summer. By the 1920s, the lower Meramec River was the main recreational spot for thousands of St. Louis visitors. Canoes began to appear on the river for fun-seekers and fishermen alike. People swam and spent their evenings at open-air dance pavilions and spent their money at clubhouses and restaurants.

Staff outside the grand Meramec Highlands Inn

The former Steiny's Inn, now the offices for the Route 66 State Park.

But once again, the good times didn't last. The Depression brought tourist traffic to a standstill. The recreation areas became neglected and abandoned beaches became overgrown. The lodges were empty and the clubhouses fell into disrepair. One after another closed its doors, mostly never to re-open. After the war, when cars replaced trains and streetcars, travelers began to seek out distant places like the Grand Canyon and Yellowstone, and the Meramec River beaches and lodges disappeared for good.

Along Route 66, the highway once passed a resort called **Sylvan Beach**, which was a privately owned amusement park with free picnic grounds and softball diamonds. The riverside was lined with cabins built on stilts so they stayed high and dry when the frequent spring floods arrived.

One remaining hot spot – although it's no longer a business – was a place called **Steiny's Inn**. Opened in 1935 as the Bridgehead Inn, the roadhouse featured a bar, dance floor, and several overnight rooms on the second floor. The place had an excellent reputation and was popular with locals, as well as Highway 66 travelers.

The restaurant was located on the east side of the bridge that spanned the Meramec River and its closest competitor, owned by Edward Steinberg, was located on the west side. In 1946, a spectacular fire left Steinberg's place in ruins and, instead of rebuilding, he bought the Bridgehead Inn and re-named it Steiny's Inn.

The place was purchased by William and Jeanette Klecka in 1972, and they reopened it with its original name. However, in 1980, the Bridgehead Inn moniker was changed again and it became known as Galley West. Today, the building still stands and serves as the offices and visitor's center for the **Route 66 State Park.** It looks much as it did back in the 1940s.

The roadhouse did stop serving food and drinks in the middle 1980s, though, when a catastrophe in a nearby town became publicly known. That little settlement was known as Times Beach and it was a place that gained national infamy at the same time the restaurant was closing its doors.

Times Beach: Modern-Day Ghost Town

The city of St. Louis has always been unlike other major American cities. It is a large sprawling region of suburbs and interconnected towns that make up the metropolitan city as a whole, making it an impossible place to live if you do not own an automobile. With the Mississippi River as the eastern border of St. Louis, the settlers who came here originally had nowhere to go but to the west and the city expanded in that direction. After all of these years, and despite the amount of construction and development that has occurred, once you leave the western suburbs of St. Louis, you enter a rugged, wild region that is marked with rivers, forests, and caves.

Housing plots in the new resort town of Times Beach were part of a newspaper promotion to encourage people to move to the river community — no one had any idea about the problems the town would face a half-century later.

Traveling west on Route 66, motorists soon began to leave the buildings and houses behind. As they reached the Meramec River Valley, they found an area dotted by oddities, including one oddity that can no longer be found on any road map — the town of Times Beach. The former resort community vanished without a trace in 1985. However, its disappearance was a very public one.

Times Beach was started in 1925 along the Meramec River as a promotion for the now defunct *St. Louis Star-Times* newspaper. After purchasing 480 acres of flood plain that had been used for farming, the owners of the newspaper started an unusual campaign to increase the newspaper's circulation. They began offering building lots in the new town for only $67.50

and each one came with a six-month subscription to the newspaper. There was one small catch: to utilize the property, and build a house on it, required the purchase of a second adjoining lot to go with it.

Believe it or not, there were a lot of takers. It was a great location for a summer resort and most of the original structures were cottages that were raised on stilts since the area was prone to flooding. By 1930, residents were building more substantial homes as the placed changed from a resort to a real community. This, along with a growing business district, gave the town a feeling of stability. However, the Great Depression, followed by gas rationing during World War II, combined to make the summer cottages impractical. They were sold off, or abandoned, and the town deteriorated into a low income community of mobile homes and crumbling houses.

In the early 1970s, the unpaved roads in town created a dust problem for Times Beach and so the community hired a waste hauler, Russell Bliss, to blacktop the roads with waste oil. A few years later, the roads were actually paved, but by then, the damage was done. What the city did not know was that Bliss had gotten his waste oil from a subcontractor who had operated a chemical plant in Verona, Missouri – a plant which had produced Agent Orange for the military during the Vietnam War. The waste from the plant contained levels of dioxin that were some 2,000 times higher than the poisonous content in the Agent Orange that had been used to defoliate the jungles of Southeast Asia during the war. And it had been generously sprayed all over Times Beach.

In the fall of 1982, an investigative reporter turned his attention to Times Beach after establishing a link between Bliss and the death of dozens of horses at a stable where he had also sprayed waste oil. This investigation was quickly followed by one launched by the Environmental Protection Agency. Soon, stories began to appear in the press about high levels of dioxin being discovered in the soil. Needless to say, panic spread through the town and every illness, every miscarriage, and every death of an animal was attributed, rightly or wrongly, to the dioxin. On December 5, 1982, the worst flooding in the town's history forced an almost complete evacuation. Days later, the EPA notified residents and town officials, "If you are in town it is advisable for you to leave and if you are out of town, do not return."

In a matter of days, the largely unknown town of Times Beach, Missouri, dominated national headlines and became a grim example of deadly environmental poisoning. By 1985, the mandatory evacuation was completed, negotiated buyouts were underway, and the town site was quarantined.

The empty town, left untouched since the day the population walked away, remained hauntingly alongside the interstate until 1992, when it was finally demolished. All traces of Times Beach, aside from the memories, have since been obliterated. In 1996 and 1997, an incinerator built at the site burned tons of contaminated soil and materials. When completed, the property was

In its final days, Times Beach became a U.S. 66 "ghost town."

certified as clean and was turned over to the state of Missouri. Today, what stands at the site of the ghost town is an abundance of woods, a wild bird sanctuary, and the idyllic Route 66 State Park, which commemorates the Mother Road.

Legends of "Zombie Road"

Not far from Times Beach – and a short distance off old Route 66 – is a ramshackle roadway that has become a place of legend in the region. The broken roadway, which has been dubbed "Zombie Road" (a name by which it was known at least as far back as the 1950s), was once listed on maps as Lawler Ford Road and was constructed in the late 1860s. The dirt and gravel road, which was paved at some point years ago, is now largely impassable by automobile. It was originally built to provide access to the Meramec River and the railroad tracks located along its banks.

In 1868, the Glencoe Marble Company was formed to work the limestone deposits in what is now the Rockwoods Reservation, located nearby. A sidetrack was laid from the deposits to the town of Glencoe and onto the road, crossing the property of James E. Yeatman. The sidetrack from the Pacific Railroad switched off the main line at Yeatman Junction and at this same location, the Lawler Ford Road ended at the river. There is no record as to where the Lawler name came from, but a ford did cross the river at this point into the land belonging to the Lewis family. At times, a boat was used to ferry people across the river, which is undoubtedly why the road was placed at this location.

As time passed, the narrow road began to be used by trucks that hauled quarry stone from railcars and then later fell into disuse. Those who recall the road when it was more widely in use have told me that the narrow, winding lane, which runs through roughly two miles of dense woods, was always enveloped in a strange silence and a half-light. Shadows were always long, even on the brightest day, and it was always impossible to see past the trees and brush to what was coming around the next curve. I was told that if you were driving and met another car, one of you would have to back up to one of the few wide places, or even all the way to the beginning of the road, in order for the other one to pass.

Strangely, even those that I talked with, who had no interest in ghosts or the unusual, all made sure to tell me that that Zombie Road was a spooky place.

Thanks to its secluded location, and the fact that it fell into disrepair and was abandoned, Lawler Ford Road gained a reputation in the 1950s as a hangout for local teenagers to have parties, drink beer, and as a lover's lane. The road saw quite a lot of traffic in the early years of its popularity and occasionally still sees a traveler or two these days. Most that come here now are not looking for a party. Instead, they come looking for the unexplained.

Lawler Ford Road has gained a reputation for being haunted.

Numerous legends and stories sprang up about the place, from the typical tales of murdered boyfriends and madmen with hooks for hands to more specific tales of a local killer who was dubbed the "Zombie." He was said to live in an old dilapidated shack by the river and would attack young lovers who came there looking for someplace quiet and out of the way. As time passed, the stories of this monster were told and re-told. Eventually, the name of Lawler Ford Road was largely forgotten and it was replaced with "Zombie Road," by which it is still known today.

There are many other stories, too, from ghostly apparitions in the woods to visitors who have vanished without a trace. There are also stories about a man who was killed here by a train in the 1970s and who now haunts the road and of a mysterious old woman who yells at passersby from a house at the end of the road. There is another legend about a boy who fell from the bluffs along the river. His body was never found. There are also tales of vanishing soldiers, Native American spirits, figures in black robes, and the standard boogeymen that lurk around secluded spots all over the country.

But is there any truth to these tales, or any historical events that might explain how the ghost stories got started? Believe it or not, there may just be a kernel of truth to the legends of Zombie Road.

The region around Zombie Road was once known as Glencoe. The unincorporated community was on the banks of the Meramec River and many of its current residents live in houses that were once summer cottages. Other nearby houses are from the era when Glencoe was a bustling railroad and quarrying community. However, the days of prosperity have long since passed it by, and years ago, the village was absorbed by the larger town of Wildwood.

There is no record of the first inhabitants in the region, but they were likely the Native Americans who built the mounds that existed for centuries at the site of present-day St. Louis. The mound city that once existed there was one of the largest in North America and at its peak, boasted more than 40,000 occupants. It is believed that the Meramec River Valley provided a hunting ground for the inhabitants and that the area around Glencoe, because of plentiful game and fresh water, was a stopping point for the Indians as they made their way to the flint quarries in Jefferson County.

After the Mound Builders vanished from the area, the Osage, Missouri, and Shawnee Indians came to the region and also mined the flint quarries for scrapers, weapon points, and other stone tools. They also hunted and fished along the Meramec River. The Shawnee had been invited into what was then the Louisiana region by the Spanish governor. Many of them settled west of St. Louis and were, for a time, major suppliers of game to the settlement.

The area around what would be Glencoe became a major travel stop for travelers, hunters, Native Americans, and settlers. With the sheer number of native people who passed through, it might explain why sightings of Native American ghosts have been so prevalent along Lawler Ford Road. Since the shallow point in the river at the end of the road made such a convenient crossing spot, the road was likely built over an existing Indian trail. Over the course of a century or more, native inhabitants used the trail, the river crossing, and the surrounding forest. Perhaps their time here has left a memory behind on this place in the form of a haunting.

The first white settler in the area was Ninian Hamilton from Kentucky. He arrived near Glencoe around 1800 and obtained a settler's land grant. He built a house and trading post and became one of the wealthiest and most influential men of the period. In those days, the Meramec River bottoms were heavily forested and made up of steep hills and sharp bluffs. The river flooded frequently and the fords that existed were only usable during times of low water. There were no bridges or ferries that crossed the river, except for one that was operated far to the southeast. The trappers and traders that traveled west of St. Louis, like the Indians before them, came on horseback along the ridge route that later became Manchester Road. It skirted the Meramec and was high enough so that it was not subject to flooding. Because of this, it passed directly by Hamilton's homestead and the trading post that he established there. With the well-used trail just outside his backdoor, as well as nearby fish, game and the availability of fresh spring water, Hamilton's post prospered.

Hamilton later built some gristmills near his trading post, which was an important resource for settlers in those days. One of the mills that Hamilton started was later replaced by a water mill for tanning leather by Henry McCullough, who had a tannery and shoemaking business that not only supplied the surrounding area but also allowed him to ship large quantities of leather to his brother in the south. McCullough was also a Kentuckian and purchased his land from Hamilton. He later served as the justice of the peace for about 30 years and as a judge for the county court from 1849 to 1852. He was married three times before he died in 1853, and one of his wives was a sister of Ninian Hamilton. That wife, Della Hamilton McCullough, was killed in 1876 after being struck by a railroad car on the spur line from the Rockwoods Reservation.

It has been suggested that perhaps the death of Della Hamilton McCullough is responsible for one of the great legends of Zombie Road. The story of this phantom states that an eerie female specter has been seen roaming the site of the former tracks. There are no recent records of anyone being struck by a train – only the unfortunate Della McCullough. It seems that she has never left the area where she died.

The railroads would be another vital connection to Glencoe and to the stories of Lawler Ford Road. The first lines reached the area in 1853 when a group of passengers on flatcars arrived behind the steam locomotive called the "St. Louis." A rail line had been constructed along the Meramec River, using two tunnels, and connected St. Louis to Franklin, which was later re-named Pacific, Missouri. The tiny station house at Franklin was little more than a shack in the wilderness at that time, but bands played and people cheered as the train pulled into the station.

Around this same time, tracks had been extended along the river, passing through what would be Glencoe. The site was likely given its name by Scottish railroad engineer James P. Kirkwood, who laid out the route. The name has its origins in Old English as "glen" meaning "a narrow valley" and "coe" meaning "grass."

Only a few remnants of the original railroad can be found today. The old tracks can still be found at the end of Zombie Road, and it is along these tracks where Della McCullough's ghost is said to walk. Her translucent figure in white strolls to the end of the abandoned line, and then disappears. If anyone tried to approach her before she reaches the end of the line, she will vanish before they come too near.

One of the first passengers to make the trip west on the rail line from St. Louis was probably James E. Yeatman. He was one of the leading citizens of St. Louis and was the founder of the Mercantile Library, president of Merchants

Bank, and an early proponent of extending the railroads west of the Mississippi. He was active in both business and charitable affairs in St. Louis and was a major force behind the Western Sanitary Commission during the Civil War. This large volunteer group provided hospital boats, medical services, and medical care for the wounded on both sides of the conflict. The world's first hospital railroad car is attributed to this group.

After the death of Ninian Hamilton in 1856, his heirs sold his land to A.S. Mitchell, who, in turn, sold out to James Yeatman. He built a large frame home on the property and dubbed it "Glencoe Park." The mansion burned to the ground in 1920, while owned by Alfred Carr and Angelica Yeatman Carr, the daughter of James Yeatman. The Carrs moved into the stone guesthouse on the property, which also burned in 1954. It was later rebuilt and restored and still remains in the Carr family today.

The village of Glencoe was laid out in 1854 by Woods, Christy & Co., a large dry goods company in St. Louis, and in 1883, it contained "a few houses and a small store, but for about a year has had no post office." At the time the town was created, Woods, Christy & Co. also erected a gristmill and sawmill at Glencoe that operated until about 1868.

One of the many prominent St. Louis citizens who traveled through Glencoe during the middle and late 1800s was Winston Churchill, (not the British statesman, but the American author) who went on to write a number of bestselling romantic novels in the early 1900s. One of the most popular, *The Crisis*, was set partially at Glencoe. The novel, which Churchill acknowledged was based on the activities of James E. Yeatman, depicts the struggles and conflicts in St. Louis during the critical years of the Civil War. It is believed that Angelica Yeatman Carr was his model for the heroine, Miss Virginia Carvel. The first edition of the book was published in 1901 and was followed by subsequent editions. Copies can still be found on dusty shelves in used and antiquarian bookstores today.

In 1868, the Glencoe Marble Company was formed and the previously mentioned sidetrack was added to the railroad, running alongside the river. The tracks ran past where Lawler Ford Road ended and it's likely that wagons were used to haul quarry stone up the road.

During the Civil War, the city of St. Louis found itself in the predicament of being loyal to the Union in a state that was predominately dedicated to the Confederate cause. For this reason, men who were part of what was called the Home Guard were picketed along the roads and trails leading into the city with instructions to turn back Southern sympathizers by any means necessary. As a result, Confederate spies, saboteurs, and agents often had to find less-trafficked paths to get in and out of the St. Louis area. One of the lesser-known trails led to and away from the ford across the Meramec River near Glencoe. This trail would later become known as Lawler Ford Road.

"Zombie Road" today

As information about the trail's existence reached the leaders of the militia forces, troops from the Home Guard began to be stationed at the ford. The trail led across the river and to the small town of Crescent, which was later dubbed "Rebel Bend" because of the number of Confederates who passed through it and who found sanctuary there.

After the militia forces set up their lines, the river became very dangerous to cross. However, since there were so few fords across the Meramec, many attempted to cross there anyway, often with dire results. According to the stories, a number of men died there in skirmishes with the Home Guard. Could this violence explain some of the hauntings that are now said to occur along Zombie Road?

Many of the people who claim to have experienced the strange happenings along the old road speak of unsettling feelings and the sensation of being watched. They also tell of eerie sounds, inexplicable noises and even disembodied footsteps. Many have spoken of being "followed" as they walk along the trail, as though someone is keeping pace with them just in the edge of the woods. Strangely, no one is ever seen. In addition, it is not uncommon for visitors to also report seeing shapes, shadows, and presences in the woods. On many occasions, these shapes have been mistaken for actual people until the hiker goes to confront them and finds that there is no one there. It's possible that the violence and bloodshed that occurred here during the Civil War has left its mark behind on this site, as it has on so many other locations.

Visitors to Lawler Ford Road today will often end their journey at the Meramec River and the riverbanks have also played a part in the legends and tales of Zombie Road. It was at Yeatman Junction that one of the first large scale gravel operations on the Meramec River began. Gravel was taken from the banks of the Meramec and moved on rail cars into St. Louis. The first record of this operation is in the middle 1850s. Later, steam dredges were used, supplanted by diesel or gasoline dredges, in extracting gravel from the channel and from artificial lakes dug into the south bank. This continued, apparently without interruption, for several decades.

The quarries were used until the demise of the gravel operation in the 1970s. The last railroad tracks were removed from around Glencoe when the spur line to the gravel pit was taken out. Some have cited the railroads as the source for some of the hauntings along Zombie Road. In addition to the wandering spirit that is believed to be Della McCullough, it's possible that some of the other restless ghosts may be those of accident victims along the rail lines. Sharp bends in the tracks at Glencoe were the site of frequent derailments and accidents. It finally got so bad that service was discontinued on the tracks that led around the bend in the river. It has been speculated that perhaps the victims of train accidents may still be lingering nearby and might explain how the area got such a reputation for tragedy and ghostly haunts.

Many visitors also claim to have had strange experiences near the old shacks and ramshackle homes located along the beach area at the end of the trail. One of the long-standing legends of the place mentions the ghost of an old woman who screams at people from the doorways of one of the old houses. However, upon investigation, the old woman is never there. The houses here date back to about 1900, when the area around Glencoe served as a resort community. The Meramec River's "clubhouse era" lasted until about 1945. Many of the cottages were then converted to year-round residences but others were simply left to decay and deteriorate in the woods.

This is the origin of the old houses that are located off Zombie Road but it does not explain the ghostly old woman or the other apparitions that have been encountered. Could they be former residents of days gone by? Perhaps this haunting on the old roadway has nothing to do with the violence and death of the past but rather with happy memories from the time the area was a resort community. Perhaps some of these former residents returned to their cottages after death because the resort homes were places where they knew peace and contentment in life.

Whatever the reason behind the reputation of the road, it is a strange place. When I first began researching the history of Lawler Ford Road, I confess to believing that "Zombie Road" was nothing more than an urban legend run amok, created by the vivid imaginations of several generations of teenagers. I never expected to discover the dark history of violence and death in the region or anything that might substantiate the tales of ghosts and supernatural occurrences along this wooded road. It was easy to find people who believed in the legends of Zombie Road, but I never expected to be one of those who came to be convinced that something truly strange was taking place there.

Fright Nights

A few miles along the highway from the site of Times Beach is the Route 66 community of Eureka. A trading center that was already well-established before the Civil War, Eureka managed to escape the fate of "death by bypass" because its business center was so close to the site of the new interstate. The frontage road has attracted gas stations, convenience stores, shopping centers, hotels, and every kind of fast food chain imaginable – all of which depend on nearby **Six Flags St. Louis**. The amusement park, which started as Six Flags over Mid-America in 1971, effectively closed down other parks (like Chain of Rocks) with its superior rides and attractions and its single admission price.

Strangely, Six Flags has a few ghostly stories connected to it. One of them is part of the history of the **Six Flags Ramada Inn**, a portion of which was once a barn on the property of the St. Louis Children's Industrial Farm. The farm was established in Eureka in 1898 to give children from St. Louis tenement neighborhoods a chance to experience life in a rural setting. A stone barn that was located on the property has been incorporated into parts of the hotel's restaurant, lounge, and meeting rooms. According to legend, the ghost of a young woman who fell to her death in the old barn now haunts the hotel. She has been seen running in the hallways and wandering the building for many years.

Inside of the amusement park itself there are also a number of eerie tales. Many years ago, I worked at Six Flags for two seasons during the Halloween "Frightfest" (telling ghost stories several times each day) and heard many tales from employees at the park. Most of them centered on the park's **Palace Theater**, where footsteps were frequently heard, unexplained voices were encountered and staff members were often touched by unseen hands. A ghostly woman was often seen walking between the Palace and the Empire Theater, which was nearby. There was also the ghost of the **Mine Train Roller Coaster**, which had a habit of opening and closing the gates and causing the ride to behave erratically. Workers swore that these things only happened when one of them expressed a disbelief in the ghost.

The Town Named for a Railroad

At the exit for Six Flags, travelers can leave the interstate and get onto Route 66 by simply following Allentown Road under the interstate and turning west. The old route is plainly marked as Highway 66 along this route as it runs alongside the railroad tracks. High stone bluffs on the other side of the road help to keep the interstate out of sight and mind. Straight ahead is the town of Pacific, but first the highway passes the remains of motels and gas stations that once made a decent living from the Mother Road, but have vanished with time.

In 1852, the Pacific Railroad Company laid out a town along its line and called it Franklin. It was to be the new railroad's first headquarters west of the Mississippi River. That same year, on July 19, the first train made its inaugural run from St. Louis to the end of the line at Franklin, where a great celebration was held. With scores of workers needed to extend the line to the west, people flocked to the area and the small community grew. In 1859, the town was officially incorporated and it was changed to Pacific to honor the railroad company that had brought prosperity to the region.

The town began to grow, with most of the development along the rail line, but it almost didn't survive the Civil War. On October 2, 1864, Confederate raiders, under the command of General Sterling Price, attacked the little railroad town. When they left, Pacific's bridges, depot, ice house, and railroad supply houses were left in ashes.

In spite of the wreckage from the war, Pacific continued to thrive. In the 1870s, in the sandstone bluffs just north of downtown, silica mines opened, bringing further wealth to the community. In those days, silica sand was used to make fine glassware and the local deposits were especially rich. The caverns are still visible today in the bluff along the north side of Route 66. Some mines remain in operation today along the Meramec River.

The next great event in Pacific's history was the arrival of U.S. 66 in 1932. With so many different alignments coming out of St. Louis, Pacific wasn't on the original route from the city. When the next alignment opened, a number of businesses appeared to cater to the new traffic that was coming through town.

One of the first was the **Red Cedar Inn**, which was built by brothers Bill and James Smith in 1934. The inn was constructed from red cedar logs that were cut from the family farm in nearby Villa Ridge. The logs were cut by hand, hauled to the site on a Ford Model AA truck, and the inn was erected on a foundation that had been dug using mule power. Soon after the inn's opening, a bar was added to the structure, nearly doubling the business. During the early years, the inn also offered gasoline service from two pumps out front, but that didn't last for long. Focusing on the restaurant service, James hired his son, James, Jr., as manager and the roadhouse thrived. In

The old Red Cedar Inn was a highway tradition for years.

1935, James, Jr. hired a young woman named Katherine Brinkman to wait tables and it turned out to be the best idea he ever had. The two soon fell in love and were married in 1940. The couple eventually purchased the business from James's father in 1944.

Alongside their own son, James, and their daughter, Ginger, the couple ran the place until James, Jr. retired in 1972. In 1987, Ginger and her father re-opened the Red Cedar Inn, with help from Katherine. She stayed around to bake the restaurant's wonderful brownies, which made the inn legendary along Route 66.

The inn was a classic example of the family-run businesses that thrived during the glory days of Route 66. Unfortunately, when the highway officially came to an end, many of them were unable to survive. The Red Cedar Inn, handed down from generation to generation, stayed alive much longer than most, but it closed down in 2005 and, sadly, has never re-opened.

On to Gray Summit

As Osage Street becomes U.S. 66, a traveler can't help but notice the bluffs that loom over the highway. On the bluffs directly above is a scenic overview called **Jensen Point** in honor of Lars Peter Jensen, the first president of the Henry Shaw Gardenway Association and manager of the Missouri Botanical Garden Arboretum for 18 years. Stone stairs that were carved in the steep hillside by Civilian Conservation Corps workers in 1939 have vanished over time but a large pavilion of stone and wood that was built on the natural rock ledge at the summit stood for decades.

West of Pacific, Route 66 climbs slowly from the valley and rises toward the town of Gray Summit. On the left side of the highway is the entrance to the Missouri Botanical Garden Arboretum and Nature Preserve. Surrounded by a low stone wall and groves of pine and spruce trees, the Arboretum was created from empty farmlands in the 1920s. Located on the Ozark Plateau, the Arboretum's natural landscape and managed plant collections cover four square miles on both sides of the Meramec River.

Fading buildings and businesses line the highway as the road stretches into Gray Summit, a small town that was founded in 1845 by Daniel Gray of New York. He built a hotel in town that same year, marking the first of the businesses that followed the railroad to the area. In time, Gray Summit became the highest point on the Missouri Pacific Railroad between St. Louis and Kansas City, and a railroad tunnel still runs beneath the town.

While in town, travelers can stretch their legs as they stroll among the Missouri wildflowers at the **Shaw Nature Preserve**, which is run by the **Missouri Botanical Garden**. The reserve was established in 1925, when air pollution in St. Louis threatened the plant population. The reserve includes a visitor's center, historic mansion, and 14 miles of hiking trails. Another stop in Gray Summit is **Purina Farms**, which allows visitors to pet and feed farm animals and provides a close-up look at livestock, sheep-shearing, cow-milking, and care for household pets.

The Gardenway Motel's classic neon sign — a part of Route 66 history

Winding along the road, at the intersection of Route 100 and U.S. 66 are the ruins of what was known as the "new" Diamonds Restaurant and the **Gardenway Motel**. The Colonial-style motel was opened by Louis B. Eckelcamp in 1945, adjacent to his home and the nature preserve. By 1954, the Gardenway was advertising "Twenty-Five Modern Cabins with Tile Baths." It would eventually boast 41 guest rooms and had an iconic neon sign that was a stark contrast in style to the motel's sprawling Colonial architecture. Unfortunately, the sign died long before the motel did, although the Gardenway finally faded away in October 2014.

The "new" **Diamonds Restaurant** never made it that long, though. Its last gasp came a number of years before, unable to keep up with the fast-moving traffic of Interstate 44. But this was not the first incarnation of the Diamonds Restaurant. The original had been a favorite stopping spot for Route 66 bus and auto travelers, starting back in the 1920s – and may have been a favorite spot for traveling ghosts, too.

Legends of Diamonds & the Tri-County Truck Stop

Although Route 66 has officially been gone for many years now, the memories remain and so do many of the old sites. Along the old highway are abandoned diners, broken and faded neon signs for businesses that have long since vanished, and even abandoned motor courts that seem to still be waiting for the road-weary traveler to check in for the night.

And in many of those now empty places, the ghosts of the past remain too.

One such place is the old Diamonds Restaurant, which was once a Missouri fixture on the "Mother Road." The restaurant actually started as a fruit and vegetable stand in 1927. An enterprising young man named Spencer Groff started the stand to get a share of the money being spent by Route 66 travelers. He did so well that the stand was eventually expanded into a restaurant and mercantile store that he called "The Diamonds." The reason for the name was simple: it had been designed into the shape of a baseball diamond. Groff sold gas from Phillips 66 pumps and rented 25 cabins for tourists across the road. The eatery, which gained fame as "The World's Largest Roadside Restaurant," offered dozens of tables and three U-shaped lunch counters with attendants. The menu ranged from burgers to turkey dinners with all of the trimmings. In time, it became a regular stop for all cross-country bus services, literally delivering customers right to the Diamonds' front door.

In 1947, the place was devastated by fire and Groff decided that he'd had enough. He turned over the business to one of his longtime employees, who rebuilt the place. It wasn't long – thanks to Route 66 – before the Diamonds was thriving again. It stayed busy into the 1960s. Unfortunately, though, the completion of the interstate brought about the end of the old highway. After Interstate 44 was opened in 1968, a new Diamonds was built near the interstate. The owners of the Diamonds picked up everything, lock, stock, and vintage sign, and moved the business two miles east to cash in on sales from the new interstate. But it did not survive. In fact, all that remains of the "new" Diamonds is the old sign. The building has long since been torn down.

Ironically, though, the original building still stands today. After the Diamonds departed, the place became the Tri-County Truck Stop. It was a couple of miles off the beaten path, but in those days, before newer and more accessible truck stops opened along the interstate, the former Diamonds was the only game in town. What was once a must-stop on Route 66 became an all-hours restaurant that catered to truckers, the late night bar crowd, and seedy drifters who were floating from one place to the next. The second floor of the building was renovated into sleeping rooms and showers and while this had been done as a service for truckers, the second floor attracted hitchhikers and prostitutes. Robberies and violence became common and it was frequented by police officers making arrests and breaking up fights.

It was in the early 1970s that stories of ghosts first began to emerge from the Tri-County Truck Stop. Employees and customers began telling of being touched by unseen hands, hearing voices, and seeing shadowy figures that shouldn't have been there. Over the course of the next two decades, eerie accounts were told of inexplicable sights and sounds in the basement and seeing apparitions in dimly lit rooms. Objects moved about on their own, lights and appliances turned on and off, and staff members told of frequent sightings of a man wearing a plaid shirt and tan pants that would appear and disappear at random. Others claimed to see the spirits of a man and a woman that were covered in blood, leading some to believe that this may have been the spectral reenactment of a murder from the building's notorious past. No records exist to say that anything like that ever happened, but the reputation of the truck stop in the late 1960s and early 1970s makes just about anything possible.

And stories got even wilder. Rampant tales of ghosts in the 1990s had local residents claiming that the ghosts of the building were actually spilling out of the place and haunting other nearby places. They claimed that ghosts had infiltrated their homes and that a new incident had started to occur on Highway 100. According to some, a hitchhiker was now being picked up on

The end of the road for the Tri-County Truck Stop

that surrounding roadway who would vanish out of the car without opening the door. He always asked to be dropped off at the Tri-County Truck Stop before he disappeared.

In time, competition from more modern, safer truck stops finally closed the doors of the Tri-County Truck Stop and its restaurant. The place remains today, a ghost in its own right, a vacant and abandoned shell of what it once was. The windows have been boarded over and the excitement of yesterday is now long gone. One has to wonder what will happen to the place now that time has passed it by.

And what will become of the ghosts?

Reminders of Route 66

Just a mile or so further down the road is the site of the old **Sunset Motel**, with its classic yellow sign. Built in the early 1940s, the 12-unit motel was one of the more distinctive motor lodges of the era. The Sunset was built from beige brick and was laid out in a V shape, in which the exterior center of the V served as a community era with ice and vending machines. One of the more unusual aspects of the motel was that it was built so that each unit had two entrances, one in the front that overlooked the landscaped grounds, and one in the back, which offered access to the parking lot and driveway. The hotel stands today much as it did eight decades ago. The original eye-catching sign remains intact and over the years has become a popular Route 66 photo stop. In days past, the motel offered "Twelve Units, Twelve Baths, Panel Ray Heat, Beautyrest Mattresses, and Quiet," but, sadly, the place is very quiet these days. The sun truly set on the motel back when Interstate 44 put it out of business.

A little further along the road was the former site of the **Villa Courts**, although you wouldn't know it if you were to see the place today. The Villa Courts opened in 1928 when a man named Stropman built at auto camp on the property and dubbed the Route 66 rest stop "Stropman's Camp." It was a pretty primitive spot, but not as primitive as most other tourist camps that were popping up along the road. Stropman's offered more than just a safe place to park your car for the night. A small building was constructed at the front of the camp, that later offered gasoline from two pumps. There was also a small grocery store that carried everything an auto traveler might need for the night, as well as necessities for the next day's journey. There was also a community restroom that gave travelers a chance to freshen up prior to setting off the next morning. Stropman's was only two miles away from the Diamonds, which offered great food, and many guests chose to make the short trip there for supper.

No one seems to known when Stropman's ownership ended and the name was changed to Villa Courts. The place was purchased by the Guffey family in 1976 and they changed the name of the store from Villa Courts Grocery to Villa Ridge Foods. By this time, the small cabins were no longer used for overnight stays, but were rented out by the month. In the early 1990s, the cabins were closed altogether and now used for storage. Villa Ridge Foods, or "Guffey's," as the locals call it, remains an important part of the lives of nearby Villa Ridge residents, although travelers of yesterday would hardly recognize it now.

Not far from the former Villa Courts is another Route 66 landmark that is unrecognizable today. The **Pin Oak Motel** was built around 1940, and was named for the beautiful trees that have long dominated the local landscape. The Pin Oak was originally laid out with two sets of two buildings. The buildings were joined by common carports and faced each other across a courtyard. When it was built, it offered only eight units, but by the 1950s, more units had been added and the carports were enclosed. Eventually, the room count grew to 28.

The Pin Oak was billed as "a better court for better people" and advertising that it had "clean, ultra-modern units." In the early 1960s, it boasted air

The Pin Oak Motel in the 1940s

conditioning, free TV, and new carpets. In 1967, though, when Interstate 44, bypassed the area, the Pin Oak, like so many other motels, fell on hard times. Over time, the "better court for better people" has been converted into self-storage units and is a shadow of its former self.

From these reminders of the old highway, U.S. 66 continues to meander north and south of Interstate 44 until it enters the town of **St. Clair**. Established in 1849 as a railroad community for the St. Louis & San Francisco Railway, it was first called Traveler's Repose by one of his early settlers. The name was changed to St. Clair in 1855, when it became a center for zinc and lead mining.

St. Clair was once home to the vintage **Arch Motel**, which has been gone for many years now. Until recently, however, the motel's old sign remained on the site and was a popular photo stop. A few years ago, it was also removed and is now in storage, waiting for a new location.

One Route 66 site that does remain – although it no longer serves its original purpose – is the former **Skylark Motel**. The motel was opened by Charlie Johnson in the middle 1950s. Johnson had originally owned the Mo-Tel Cabins, which he built in the 1940s, but he and his son, Robert, decided to build the new place west of town.

Using facets of a streamlined modern style, they built a unique place. An unusual two-story, white stucco building housed the office and several guest rooms. Carports were built at the rear of the property for traveler's convenience, and additional rooms were located in a ranch-style structure that was just west of the original building. The most exceptional aspect of the motel's architecture was the glass-block tower at the west end of the main structure. The tower was spectacularly illuminated at night with multi-colored

The Skylark Motel, with the glass tower (left side) that was illuminated at night.

lights that were within the structure. The tower's light would be splashed across the front of the white stucco building in a dazzling array. A billboard-sized neon sign at the front of the property was also an attention-getter. The Skylark was perfectly perched on the crest of a hill so that at night, when the tower was lit and the neon sign was on, it could be seen for miles down the highway in both directions. The motel also had a playground, TV in every room, and air conditioning.

Although the giant neon sign out front is gone and the tower is dark today, it's not as hard as you might think to imagine what the Skylark once had to offer. The main building has since had an addition built to its east side, and the property now serves as the local VFW Hall, but the memories are still standing for us to enjoy.

About 10 miles southwest of St. Clair, Route 66 brings travelers to Stanton. Once an unincorporated community that became a favorite highway stop due to its proximity to nearby attractions, the small town almost seems smaller today than it did back in 1946, when Jack Rittenhouse included it in his *A Guide Book to Highway 66.* At that time, the tiny town was home to only about 115 people and Rittenhouse described it as having a AAA garage, a gas station, a store, a few cabins, and a good café called Wurzburgers. There isn't a lot more than that in town today, but people who come to the area don't come for the amenities – they come because they want to see the cave.

Meramec Caverns: Missouri's Most Famous Cave

While traveling on Route 66 in days gone by (or even Interstate 44 today), for many miles in both directions, travelers encountered barns, signs, and billboards extolling the finer points of one of the Mother Road's most famous tourist attractions – Meramec Caverns.

Located just three miles off Route 66, down a twisting road outside of Stanton that winds to the Meramec River, the cave was commercially developed in the 1930s by Lester B. Dill, a Missouri farm boy with the cleverness of P.T. Barnum. "I have put more people underground and brought them out alive than anyone else," Dill often boasted and no one could dispute the claim.

Lester Dill was born in 1898 and was the second of nine children. He was only six years old when his father, Thomas Benton Dill, ventured into Fisher's Cave, across the Meramec from the family farm, for the first time. By the time he was 10, Lester, guided by a kerosene lamp, was taking tourists from St. Louis on guided cave tours. Over the years, Dill continued to explore the many caves of the Meramec Valley. Later, Dill and his wife, Mary, followed the oil boom to Oklahoma, dabbled in Florida real estate, and then moved to St. Louis, where Lester worked as a carpenter. In 1928, when his father was appointed the first superintendent of the new Meramec State Park, where Fisher's Cave was located, Lester came back to the area. He signed a contract with the state and launched a cave-guiding business, complete with souvenirs and homemade food.

Lester Dill

A few years later, when the state contract expired, and with the country in the midst of the Great Depression, Lester began searching for his own cave to develop. He finally decided to lease Saltpeter Cave, which was just a few miles downstream from the park. Spaniard Hernando De Soto was said to have discovered the cave in 1542, and a couple of centuries later, it was explored by a French miner named Jacques Renault. During the 1800s, the cave was used by saltpeter miners for storage and shelter, and legend had it that escaped slaves were sheltered there as they made their way to safety in the northern states. There were also stories that outlaws, including the famous Jesse James gang, found refuge in the cave and may have even left some of their ill-gotten gains hidden somewhere inside.

The legends of the cave were important to Lester, but even more important was the cave's proximity to Route 66, America's most traveled highway. Dill knew that if he got the word out about the wonders of the cave, the tourists would beat a path to his door. He renamed the new attraction "Meramec

The early entrance to Meramec Caverns as a commercial cave.

Caverns" and hired a local sawmill crew to construct a road to the cave. Meramec Caverns opened on Decoration Day (Memorial Day) 1933, and a total of six visitors paid 40-cents per person to follow Lester Dill through the damp passageways. It was not a great start, but Lester was not worried. He eventually bought the property and put almost every cent that he earned into improving and promoting the show cave.

Throughout the bleak years of the Depression, tourist traffic was sparse, so Lester hosted public dances in the spacious cave as a way to earn a little extra money. The cave had been used in such a manner since 1895. At that time, a man named D.N. Gideon and his partner, Joseph Schmuke, began holding parties and dances in what became known as the "Ballroom" section of the cave. The events reached a wide audience. Gideon and Schmuke connected with A. Hilton, the passenger traffic manager of the Frisco Railroad, and he eagerly promoted the events as a way to fill seats on trains that ran between St. Louis and Springfield. Gideon and Schmuke made so much money that they continued to offer summer dances at Saltpeter Cave until 1910. Lester Dill started the dances again as a way to earn extra money during the leanest years in the cave's history.

For the first three years of the cave's operation, the entire Dill family, including the children, worked day and night. They even lived in a tent at the site. They battled treacherous ice on the steep road between Route 66 and the cave entrance, and in the spring, built brick dikes to hold back the river and keep it from turning the parking lot into a lake and flooding the cave entrance.

Visitors that managed to make it to the cave always left with a Meramec Caverns sign tied to their bumper. School children that were hired by Lester saw to it that a sign was attached to the bumper of each and every automobile that stopped at the cave. Later, the job became easier when adhesive was developed for the backs of the bumper signs. In 1940, while he was exploring an unknown part of the cave, Lester found some rusted guns and an old chest, which he claimed had belonged to none other than Jesse James. Immediately, the phrase "Jesse James' Hideout" was added to the bumper stickers.

One of the famous Meramec Caverns barns, which dotted the landscape along U.S. 66, directing travelers to the cave.

Besides the millions of bumper stickers attached to cars and the brochures handed out to tourists, Lester promoted the cave by posting signs, mostly painted on barns, along highways in as many as 40 states. Lester and his crew scoured the countryside, especially along Route 66, searching for just the right barns for their eye-catching signs. To entice the farmers who owned the barns, Lester handed out watches, pints of whiskey, and free passes to the cave. There were very few of the farmers who turned him down, and soon Meramec Caverns barns were appearing along wide-open stretches of U.S. 66.

During World War II, when gas rationing hit, Lester traveled to Fort Leonard Wood, a large basic training camp, and convinced the army to convoy troops to the cave for maneuvers. Hundreds of soldiers camped in the river bottom and marched into the cave in full battle dress. Every night, Lester threw dances for the soldiers in the cave and gave special rates to anyone in uniform.

Francena, one of Lester and Mary's daughters, later married one of these soldiers, Rudy Turilli, a handsome Italian from New York. After the war ended, Rudy became the general manager of the cave and handled most of the promotion and publicity. It was Turilli who discovered a man named J. Frank

Dalton, who raised eyebrows in 1949 by declaring that he was actually Jesse James. It was another man, he claimed, who had been killed in his place in 1882. Turilli brought the old man to live in a cabin near the entrance to the cave and reporters from all over the country came to Meramec Caverns to interview him. The old-timer told wonderful stories and showed off his guns for several years, finally passing away at the age of 104 in 1951. There was no way to calculate the amount of publicity that J. Frank Dalton brought to the Meramec Caverns.

In the early 1950s, during a time when Americans were preoccupied by the Cold War, Meramec Caverns became known as the "safest bomb shelter in the world" when Lester offered the cave to the government as a haven from atomic blasts. He created a passage in the cave to be used as a shelter and stocked it with rations and thousands of gallons of water. Visitors paid to visit this part of the cave and as an ominous incentive to return, were given tiny cards with the admission tickets – cards that promised them a spot in the fallout shelter if the "Big One" ever hit.

Lester Dill never missed an opportunity to promote the caverns and celebrities, including singers Kate Smith and Pearl Bailey and canine star, Lassie, toured the "world's only five-story cave." In 1960, Lester dubbed a small nook in the cave the "Honeymoon Room" and managed to get it featured on the *Art Linkletter Show.* For the show, Dill dressed a honeymoon couple in leopard skins, confined them to the room and promised them a free trip to the Bahamas if they could find a hidden key within 10 days. Each time a tour group passed, the caveman couple were required to act out a skit. The humiliation – and the publicity – lasted the full 10 days since Lester didn't actually hide the key until day 10.

Toasted on network television shows and in the press as "America's Number One Cave Man," Lester Dill died in 1980. Despite the passing of the man who put Meramec Caverns on the map, the cave remains in family hands and continues to draw big crowds every summer. The cave was an icon on Route 66 and remains a permanent attraction after all of these years.

And it seems apparent today that a little of the cave's colorful history has remained behind in other ways, as well. Stories of strange happenings began to be told at Meramec Caverns in the late 1940s. The guides don't offer these stories voluntarily, but will usually relate odd events when asked. Many of the tales seem to connect to events of the past, perhaps repeating themselves over and over again in a ghostly manner. Many staff members and visitors speak of hearing voices and footsteps in the cave when no one is there. Such events could be dismissed as echoes encountered by people who are not familiar with the acoustics of caves, but what about the reports from experienced cavers? Others tell of the sounds of music and laughter, perhaps lingering remnants of the parties held in the cave in the late 1800s, early 1900s, and into the Great Depression.

One cave guide related the fact that the last tour group of the day often hears mysterious voices coming from the dark corridors of the cave. In busy attractions like Meramec Caverns, it's not uncommon to hear the sounds of the cave tour in front of you or behind you, but what about when it's the last tour of the cave? Why do visitors hear voices from a tour that simply isn't there?

A few people who have visited Meramec Caverns have reported the apparition of a smiling man who has been seen in the cave. He is there one moment and gone the next. Lights flicker in the cave when this ghost puts in an appearance, even when there is no one near the switch. Some have suggested that this ghost is the spirit of Lester Dill, never having truly left the cave that he loved so much. It seems that he is still there, watching over his beloved cavern, even after death.

The Man Who Would Be Jesse James

The word "weird" is used to describe a lot of things in this book, from roadside attractions to unusual people, but perhaps one of the weirdest attractions on old Route 66 is the Jesse James Wax Museum in Stanton. It's mostly because the place is not exactly what most visitors think it is before they walk in the door. It's not so much a tribute to the infamous Missouri outlaw and bank robber, Jesse James, but the man who claimed to be Jesse James -- a fellow named J. Frank Dalton.

The roots of the future museum date back to 1949, when Dalton arrived at Meramec Caverns. The shrunken old man was carried on a stretcher to a room filled with party cake and candles. The bedridden man claimed to be celebrating his 102nd birthday – and he also claimed to be Jesse James.

There is no question that Jesse James was one of the most famous outlaws in history. Born and raised in Missouri, Jesse rode with Quantrill's Raiders during the Civil War and unable to surrender after the war ended, he, his brother, and their gang of cousins and friends wreaked havoc with banks and trains all over the Midwest. He remains an intriguing man, portrayed as both a cold-blooded killer by Pinkerton detectives and a "Robin Hood" rebel by friends and neighbors; he became a legend over the years. It's little wonder that the grave itself had trouble keeping Jesse James in it. History states that Jesse was shot to death by Robert Ford on April 3, 1882 – shot in the back while straightening a picture on the wall. But the official account of Jesse's death was just too mundane for his admirers to accept. In 1902, Jesse's body was actually exhumed and reburied to make sure it was safe. Less than five decades later, nearly a dozen old men came out of the woodwork, each of them calling the corpse a counterfeit and each claiming to be the authentic

Jesse James. One by one, most of their stories were shot full of holes, but one of them managed to capture the attention of Rudy Turilli, the son-in-law of Meramec Caverns owner Lester Dill.

Rudy had been fascinated by the legend of Jesse James for more than 20 years. When all of the old men came forward claiming to be Jesse, he discredited all of them – except for J. Frank Dalton. By 1948, Rudy was heir apparent to the caverns and proven to his father-in-law that he was a skilled promoter of the cave. He and another fellow participated in a stunt to promote the cave that made national news. The two men climbed the Empire State Building and threatened to jump off unless everyone in the world went to Meramec Caverns! The authorities eventually talked them down. Rudy and his friend spent nine days in jail but the story made newspapers all over the country.

When Dalton's claim on the "Jesse James" name was first reported in Lawton, Oklahoma, Rudy and Lester assumed that he was another fraud. However, neither one of them was able to just ignore the story. Meramec Caverns had a huge investment in Jesse James. They had been promoting the place as Jesse James' hideout for a number of years and the discovery of a strongbox that had been taken during a James train robbery turned up in an uncharted section of the cave seemed to offer proof of the story. If Jesse was still alive, Rudy and Lester were determined to find him.

Rudy traveled to Oklahoma to meet Dalton and became intrigued by what he found. The bedridden old man who claimed to be Jesse James was winning over the skeptics. The press was starting to put its confidence into print and no interviewer seemed able to poke a hole in his story. Most interesting of all, the self-proclaimed outlaw had a reason for why he'd kept silent for so long. Dalton claimed that Robert Ford had actually shot Charles Bigelow, another James gang member, in 1882. Bigelow's brains were blown out and he was buried under Jesse's name so that the real outlaw (i.e. Dalton) could live in peace. Missouri Governor Crittenden had been in on the ruse. Dalton and the rest of the gang had made a pact to disclose their true identities only after they reached the age of 100.

Rudy, still skeptical, examined Dalton with a magnifying glass and was stunned to discover damage done to the old man's body agreed with reports or injuries sustained by Jesse James – from a mutilated tip on the left hand index finger, to evidence of severe burns on both feet, a drooping right eyelid, and bullet scars along the left shoulder, hairline, and abdomen. If Dalton wasn't Jesse James, he had groomed himself from head to toe, leaving out nothing, to make himself appear that he was. Rudy began making arrangements to bring Dalton to Stanton. He was planning a birthday celebration for the man that he believed was the legendary outlaw.

During the planning, Dalton told Rudy to try and track down some of the other living members of the gang and Rudy found John Tramell, a cook who had once rode with the gang. Rudy told the man that Jesse James wanted him to come to Meramec Caverns for his 102nd birthday party, but Tramell swore that he didn't know the man. When Rudy went back to Dalton for an explanation, he was told that since he didn't know a secret password, Tramell wouldn't talk with him. When asked why he didn't offer the password originally, Dalton said that he wanted to make sure that Rudy could be trusted. Dalton gave him the password, and this time, when he returned to Tramell, the old man agreed to come to the party.

Dalton was given a cabin on the Meramec Caverns property where he could live. He drank heavily and loved telling stories. He was friendly with just about everyone – except reporters, which he grew to hate. They bothered him day and night. Dalton asked for a six-shooter and would actually shoot holes in the ceiling of his cabin to scare the reporters away. Rudy and Lester became concerned that he might actually kill someone, so they started taking the powder out of the bullets and replacing the lead. This plan didn't work well, because Dalton picked up the bullets and knew they were light, so he demanded a full load.

While Dalton was busy fending off reporters, Rudy was working hard to secure Dalton's legitimacy. Over the years, his faith in Dalton led to him appearing on *What's My Line?* and *The Tonight Show*. Rudy appeared in newspapers and in men's magazines, where he offered $10,000 to anyone who could prove Dalton was a fraud. The story brought so much publicity to Meramec Caverns that Rudy created his own tribute to Dalton in the form of the Jesse James Wax Museum in Stanton.

Today, the museum still stands along Route 66 in Stanton. Inside, life-sized figures of Dalton, Rudy Turilli, Cole Younger, and others greet visitors. Firearms that purportedly belonged to the James gang can be found in glass cases and antiques like Frank James' bathtub and a barber chair in which Jesse received his last trim are on display. There are autopsy photographs and a computer-enhanced projection that turns a 34 year-old Jesse James into an elderly J. Frank Dalton, plus a set of 12-inch ears that allegedly prove that the lobes of Dalton and Jesse James were a perfect match.

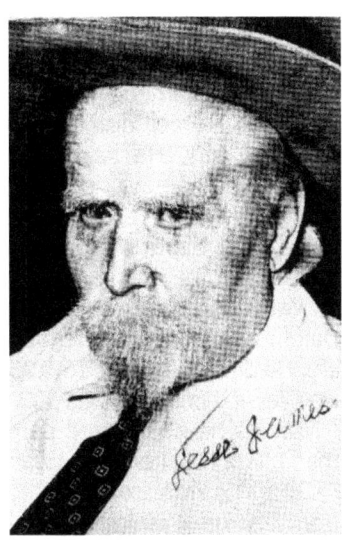

"Jesse James" after he left behind the J. Frank Dalton "alias"

Before Dalton's death, Rudy and Lester petitioned the Franklin County Circuit Court to change Dalton's name back to Jesse James. With hat in hand, Dalton was carried into the courthouse on a stretcher. However, Judge Ransom A. Breur dismissed the whole thing as a publicity stunt, which it probably was. He said: "There is no evidence here to show that this gentleman, if he was ever Jesse James, has ever changed his name. If his name has never been changed from Jesse James, he is still Jesse James in name, and there is nothing for this court to pass on. If he isn't what he professes to be, then he is trying to perpetrate a fraud upon this court."

With that, Lester and Rudy returned to Meramec Caverns and J. Frank Dalton remained a mysterious and grumpy old man for the remainder of his life. He died on August 16, 1951, during a visit to Granbury, Texas. If he really was Jesse James, he was 103 years, 11 months, and 10 days old.

Unless he was indeed perpetrating the fraud, Rudy Turilli was convinced that J. Frank Dalton really was Jesse James. But was he?

In 1995, Professor James E. Starrs (a law professor, not a forensic scientist) from George Washington University exhumed the body of Jesse James that was buried in Kearney, Missouri – only one of two gravesites of James. Based on DNA comparisons with living members of the James family, it was ruled that the body in the grave was actually that of Jesse James. Not surprisingly, though, there was a lot of controversy about the findings, the quality of the evidence and why distant relatives were used for the tests when Jesse's mother, Zerelda, was buried nearby. Supporters of the J. Frank Dalton claims scoffed at the findings and swore to produce their own tests of Dalton's remains.

As far as I know, though, that has never been done. As of this writing, the truth –or fiction – of the story of J. Frank Dalton remains a mystery.

The Town Named for Liquor

South of Stanton, the old highway remains just off the interstate all of the way through the town of Sullivan, where George Hearst, father of publishing giant William Randolph Hearst, was born. Sullivan was founded in 1856 by Stephen and Dorcas Sullivan, who came to Missouri from South Carolina. They had learned of the Meramec River and the surrounding area from none other than frontiersman Daniel Boone. They settled in the region, built a cabin, and cleared a large piece of land for farming. A large portion of their land later became the site of the original town of Sullivan. When Stephen heard about the plans of the St. Louis & San Francisco Railroad Company to extend the southwest branch from Franklin (Pacific) to Rolla, he donated property to the railroad, along with a building to be used as a depot. Soon after, people began migrating to the area, working as farmers, railroad men, and mining the local mineral deposits.

Bourbon Lodge, a favorite stopping spot on U.S. 66

The mining of lead, iron, zinc, and copper helped the economy of Sullivan to thrive until the late 1870s. Even after an end to the mining, the last days of the railroad, and the fading of Route 66, Sullivan has remained an attractive town for locals and visitors alike.

A few miles away on Route 66 is the town of Bourbon, which is believed to be the only town in the United States named for bourbon whiskey. The town got its start when the construction of the railroad began in the 1850s, following the Old Springfield, or "Wire" Road. As settlers and railroad workers came to the area, there were many Irish immigrants among them and they brought along a thirst for whiskey. An enterprising businessman named Richard Turner opened a general store near the railroad construction site and began selling a bourbon from the front porch of his store. Since the store had no official name, the workers dubbed it the "Bourbon Store." A small town grew up around the store and the name "Bourbon" stuck. A post office was opened in 1853, and the town was given the designation of "Bourbon in the Village of St. Cloud." Wealthy land owners had planned a village about a half-mile from the store, but it never actually came about, so the name "Bourbon" was applied to the store, homes, and other businesses that sprang up nearby.

With the arrival of U.S. 66 in 1926, auto courts, cafes, and service stations began popping up all along the highway in the area. In 1932, Alex and Edith Mortensen opened what became the most popular spot in the town's history, the **Bourbon Lodge**. This small, fledgling operation included a café and three overnight cabins. The café featured a 25-cent breakfast that included eggs, bacon, toast, and coffee. The cabins, which offered running water, were rented for 50-cents a night. A Phillips 66 service station was later added, as was a fourth tourist cabin. By 1939, the Mortensens were charging $1 to $1.50 per night for the cabins, which now also had showers and indoor toilets. They eventually sold the lodge in the early 1940s and moved a half-mile west on Route 66, where they operated the Hi Hill Cabins and Station until 1947.

Many of the old Bourbon Lodge structures still stand today, including the lodge and café, which is now a private residence. The service station and a couple of the cabins were still standing last year, in various states of disrepair.

"The Mammoth Cave of Missouri"

After leaving Bourbon, the highway continues into the countryside past the cutoff to Leasburg, just above Onondaga Cave. Formerly owned by Lester Dill, Onondaga was considered one of the country's most magnificent caves because of its huge formations, gigantic rooms, and amazing colors of cave rocks. Lester Dill turned it into a major tourist attraction, but it actually got off to a very treacherous start – which in the 1930s turned into a shooting war.

In the 1880s, the future cave attraction was seen as little more than a water-filled hole. In 1881, the spring that poured out of the mouth of the cave was harnessed to power the William Davis Grist Mill. No one thought to actually enter the wet confines of the cave until 1886. That summer, a drought lowered the water levels and mill workers Charley Christopher, John Eaton, and Mitius Horine decided to go inside using a small rowboat. They squeezed their way to the onyx center of the cave and couldn't believe what they saw. Two of the men, Christopher and Eaton, immediately made plans to purchase the cave, but once they owned it, they couldn't decide what to do with it. The onyx market was at its peak, but neither man had the money to mine the cave. They finally decided to open it as a tourist attraction and called it the "Mammoth Cave of Missouri," swiping the name of the famous cave in Kentucky.

Unfortunately, though, the tourist market turned out to be difficult to break into, and in May 1902, Eaton sold his shares in the cave to Eugene Hunt Benoist of the Indian Creek Land Company. Christopher bailed out soon after and sold his half of the cave to a St. Louis mining concern that was headed by George Bothe, Sr. Bothe had the wealth and equipment to mine the cave, but while he was completing his core tests, the onyx market collapsed. Builders had been using Missouri onyx as a substitute for marble but they soon discovered that the onyx became soft once it was taken from its natural environment. Bothe soon realized that he was now stuck with what appeared to be a worthless hole in the ground.

But the cave came into its own in 1904, the year the World's Fair came to St. Louis. Bothe did whatever he could to snag sightseers for the cave. A "Name-the-Cave" contest earned Onondaga its name – Iroquois for "Spirit of the Mountain" – and the Frisco Railroad brought visitors on an 80-mile excursion train ride to see the cave for themselves. The train fare cost $1.60, with an additional 75-cent buggy ride from Leasburg to the cave and back again. Another $1 bought a ticket inside, which was pretty pricey for the time. Visitors were floated into the cave in flat-bottom boats. The boat ride ended after a short distance and then visitors walked during the rest of the five-hour tour. Afterward, anyone too exhausted to make the trip home could spend the night in the Davis Grist Mill, which had recently been partitioned into sleeping rooms.

After the World's Fair, Onondaga's popularity began to grow. In 1910, Bothe sold the cave to his niece, Catherine Weinborg, and she sold it to Bob Bradford three years later. Bradford finally built a proper road to reach the cave, which brought more business in the 1920s.

And then, in the early 1930s, the Mook brothers made their unwelcome arrival in the area. The two men, William and Lee Mook, began leasing property near Onondaga with the intention of opening a resort for doctors. But then they learned that the cave actually ran underneath their property. Late at night, they entered the cave through a remote sinkhole and dug a passage into "their" section of the cave. They decided that their land extended to the halfway point in the cave's "Big Room" and put up a barbed wire fence to separate the caves. They named their half of the cave Missouri Caverns and opened tours of their own in 1932.

One of the cave's most popular attractions was the "Lily Pad Room"

The entrance to Missouri Caverns was closer to Route 66 than the entrance of the Onondaga Cave. The Mooks used this advantage to steal as much of Bradford's business as they could. Erecting a sign that read "Cave – Drive-in," they sidetracked visitors into their parking lot. On other occasions, they hired people to fake auto breakdowns in front of Missouri Caverns so that no cars could get past them to Onondaga Cave. It was common for arguments to break out at the barbed wire fence in the cave and guides often encouraged their respective customers to throw rocks and hurl insults at the other tour group.

Bob Bradford met these challenges with patience but, occasionally, his temper got the best of him and once, he threatened Lee Mook with a gun. On calmer days, Bradford won customers with his new "Submarine Room." The attraction was behind Onondaga's "Lily Pad Room" in a nook that naturally filled with water. Bradford built a gangplank into the area and drained most of the water so that visitors could view beautiful crystals that formed below the waterline. He was forced to re-drain the Submarine Room every three weeks so that it maintained its postcard-perfect view.

Violent encounters at the barbed wire fence grew more common – and more ridiculous. In 1934, Missouri senatorial candidate Harry S. Truman toured Missouri Caverns with an entourage of Democrats. On the same day, a group of Republicans toured Onondaga Cave. The two parties met at the barbed wire fence and spent most of the afternoon ridiculing each other to the point that some of the men came to blows.

On May 7, 1935, the Supreme Court ruled on the dispute between the two caves. The Mooks – and their fence – could stay. The news of this was made slightly more palatable to Bob Bradford because William Mook had died the previous November.

Missouri Caverns and Onondaga Cave operated next to each other into the 1940s. In time, Onondaga Cave emerged as the prominent attraction. In 1937, Bradford built the Cool Room, a motel that sat on the banks of the Lost River, immediately outside of the cave's entrance. The bedrooms and the recreational area of the motel were chilled by genuine air from Onondaga Cave.

World War II closed Missouri Caverns. By July 1945, both Lee Mook and Bob Bradford were dead. Bradford's widow sold Onondaga Cave to Barnard Hospital. Charles Rice, the hospital's director, had already inherited Missouri Caverns from the Mooks. He retired from the hospital on the day it was announced that he owned both halves of a very troubled cave.

Rice spent the next few years working to put Onondaga back together again. He tore down the barbed wire fence, demolished the old grist mill, and ran electric lights into the cave for the first time. He laid new cave trails and greatly improved every aspect of the attraction. Improvements were still underway when Rice died in 1949.

Four years later, Lester Dill and Lyman Riley bought the cave from Rice's family. By 1953, Dill and Riley were known as the "King Cavemen of Franklin and Crawford Counties." Lyman was a native of Sioux City, Iowa, who worked as a schoolteacher until he met his wife, Velma, at a show cave. He stayed in the business and hooked up with marketing genius Dill, who had brought "Jesse James" (J. Frank Dalton) to Missouri and had painted ads for Meramec Caverns on barns across the Midwest. Both men had managed the cave together for Charles Rice and knew that Onondaga offered things that were unique among other Missouri show caves.

They were also quick to make changes when they were needed. When Dill took over the cave, they were still bringing people into the place by boat. The guide stood at the front and pulled the boat along, but one day, a boat tipped over and a young girl fell into the water and drowned. Needless to say, they immediately made plans to stop the boat trips.

Dill fashioned a dry entrance to Onondaga Cave, but the loss of

When Lester Dill took over the cave, guests were still being taken inside by boat. After a boat tipped over and a young girl drowned, a dry entrance was immediately built.

the boats left him without a promotional gimmick. Watching television gave him a new idea and he decided to cash in on the popularity of Daniel Boone. The famous frontiersman had spent the later years of his life in Missouri and had traveled on the Meramec River, so Lester decided to tout the cave as Daniel Boone's discovery. The new "legend" had it that Boone had chased a bear into the cave and discovered its natural wonders. He renamed the grounds Daniel Boone Park, and when I was a kid, I remember stopping at the cave and posing for pictures at a wooden cut-out where you could stick your face through so that the finished photo showed you wearing a buckskin outfit and coonskin cap.

In 1967, Lyman Riley sold his interest in the cave to Lester Dill. That same year, the cave faced a fatal threat when Congress authorized construction of a dam across the Meramec River. The dam would potentially provide flood control and area recreation, but studies also showed that it would flood 80 percent of Onondaga Cave. Dill joined the opposition to the plan, and eventually, the dam project was dropped. After Lester Dill died in 1980, Missouri made Onondaga a state park.

Onondaga Cave today is a beautiful place and stands as one of the most exciting of Missouri's show caves. In spite of this, it has a weird feel to it – wavering between the solemnness of a state park and the cave's quirky, commercial past. Many of the 2,200 concrete steps that were installed by Charles Rice now crumble next to a newer, less-intrusive cave trail. Copper coins that were removed years ago have left the "Lily Pad Room" pools an eerie bluish color. Even after all of these years, an echo of the past still remains at Onondaga Cave. Daniel Boone may have departed decades ago, but some of the weirdness can still be found.

Flying to Cuba

Just down the road from Onondaga Cave is the town a Cuba, a once-important stop on Highway 66. Cuba had its beginnings in 1857, when two men, M.W. Trask and W.H. Ferguson, surveyed the town site in anticipation of the St. Louis and San Francisco Railroad coming through the area. Responsibility for naming the town fell to George Jamison and Wesley Smith. Smith suggested naming the town "Cuba" as a show of support for Cuban citizens, who were then under Spain's oppressive hold. Jamison wanted to name the town for his wife, Amanda, who already had a post office named after her just a mile and a half from the town site. Legend has it that the issue was finally decided by letting a stick stand on end. Whichever way it fell determined the name of the town – Cuba won.

Before the railroad arrived, many people in the area made their livings working in the iron ore industry and as farmers. With the arrival of the railroad in 1860, Cuba became a major shipping point, especially for apples, which were vital to the town's economy into the 1930s. Apple orchards were planted in abundance and the community became known for its quality fruit. The town became known as the "Land of the Big Red Apple," and by the start of the twentieth century, Cuba was the largest producer and distributor of apples in Missouri.

When Route 66 came through in 1926, things really began to thrive. Cuba moved away from the railroad tracks and closer to the new highway. The community embraced Route 66 and its economy began to be based on the endless parade of tourist traffic. Motels, diners, and service stations seemed to pop up overnight.

The interstate bypassed Cuba in the late 1960s, but the town never abandoned Route 66. They remain proud of their heritage and have worked hard to retain the flavor of the highway in their community. It has been dubbed the "Gateway to the Ozarks" and "Mural City," and remains a must-stop town for U.S. 66 travelers.

One of Cuba's long-time Route 66 icons was the **Midway**, a restaurant and a garage with a car showroom. Allyne Earls leased the Midway for 10 years and finally bought the building in 1944. She put in 24 bedrooms and four bathrooms on the second floor and expanded the restaurant into the garage. By the time she finished remodeling, she had 36 people on staff. During World War II, the rooms were filled with Fort Leonard Wood soldiers and their wives. As many as 600 soldiers were fed every day at the Midway. A T-bone steak, fries, vegetable, and a salad cost only $1.20. If money was

The Midway, a long-time Route 66 icon in Cuba.

tight, a hamburger was just 12- cents. For 38 years, the Midway was open 24-hours a day. When Allyne finally sold the place in the 1970s and the new owner asked for the keys, she couldn't find them. The doors to the Midway had never been locked. In time, the building was converted into a business mall and in 2011, was torn down.

A remaining landmark is the **Wagon Wheel Motel**, one of the most recognizable spots in town. Originally known as the Wagon Wheel Cabin Court, it was built by Robert and Margaret Martin, and constructed by a local stone mason. It started out as a nine-room motel and the Ozark stone and the brick trim around the windows gave the place its classic "rocked" look, which was so popular around the region. The Wagon Wheel once boasted "all modern steam heated, fireproof cottages," according to the postcards that were sold on site. In the 1930s, rooms rented for $1.50 per night. By 1946, the motel had expanded to 14 units, a number that grew to 18 when the attached garages were enclosed and converted into rooms. A service station and a 24-hour café were also added to the property, but they operated independently from the motor lodge.

The Wagon Wheel Motel is a former cabin court that still offers a nostalgic place to stay for Route 66 travelers.

When Interstate 44 bypassed the area in the late 1960s, the future of the Wagon Wheel looked grim, but the motel managed to hang on. The place had several owners over the years (including a man named Mathis, who designed the distinctive neon sign) but Harold and Pauline Armstrong have run the Wagon Wheel for the last 40 years or so, continuing to offer clean rooms at a great price for the nostalgic Route 66 adventurer.

Roadside Rocking Chair

After Cuba, Route 66 becomes a country road and travels to the small town of Fanning – a small town with a very large attraction. On the edge of town is the U.S. 66 Outpost and General Store, and while this is a fun little place to pick up highway souvenirs and drinks, it's not the main attraction. The main reason for stopping here is hard to miss – it's a gigantic rocking chair, now known as the **Red Rocker**. Erected on April Fool's Day 2008, the chair stands on rockers that are each 31 1/2 feet long and each weigh a ton. It's built of steel pile and had to be lifted into place by two cranes.

The chair was conceived by Outpost owner Dan Sanazaro as a way to entice customers into his shop, which he had opened two months earlier. It was designed by a friend with no formal engineering training and was built by the owner of a local welding company. Dan recalled a giant rocking chair that he had seen as a kid on a family road trip and wanted one for himself. He knew of 34-foot tall rocker in Franklin, Indiana – called "Big John" – and he knew he had to make one bigger.

At over 42 feet tall, Dan's chair, which was originally called "The World's Largest Rocking Chair," not only towered above Big John in Indiana, but was also taller than the previous record holder in Alabama. In order to be certified by Guinness as the World's Largest Rocking Chair, it had to do one thing – rock. It was designed to do just that when it was first built, but the massive chair was so terrifying when it was in motion that Dan eventually had it welded securely to its base.

Unfortunately, the chair wouldn't be able to hang onto its world record status. Just as Dan Sanazaro's chair had beaten out others that once held the designation for World's Largest Rocking Chair, the Missouri chair lost out on the Guinness designation in the Fall of 2015 when a new rocker was built in Casey, Illinois. But Dan didn't let it phase him. He hired a local painting company, Brown & Son, and they gave it a bright red patina to go with its new name of "Red Rocker."

But whatever color it is, there is no way that a traveler can miss this modern Route 66 roadside oddity.

Wine, Women & Song

As Route 66 winds along, it ends up just four miles east of St. James at the the small, unincorporated community of Rosati. Settled in 1845, the town was first called "Knobview," for the three high hills that overlook the area from the east.

The first store there was built by the first resident of the area, Thomas Kinsey, Jr. A short time later, a U.S. survey of the region was conducted and when it was completed, land was offered to any company that would build a railroad through that part of Missouri. In the summer of 1850, the Pacific Railroad arrived at Knobview and the general store became known as Kinsey's Station. It also housed the settlement's first post office. The railroad began selling off its excess land at reasonable prices and a number of Italian immigrants were attracted to the region. New homes, services, and businesses sprang up, including two more stores, a saloon, a canning plant, a new post office, school, and a church. In 1906, the St. Anthony Catholic Church was built, and in 1934, the town was renamed after the first bishop of the Roman Catholic Archdiocese of St. Louis, Italian-born Joseph Rosati.

Many of the Italians turned to farming and attempted to plant grape varieties from Italy, but after having no success, they switched to Concord grapes, which became the predominate crop for many decades. By the 1930s, more than 250,000 vines were producing grapes along Route 66. Along this stretch of Route 66 every September, grape stands used to dot the landscape and offered tourists the chance to purchase bags of grapes and jugs of fresh juice. A few of these stands migrated over to Interstate 44, but there are not nearly as many today as there were in the past.

By the 1970s, fewer contracts were being filled by Welch's for purchasing Concord grapes and by the 1990s, they had stopped altogether. The locals adapted, though, and started replacing their vines with wine grape varieties. Thanks to this, wine-making has become a major business in the area and several wineries have opened in the area, including the **St. James Winery**, which ships its excellent product all over the Midwest.

Just a few miles from Rosati is the town of St. James, which is known as the "Forest City of the Ozarks." Founded in 1859 by John Wood, he bought land in the area in anticipation of an extension of the St. Louis & San Francisco Railway. Intended as a shipping point for the nearby Meramec Iron Works, which had previously shipped its product by wagon train, Wood saw a great opportunity for a town, which he originally called "Scioto." It was changed to St. James within a year and the iron ore mines provided the first employment in town.

When the Civil War began, the town fell under Union Army control and fierce fighting with Confederate sympathizers took place in the area. A detachment of German immigrant volunteers, who were encamped near the town, was so impressed by the area that they moved to St. James when the war was over. Their German influence can still be felt in the town. By the 1870s, St. James turned to lumber, farming, and wine making. The Italian immigrants who came to Rosati and the surrounding area, largely fleeing from poor working conditions in Chicago, started the vineyards and wineries around St. James.

When Route 66 came to St. James, the town became a tourist destination and was popular for the grapes, rich forests, Meramec Springs, and its proximity to the rivers of the Ozark region. **Finn's Motel** was one of the early U.S. 66 resting spots and it remains open today, although the vintage neon sign that could once be famously found on the premises has been moved away.

The old Finn's Motel sign was classic neon.

A one-time classic spot in St. James was the **Rock Haven Cabin Court**, a classic example of the late 1920s and early 1930s motor court – simple overnight rest stops for travelers and businessmen. Opened soon after U.S. 66 was designated as a highway, Rock Haven offered six small "modern" cabins that were built from native sandstone slabs called "giraffe rock." This kind of rock was common in the region and was used to build everything from homes to motels, restaurants, and service stations. Indoor plumbing was not typical in the early motor courts and Rock Haven, like most others, provided a community washhouse with hot and cold running water for showers.

In 1950, Frank and Ruth Waring purchased the Rock Haven and that summer, added a wooden double cabin, a restaurant, and a new Standard Oil

The Rock Haven Court offered six modern cabins, along with a restaurant and service station.

filling station. In 1954, they sold it to Rudy Gilder, who operated the motor court until the interstate bypassed it in the late 1960s. After being converted to a tavern and nightclub in the 1970s, the restaurant building, although now altered, still stands today as a private residence. In 1988, all but one of the cabins were torn down, leaving only a small glimpse into the history of auto travel on Route 66.

A Stop at the Mule Trading Post

Just a few miles down the highway from St. James is the **Mule Trading Post**, one of Route 66's most popular tourist stops. To many travelers along old Route 66, a mule must have seemed like an unusual mascot to see on roadway signs, directing them to a tourist stop known as the Mule Trading Post. Oddly, though, mules have long been associated with Missouri, starting back during World War I when the state furnished most of the mules for the army. And like its stubborn namesake, the Mule Trading Post had survived nearly 70 years along Route 66, refusing to give in to the changing times and interstate bypasses.

Founded in 1946 on the three-lane alignment of Route 66 in Pacific, Missouri, the Mule was the brainchild of Frank Ebling. He started the place as a combination restaurant and gift shop, but soon dropped the food when he realized how much money he was making selling the roadside trinkets. By 1955, the Mule was among one of the largest sellers of souvenirs in the Ozarks. When the new interstate blew past Route 66 between St. Louis and Pacific, Ebling didn't hesitate. He built a new place east of Rolla and moved the Mule further west on the highway. He settled down in 1957, and the Mule has not moved since.

Mule Trading Post

    The gift shop sold every type of kitschy souvenir imaginable – ashtrays, plates, state spoons, cups and saucers, shirts, Indian knick-knacks, fake wood religious plaques, fireworks, and much more. Herb Baden was the next owner of the store. He was an Ozark souvenir wholesaler who got into the trinket business in 1955. He surprised himself by being a natural at the business. For seven years, he worked for Lugene's Wholesale Souvenir Company in Branson, Missouri, and logged thousands of miles selling ashtrays and souvenir pencils. His biggest accounts were Route 66 items, Lake of the Ozarks, Meramec Caverns, Onondaga Cave, but his biggest retail client was the Mule Trading Post.

    After months on the road, Baden realized that he wanted to spend more time with his family and so he took a job running a Stuckey's Pecan Shop in Illinois. He ran the Stuckey's for four years and then decided that he wanted to be his own boss. When the Mule Trading Post went up for sale, he knew it was what he wanted. He knew the business was good because Ebling was a huge buyer of souvenirs from him in the past.

    He bought the Mule in 1966 and quickly began learning more about the business than he'd ever dreamed. He knew all about the souvenir market, but he didn't know much of anything about the advertising needed to make the trading post work. Unlike the majority of Route 66 tourist spots, the Mule had the best luck when it positioned its billboards to catch travelers who were motoring east. They discovered that most people didn't buy their souvenirs until they were headed home. For the Mule, this meant people returning to heavily populated areas in Illinois, Ohio, Indiana, and Michigan.

    Baden also realized that the Mule trademark created by Ebling was really important to people. Tourists loved the cartoon jackass and actively looked for him on the road. There were 40 blue and yellow signs along Route 66. All of them were the same except the message on each sign. All of the trading post's signs stretched between Rolla and Joplin and all were in Missouri – even though people swore they saw them in Texas, Oklahoma, and even California. The "sightings" happened so often that the staff just decided to go along with it and when people claimed to see a Mule sign where none existed, the staff laughed and said they had forgotten about that one.

As odd as it seemed, the Mule's charmed life continued through changes in highway access. When Interstate 44 bypassed the Mule and destroyed most of the neighboring businesses, the Mule experienced an increase in sales. In the 1970s, when the supply of Ozark hand-woven baskets ran out, Baden found his customers already looking for cheaper items. He soon found that anything with "Missouri" or the "Ozarks" on it sold very quickly.

Over the years, the Mule attracted more than its share of unusual visitors. Barry Goldwater stopped in soon after his presidential campaign hit the skids. Jack Klugman came in one afternoon, signed autographs, and then bought some fireworks. On one occasion, an escaped mental patient appeared at the counter and announced his plans to commit suicide in the store. Baden called the highway patrol and put a stop to the plan.

But by far, the Mule's weirdest contribution to Route 66 lore was its Piano-Playing Chicken, who was a regular attraction at the trading post in the 1960s. The chicken was one of many developed by a Lake of the Ozarks man named Al Lechner. He put together coin-operated machines with a live chicken and a small piano inside. You put in a quarter and the chicken got the signal to peck on the piano. The minute it stopped, the machine distributed some feed. People loved it, but one hot summer, the Humane Society put an end to the program.

Today, the Mule Trading Post survives as it has always survived – with a stubbornness that simply doesn't allow it to quit. Back scratchers, shirts, and kitschy souvenirs are still on hand. Above the store's main entrance, a neon rendition of the Mule's trademark still waggles its ears, reminding everyone of the trading post's early days.

On Past Rolla

Just down the road from the Mule Trading Post is the town of Rolla, home to a branch of the University of Missouri. The town had started back in 1855 when a group of contractors who were constructing the St. Louis & San Francisco Railway selected the area for supply warehouses and a railway office. Anticipating the arrival of the railroad, nearly 600 people moved to the area over the next six months. According to legend, a local resident, George Coopedge, who was homesick for his native North Carolina, suggested the name of Raleigh for the new town. The name was accepted and city leaders ended up spelling the name of the new town the same way that Coopedge pronounced it – hence, "Rolla" was born.

On January 1, 1861, the first train arrived in Rolla, but the outbreak of the Civil War prevented westward expansion of the line for the next several years. However, the town did become an important transportation hub as supplies were shipped from the east and loaded onto wagons heading west. During the war, Rolla served as a military post with as many as 20,000 Union troops stationed in the surrounding area.

When U.S. 66 came through Rolla, it replaced Route 14, a gravel road that was usually only open to travel in good weather. Work began on the concrete slab in 1928, and the stretch of road between Rolla and Lebanon became the last piece of road to be paved in Missouri. When the concrete two-lane road finally opened in 1931, Rolla commemorated the event with a public celebration, complete with a parade. The locals certainly had cause to celebrate because the new road resulted in a booming business for the town's cafes, service stations, and motels.

After the loss of Route 66, Rolla still managed to thrive. Many of its smaller businesses died out after Interstate 44 replaced the old highway, but thanks to the university, it came back strong. In fact, the University of Missouri has managed to develop one of the town's premiere roadside attractions – a half-scale version of **Stonehenge**, which was built by students from the college.

Touted as being the oldest still-operating business on Missouri's stretch of Route 66, the **Totem Pole Trading Post** has been in Rolla since 1933. Harry Cochrane opened up the first Totem Pole Trading Post on Arlington Hill, about 10 miles west of the present-day location. He built a small building with an eye-catching totem pole outside and started selling gifts and souvenirs to Highway 66 travelers. Nearby, he also set up a tourist camp for primitive overnight accommodations.

In 1950, Ralph Jones purchased the trading post and kept it going through the many changes that came to the highway after World War II. Around 1954, the state bought some of the property where the tourist camp was located, and cabins had to be moved to allow for an extra set of highway lanes to be built. In 1967, the state announced that it was taking over the entire property in order to build service roads for the new interstate. The Jones family closed down the trading post, but only for a short time. They moved to a new location, closer to Rolla, bringing along the original totem pole, which can now be seen in the current location's gift shop. As luck would have it, old Route 66 was located behind the building and the new interstate was out in front.

In 1977, Ralph's son, Tim, along with his wife, Alice, took over the trading post. Unfortunately, a short time later, they were closed again. The interstate was being moved and would effectively wipe out the store's driveways. With the same fighting spirit that his father possessed, Tim moved a little over three miles east to a third location in a former Shell service station, where the trading post remains today. Even after all of these hurdles, the Jones family has managed to keep the doors open and the travelers coming in. It's still a great place to find Ozarks crafts, antiques, oddities, fireworks, books, and, of course, Route 66 souvenirs.

One former U.S. 66 landmark that did not survive the passing of time was **Schuman's Tourist City**, which was opened by R.E. Schuman in 1928, hoping to capitalize on the new road through town. Originally known as Schuman's Cottage City, with 17 "clean, comfortable cottages," it later became

Schuman's Tourist City

Schuman's Tourist City, and then Schuman's Motor Inn in the 1950s. From the day the cottages first opened in 1928, Schuman constantly made improvements to the guest cabins and the grounds, adding conveniences like covered parking, steam heat, in-room radios, and telephones. By the late 1930s, Tourist City also included a service station, café, and a two-story hotel that could accommodate up to 200 guests. It was billed as offering "all the facilities of a fine city hotel combined with the conveniences of an ultra-modern motor court." In 1931, after Schuman's was robbed by an armed gunman, the owners hired a guard to patrol the grounds at night. An advertising postcard noted that "all parts of the court and all floors of the hotel" were carefully patrolled and kept safe.

R.E. Schuman became a prominent businessman in the Rolla area and owned several other businesses, including the Central Missouri Hatchery,

The decaying entrance to Larry Baggett's Tribute to the Trail of Tears. Since his death in 2003, his labor of love has slowly crumbled away.

which turned out thousands of baby chicks each week. He also owned a commercial flower garden, located next to the motel. As Schuman's Motor Inn, the place survived well into the 1960s before it closed. Today it is a distant memory for the thousands of tourists who once made the "city" a home away from home.

Tribute to the "Trail of Tears"

Not far past Rolla is one of the more unique sites on Highway 66, Larry Baggett's Tribute to the Trail of Tears, an unusual property that is decorated with a stone arch, statues, stone walls, and rock gardens. It was built by the late Mr. Baggett to honor the Native Americans who suffered and died along the infamous "Trail of Tears."

In 1830, the U.S. government passed the Indian Removal Act, which forced tens of thousands of Cherokee, Creek, Seminole, Chickasaw, and Choctaw to leave their homes in the southwest United States and relocate to reservations in present-day Oklahoma. The Cherokee, the largest tribe in the Southeast, fought exile by passive resistance, lawsuits, and national publicity. The Cherokee had established homes and communities, cultivated the land, and had a treaty with the United States to protect their land in Georgia and

Tennessee. But when gold was discovered in Georgia, the government declared their claims to property as "null and void." This resulted in a frenzied land grab and the forced removal of the Cherokee from their homes. President Andrew Jackson further made the point, "Humanity weeps over the fate of the Indians, but, true philanthropy reconciles the mind to the extinction of one generation for another."

Thanks to the fact that they had successfully resisted the government's efforts to force them out for several years, their removal was particularly brutal when it finally came. In the spring and summer of 1838, more than 15,000 Cherokee Indians were forcibly removed by the U.S. Army. Held in concentration camps through the summer, they were placed on a death march, during which they suffered from exposure, disease, and starvation. Thousands died and the Cherokee came to call the march *Nunahi-Duna-Dlo-Hilu-I* – the "Trail of Tears."

In time, history marched on. The Indians lost their "permanent homes" in the west when land was needed for expansion and the story of the Trail of Tears began to fade. But Larry Baggett had not forgotten – or rather, according to his own testimony, the ghosts of the Cherokee who once traveled the trail refused to let him forget. He claimed that he would often be awakened in the middle of the night by a knock at his door. Whenever he got out of bed to answer, though, no one would be there. Later, Baggett was visited by an elderly Native American man who told him that his house was built directly on the Trail of Tears, blocking the path. The land around his home had been a campsite during the forced march, and many of the Cherokee had camped, rested, and even died where Baggett now lived. Before he met the man, Baggett had built a stone wall next to his house and now the Indian told him that he needed to put stairs there since the spirits were unable to get over the wall. Baggett did what the old man asked and when the stairs were finished, the late-night knocking stopped.

When Baggett had bought his land, he had planned to build a campground there, but his plans changed after his wife died. He decided to build a tribute to the Trail of Tears instead. He came to believe that he was destined to accomplish this task. After surviving two heart attacks and a severe case of diabetes, Baggett firmly believed he was given a new lease on life. He gained a unique perspective about life and death, religion, astral travel, astrology, and spiritual topics. The Trail of Tears tribute seemed like a natural extension to his unusual interests for Baggett.

He set to work. At the entrance to the property, he erected a stone archway with the words "Trail of Tears" on it. It sat between a statue of himself on one side and a sculpture of water pouring out of a bucket on the other. He built stone walls, more statues, a wishing well, several rock gardens, and a sign that described the plight of the Native Americans who suffered and died on the Trail of Tears. His large stone house was constructed around three large trees.

During its busiest days, Baggett's memorial attracted attention from all over the country and turned him into a local legend. News stories and documentaries about oddities on Route 66 always featured Baggett and his shrine grew over time.

Sadly, Larry Baggett passed away in 2003 and his shrine was sold. Since that time, it has stood empty, largely abandoned. The sculptures are deteriorating – the head of his self-portrait sculpture is currently missing – and it seems the tribute to tragedy may someday fade into history.

John's Modern Cabins & Vernelle's Motel

As Highway 66 kept winding its way on southwest of Rolla, it eventually made its way past Doolittle and entered the outskirts of Newburg. It was there, along the highway that Bill and Beatrice Bayliss opened Bill and Bess's Place in 1931, which would go on to achieve legendary status as **John's Modern Cabins.**

When the tourist court was originally opened by the Bayliss family, it boasted six log cabins and a dance hall. Located just off the highway, it saw a steady stream of travelers and even locals, who took advantage of the entertainment that appeared at the dance hall. In 1941, the property was sold and changed hands a number of times over the next decade. The region was buzzing with activity around this time as soldiers and their families poured into the Fort Leonard Wood area during World War II. In 1951, the court was sold to John and Lillian Dausch for $5,000 and became John's Modern Cabins. John Dausch gained quite a reputation in the area as a colorful character, and many called him "Sunday John" because he sold beer every day of the week – including Sunday, which was in open defiance of local laws at the time.

When Route 66 was widened in 1957, the state required the cabins to be moved back from the original road. The dance hall was torn down completely. By 1965, the state was constructing Interstate 44 and more of the land from the tourist court was lost to freeway construction. The new interstate did not provide easy access to the cabins and this would prove fatal to the business.

Not long after the interstate bypassed the site, Lillian passed away and John simply lacked the energy to keep things going. The tourist court was shut down for the first time in almost 40 years. John's death in 1971 left the property abandoned for the next five years. In 1976, Loretta Ross of St. Charles, Missouri, purchased the site with grand plans to re-open the cabins, but the plans fell through. For the next 25 years, the property was left to decay. The Ross family made plans to bulldoze the remaining buildings in 2002, but the plans were blocked by Route 66 preservationist – who then, sadly, failed to do anything to save the site.

Today, John's Modern Cabins is a "ghost" tourist court. Unmaintained since 1971, the property is beyond repair. In 2011, the roof of John's large cabin, where he and Lillian lived, collapsed. Two of the newer cabins on the site have also fallen down. The court's community bath, the maintenance building, and all six of the original cabins do remain, but are in hazardous condition. This section of U.S. 66 is usable but is no longer maintained and the two lane road now dead-ends at a demolished bridge near what was once Arlington, Missouri. Interstate 44 has also been diverted away from its original 1967 path, now an abandoned pair of gravel roads, as part of a highway realignment in 2005.

Some of the ruins of John's Modern Cabins

John's Modern Cabins still exists, even if it can't be seen from the interstate, but there is little left here but memories. It is no longer safe to enter any of the buildings, although the exteriors remain for those with cameras and a need to document this tragically abandoned and neglected piece of Route 66 history.

Not far from John's Modern Cabins was **Vernelle's Motel**, which managed to survive seven changes to Highway 66's route over the years, but was finally doomed when Interstate 44 was realigned due to unsafe conditions. It was a sad ending for a business that had endured so many changes over the course of so many years.

Vernelle's history can be traced back to 1938 when E.P. Gasser built a store, filling station, novelty shop, and six tourist cabins on the property and named it Gasser Tourist Court. The name was changed to Vernelle's in 1952 when Fred Gasser and his wife, Vernelle, bought the place from Fred's uncle. They opened a motel and a restaurant that seated up to 100 people and became famous for its chicken-fried steak and open-faced roast beef sandwiches. At one point, they even had a petting zoo on the property, which enticed travelers to extend their stop and spend a little more of their cash.

Unfortunately, the restaurant closed in 1967 when Interstate 44 came through the area.

The motel was sold to Forest Riley a short time later, and then to Nye Goodridge in the early 1960s. His son, Ed, ran the place until its final years. Ed had once worked in the restaurant as a cook and "did a little bit of everything," while his wife, Jean, worked as a waitress. Three units were added to the motel when the restaurant was torn down, which brought the total number of rooms up to 17.

Vernelle's Motel, with its classic 1950s-era sign, endured off the beaten path, invisible from the interstate for many years, but progress marched on and today, it is only a memory.

Stony Dell Resort

As a modern-day traveler motors along State Highway D, which leads to the small town of Jerome, his wheels turn over what was once Route 66. Speeding along, an adventurer that knows where to look will notice an elaborate stone archway, near an abandoned house, with an old painted sign that offers "Gas, Food, Bait, and Hand-made gifts." This is what remains of **Stony Dell Resort**.

Although the nearby town of Arlington already existed before U.S. 66 came along, it was in the 1930s and 1940s that the community truly began to boom. It was the famous highway that gave the town life, largely thanks to its proximity to Fort Leonard Wood, which brought heavy military traffic to Route 66 during the war years.

Arlington became home to Stony Dell Resort in 1932, when it was constructed by George Prewett. It soon became one of the busiest destination resorts in Missouri at that time. Movie star Mae West visited the resort on at least one occasion and since it was a short drive from Fort Leonard Wood, it became a popular weekend hangout for the troops. Activities at Stony Dell included a large swimming pool, tennis, dancing, boating, fishing, a restaurant, service station, bus stop, and a Justice of the Peace for quickie weddings. In 1939, 10 cabins were available for rent ($1-$2 per night). One swimming pool was fed by an artesian well and the water was quite cold. The water became so popular that it was bottled and sold in the resort's gift shop. The resort was so popular that the Highway Patrol was on hand to direct traffic off Route 66 on some days. Church groups often used the resort for retreats.

Stony Dell Resort, often so busy that highway patrolman had to direct traffic to keep U.S. 66 from becoming congested with people trying to get the resort.

Arlington began to die in the late 1940s. There were fewer soldiers at the military base after the war and much of Route 66 had been rerouted to make travel faster. Jack Rittenhouse listed Arlington, in his 1947 guide, as "a small, old-style village whose main street was cut off by a new highway." As the locals drifted off, a man named Rowe Carney purchased many of the town's building, intending to turn it into another resort, but he never followed through with his plans. Arlington is a ghost town today, existing in name only, with a few scattered buildings serving as a reminder that it was ever there at all.

Stony Dell Resort managed to hang on a little while longer. From 1954 to 1967, it was run by Fred Widener, although by the 1960s it was showing signs of age and wear. Finally, in 1967, the south half of Stony Dell Resort- the entire swimming complex - was torn down to accommodate Interstate 44.

Today, only a few of the resort buildings remain as ramshackle reminders of yesterday, an era when good times and swinging music made the resort come alive.

Getting Your Kicks

Traveling southwest past Rolla and toward Waynesville, the highlands of the Ozarks begin to merge with the Springfield plateau of Southwestern Missouri. Travelers will find substantial sections of Route 66 still exist between Rolla and Springfield. The old highway remains alive in many of the towns, like Martin Springs, Doolittle, Newburg, and others.

This was an important stretch of Route 66. Just two miles west of Rolla, Martin Springs was used for watering horses and livestock, long before Route 66 was ever dreamed of. By the time the highway was created, a store was built and nearby, at the site of an old pioneer cabin, one of the first truck stops in America – the **Old Homestead** – was opened in 1925. Three years later, W.D. and Lynna Aaron built a radiator shop next door, and for many years, they operated the only tow truck service in the area. Lynna served light lunches and kept some groceries on hand to sell, and when things got busy, helped at the gas pumps out front.

This stretch of highway stayed busy for years. In 1940, M.L. Pierce opened a salvage yard and **Poe's Truck Stop** opened for business in 1953. Lou Hargis opened a skating rink nearby during World War II. Hargis was the second mayor of Doolittle, a small town that was loosely strung along about two miles of road. This wide spot in the highway was originally called Centreville, but found itself in the international spotlight on October 10, 1946, when it changed its name to honor General Jimmy Doolittle. The World War II flying hero flew his own airplane to the dedication ceremonies and landed it on the eastbound lane of Route 66.

Devil's Elbow

Perhaps one of the most eerie place names along old Route 66 is "Devil's Elbow," a quiet little community on the Big Piney River. The little Ozarks town has nothing sinister in its origins, despite the name, and its diabolical moniker came from lumberjacks who floated logs down to this treacherous point in the river. The logs often jammed up at the bend (elbow) and caused long delays, leading the men to comment that the river at this point had a "devil of an elbow."

A block east of the highway bridge that crosses the river sits the **Elbow Inn**, a roadhouse tavern that is very popular with the motorcycle crowd. The place is best known for its barbeque – and for the hundreds of women's undergarments that are nailed to the ceiling. Visiting ladies leave their bras behind at the place on a weekly basis.

The Elbow Inn is best known for its cold beer, tasty barbeque, and the hundreds of women's undergarments that are nailed to the ceiling.

But this was not the original incarnation of this place. It started out as the **Munger-Moss Sandwich Shop**, a Route 66 icon. Nellie Munger and Emmett Moss opened the place in 1936, soon after they were married. It was built on a piece of land that was right next to the bridge over the Big Piney River, making it one of the most picturesque eating spots on the highway. In 1943, Route 66 bypassed this location when a new four-lane section was built to accommodate heavy military traffic from nearby Fort Leonard Wood. The re-alignment killed the tourist traffic and business slowed to a crawl. The Munger-Moss Sandwich Shop moved, along with its new owners, to a new location, west of Devil's Elbow in the town of Lebanon.

In 1946, Paul and Nadine Thompson bought and re-opened the original location and changed the name of the place to the Elbow Inn, which they successfully operated into the 1960s. After it closed down, the café sat empty and at one time served as a private residence. It opened again, though, in 1997 and remains in operation today.

From Top:
* *Devil's Elbow Café*
* *McCoy's Store & Camp*
* *Miller's Market*

These were just some of the many businesses in the thriving community at the heyday of Route 66. The interstate would put nearly all of them out of business in the early 1980s.

Across the bridge was the site of the old **Devil's Elbow Café** and a Conoco station that was opened in 1932. The café and the station were once affiliated with the nearby **Cedar Lodge**, which was surrounded by 10 small cabins. The café was home to the local post office from 1931 to 1941, and years later, was turned into a tavern called the Hideaway. It burned down in the 1950s. A block from the café was **McCoy's Store and Camp**, a general store and motel that was built by Charles McCoy in 1941. The store sold fishing tackle and sporting goods and also rented boats that were used on the Big Piney. There were six small sleeping rooms for sportsmen upstairs. In 1948, the McCoys added seven small cabins to the property, but the place closed in 1954, and it was turned into an apartment building.

That same year, McCoy's son-in-law, Atholl "Jiggs" Miller, and his wife, Dorothy, built **Miller's Market**, which sold camping gear, dry goods and gasoline. The store served as the post office in town until 1982, when the market was sold to Terry and Marilyn Allman. They operated the place as Allman's Market until 2001, when it was purchased by Phil Sheldon. Sheldon had managed the Hideaway for a year before going into the army in 1942.

About a mile west of Devil's Elbow was **Ernie and Zada's Inn**, also known as the **E-Z Inn**. Built in the late 1930s, it quickly developed a reputation among the locals for being a wild beer-brawling, jukebox honky tonk. During the inn's heyday, it was also home to a trailer camp, several "modern" cabins, a restaurant, and a Sinclair service station. The restaurant offered lunches in the afternoon and dinner in the evening.

Ernie and Zada's or, as it was better known, the E-Z Inn.

In that part of the state, hunting and fishing was (and is) a major tourist draw. The E-Z Inn catered to sportsmen and soon became a popular stop for tourists on their way to a deer hunt and for those hoping to pull a big bass from the nearby river. Unfortunately, though, serving Falstaff beer to hunters and fishermen was not enough to keep the doors open. The E-Z Inn closed just a few years after opening, citing "a lack of business and hard times." The onetime gas station and restaurant still stand today as a private residence and a few of the cabins are still nearby.

In 1943, the main branch of Route 66 bypassed Devil's Elbow, but it was not until the 1980s that the interstate completely left the town behind. It still remains today as a relic of the road, mostly remembered only for its colorful name – and the often rowdy little bar that has a very large collection of bras on the ceiling.

Murder at Devil's Elbow

Despite its diabolical name, Devil's Elbow has no connection to the supernatural. However, there is an odd legend about a town called Mayfield, a ghost town that was located about two miles away along a rutted gravel road. Today, all that remains of the town is the Mayfield Cemetery, a collection of worn and weathered stones that are scarcely legible after all of these years.

The cemetery can be found off the gravel road, but about a mile before a traveler arrives there, he should look for a grave marker that belongs to a woman named Eliza Jane Laycocks Thomas, the wife of Henry Thomas, who died in 1897. There is no marker for Henry Thomas nearby. In fact, there are no other markers at all. This isolated grave poses a mystery that has been forever lost to time. Local legend claims that Eliza was a witch and could not be buried within the grounds of the Mayfield Cemetery, which is why she was buried all alone. The stories say that she still roams the forest near her grave, crying and moaning in anger, and occasionally cutting long ribbons into the tents of campers who sleep too close to the place where her body was laid to rest.

We will never know if there is any truth to the story of Eliza Thomas, but there is another story – one of death that involves a killer who has remained unpunished for nearly 50 years.

On October 18, 1968, three young men – Wayne Gilbert, Harold Presley, and Bobby Tryan – worked together at the Soto Service Club at Fort Leonard Wood. Gilbert was the oldest of the three, at 32, and had worked as the night manager at the club for 11 years. He was dependable and hard-working, as were the other two men, so when the day manager came to work on the morning of October 19 and found the back door unlocked and the safe standing open, he knew something was very wrong.

Military police officers were called to the scene and investigators quickly went to work. The back room of the club showed signs of a struggle and a roll of coins was found on the ground outside. The situation became more serious when it was realized that 20-year-old Bobby Tryan's 1960 Chevrolet was still in the lot. Tryan and Presley, 18, often rode to work together. Gilbert usually drove a 1964 maroon Ford – it was missing. A call was placed to the families of the three men and it was discovered that none of them had come home. What seemed to have been a simple robbery had now taken a more sinister turn.

The Missouri Highway Patrol and the Pulaski County Sheriff's Department were called into the case and advised about the robbery and the missing men. A military aircraft went up to take a look around the surrounding area for the missing car. FBI agents from Springfield and Joplin later arrived at the base. They had jurisdiction over the case since the crime had occurred on federal land. Hours passed and there was still no sign of the three men.

Later that same morning, a local man and his family were going to a farm they owned near Devil's Elbow. There was work to do and they planned to do some squirrel hunting. They turned off Route 66 onto a narrow dirt road that led to the farm and then immediately stopped the car. There were three men lying face down next to the road. All three had been shot in the head – and all were obviously dead. The family hurried to the closest store in Devil's Elbow and called the sheriff's office. A short time later, Deputy Leroy Tucker arrived at the store and the family led him back to the bloody scene. He had been alerted to the robbery at the Soto Club and the missing employees, and guessed by their uniforms that the three men had been found. He radioed the sheriff, High Patrol, and the military investigators about the discovery.

Pulaski County Coroner Charles Moss arrived at the scene at 11:15 a.m. He and the lawmen on hand investigated the scene and then Moss released the bodies to the Army pathologist, Dr. Isadora Mihalskis, who had them transported to the Fort Leonard Wood Hospital for autopsies. The autopsy revealed that the three men had all been shot multiple times in the head. The killer, or killers, had been standing above them and fired down into them while they were on the ground. Harold Presley also had a wound in his forearm, caused by a bullet passing through the head of another victim and striking his arm where he lay. There were no weapons found at the scene, but there were bullets, bullet fragments, and spent shell casings that were recovered. All of them were .32 and .38 caliber bullets and casings.

Meanwhile, investigators canvassed the area, but there were few people living near the remote site. No one had seen any cars traveling along the dirt road. Two farmers thought they might have heard gunshots around 11:30 p.m., or closer to midnight, but they assumed it was hunters or a car backfiring. Detectives had also found out that the money taken from the safe at the club amounted to $3,636.00 and as much as $1,000 of it was in quarters – which became an important point later in the investigation.

According to the cashier at the club, an 18-year-old young woman, they had closed at 10:00 p.m. the previous night. After finishing her work, she had left around 11:15. She reported that, as she was leaving, she saw Gilbert doing paperwork, Tryan was mopping, and Presley was buffing the floors. It was quiet outside when she left. The only activity that she noticed was a soldier in a nearby telephone booth and a red car that was some distance from the club. She saw nothing unusual.

As the investigation continued, though, one name began to be heard repeatedly by the detectives – Harry "Dino" Hurd. Not only did Hurd have a bad reputation, as one writer put it, as "the most dangerous man to ever set foot in Pulaski County," he had previously worked at the Soto Club and had been fired by Wayne Gilbert because he failed to do his work. Perhaps he had hard feelings toward Gilbert, who was well-liked by the rest of the staff, or perhaps he simply knew how much cash was kept on the premises and how the club operated after hours. Regardless, he soon became the prime suspect in the Soto Club murders.

Soon, the investigators had hard evidence against Hurd. A local man named McClain was working at the nearby Ramada Inn on October 19. He noticed a 1964 maroon Ford in the parking lot. McClain knew Wayne Gilbert and believed that the car in the lot belonged to him. He had heard about the robbery, so he called the police. The car was verified as Gilbert's and was searched and fingerprinted. The prints that were lifted were sent to the lab for analysis. They later came back as belonging to Dino Hurd.

In addition, Dino's brother, Chester Hurd, was reported to have used a large amount of quarters to purchase items around town. Were they part of the $1,000 in missing quarters that were stolen from the club?

According to locals, the investigators must have been getting too close. Wayne Gilbert's mother started receiving frightening telephone calls. She was threatened and warned not to pursue any further investigations and to stop cooperating with the police. The terrifying calls were repeated over several nights, even after sheriff's deputies were assigned to her for protection. She believed that Hurd, or someone he knew, was trying to convince her to not help the police.

Investigators worked hard to solve the case, but even the fingerprints were not enough to shake the alibi that was offered for him from his wife. She told detectives that Dino was home with her on the night of the murders, watching television. He never left and could not have committed the crime. The case came to a standstill and went cold. The alibi was solid and investigators had no way to break it.

But Hurd would not stay out of the news, or out of sight of investigators, for long. The early 1970s arrived with a string of murders and bombings in the Ozark hills and Dino Hurd was right in the middle of the violence.

On September 2, 1972, sheriff's deputies received a call at 6:35 p.m. about a shooting at Pat's Café on Highway Y, about two miles north of St. Robert. When officers arrived, they found two bodies on the floor of the café. They were identified as Robert Glanton and M.C. Curtis. Both men were armed with .38 caliber revolvers and a .357 Smith and Wesson. There were .45 caliber shell casings on the floor around the dead men.

According to Patricia Stump, the owner of Pat's Café, she was in the kitchen on the night of the shooting and heard five or six shots fired in the dining room. When she was asked at the coroner's inquest if she could identity the other men who arrived late and had dinner with Glanton and Curtis, she said she could not. She was then reminded of the possible penalties for withholding information while under oath, but she still refused to talk. According to sheriff's deputies, Mrs. Stump had originally told them that one of the men who fled the scene after the shooting was the "Hurd boy." Soon after making this identification, she refused to speak any further about Dino Hurd.

After several bombings, followed by the murders at Pat's Café, the FBI opened an investigation into the crime and violence taking place around Fort Leonard Wood. As a result of the new investigation, agents decided to take another look at the Soto Club case, which had stalled out years before. After pressure from federal agents, Dino's brother, Chester, agreed to testify about Dino's involvement in the murders. Hurd's now ex-wife had changed her story about Dino being home with her on the night of the murders. She now said that he was not home until well after daylight the next morning. At trial, however, Chester Hurd changed his story again, now saying that he had lied to the FBI about Dino's involvement in the murders. Regardless, a jury found Dino guilty on May 2, 1974, and he was sentenced to life in prison.

But this was not the end of the story. Hurd appealed his conviction and the Federal Court of Appeals determined that he had been sentenced under the wrong statute and could only be sentenced to 15 years for the robbery, not the murders. The Pulaski County prosecutor had to file new murder charges. On July 7, 1977, Hurd filed a motion for a new trial because of newly discovered evidence that could exonerate him. That motion was denied on February 3, 1978. Hurd filed another motion on March 9, stating that he had been denied effective counsel at trial. A hearing on this motion was held on August 30, and at the hearing, Hurd testified about his attorney's conduct at trial, and produced three witnesses his trial attorney had allegedly failed to subpoena or interview: Rachel York, a customer at a hair salon that Hurd owned; an acquaintance named Charles Bratton; and his mother, Ethel Hurd.

Rachel York testified that Hurd had been at the salon on the night of the robbery. When asked how she recalled this, York said that it was on the Friday night following her miscarriage, which had occurred on October 12 or 13. The following Friday was October 18, the night of the robbery. The U.S. attorney had not been aware of his alibi prior to the hearing. However, when he contacted a hospital in St. Louis where York's medical records were filed, he found that the miscarriage had occurred on October 9, placing York, according to her own testimony, in the hair salon on October 11, a week before the robbery. The medical records were filed into evidence on October 6, 1978.

Hurd's friend, Charles Bratton, testified that two men, that he wouldn't name, had actually committed the robbery, had divided the loot from the robbery at his home. They had discussed the robbery in his presence and Hurd's name was never mentioned. Ethel Hurd's testimony was backed up by the statement of Rachel York. She said she was also in the salon with both of them on the night of the murders – which turned out to be the wrong date.

Hurd's conviction was upheld and he finished serving his sentence for the robbery. Neither Hurd, nor the other suspect, his brother Chester, were ever tried for murder. Chester was found dead a few years later, an apparent suicide by hanging. Dino Hurd has not been seen since his release from prison, although locals have speculated that he is living in another state, under an assumed name.

The murders of the three men have never been forgotten and many who live in the Devil's Elbow area still talk about what happened on that dark night in October 1968. Some wonder if those murder charges will ever be filed, and

if they are, whether there is still a chance that justice will be found for the young men so cruelly murdered on that dirt road, just off Route 66.

The Ghosts of Fort Leonard Wood

After Devil's Elbow, the route twists through St. Robert and then on to Waynesville, home of Fort Leonard Wood. Waynesville was established in 1833 as a trading post for settlers and trappers on the Roubidoux River and was named for General "Mad Anthony" Wayne, a hero of the American Revolution. This stretch of Route 66 had deep roots. It could be traced back to the early 1800s, when the overland road was established between St. Louis and Springfield. Like much of Missouri, Waynesville declared itself "Confederate" during the Civil War, flying the rebel flag over its courthouse. However, this was short-lived due to its strategic location on the Wire Road. On June 7, 1862, Federal troops marched in, taking over the town, and building a fort to protect the roadway.

Many of the buildings in Waynesville date back to the 1920s and 1930s, including the former Bell Hotel, which was built in anticipation of the tourist trade on Route 66. It was operated by Robert Bell until 1937, using the slogan "Every Facility for the Traveler's Pleasure – Old Southern Hospitality." During the hard times of the Depression, it was tourist traffic on U.S. 66 that kept Waynesville alive.

In 1941, the construction of Fort Leonard Wood brought thousands of military and construction workers to the area, and as World War II unfolded, Waynesville became the primary place for recreation and relaxation for the men and women stationed at the base. Today, it remains a small, friendly town of the Ozarks and the gateway to one of the nation's largest military reservations.

The history of Fort Leonard Wood began with a modest groundbreaking ceremony in December 1940. The 71,000-acre fort was named in honor of Major General Leonard Wood, a graduate of Harvard Medical School and later the commander of the Rough Riders during the Spanish-American War. He later served with distinction as the governor of Cuba and as chief of staff of the U.S. Army from 1910 to 1914.

Between December 1940 and the spring of 1941, construction at the new fort continued at a quick pace. During this time, enough buildings had been erected to house the new Engineer Replacement Training Center, but when the United States entered World War II on December 7, 1941, the post quickly became one of America's main training centers. Between 1941 and 1946, over 300,000 soldiers trained at Fort Leonard Wood. At its peak, the post housed over 50,000 soldiers at a time, far more than the populations of any of the small towns in the region.

In addition to being used as a training center, the fort was also used as a prisoner of war camp for captured German and Italian soldiers. For the most part, the conditions that the prisoners lived under at Fort Leonard Wood were much better than they had enjoyed in their own armies. A former member of Rommel's Afrika Corps, incarcerated at the fort, said that the barracks were comparable to a Hilton hotel and the food was of such quality that the hotel could not have served better. The prisoners received a daily wage of 10-cents, whether they worked or not. Prisoners could receive as much as 80-cents a day (the equivalent of an Army private's wage in 1941) if they volunteered for additional work. None of the officers were expected to do manual labor. Instead they were given a monthly stipend based on their rank, which was between $20 and $40 a month. Needless to say, there were few escape attempts from Fort Leonard Wood during the war. Those most notable occurred on September 10, 1945, when a German named Rudolf Krause slipped away during a trash detail. Three months later, the FBI captured him in Orlando, Florida. His plan was to sign on as a sailor on a neutral merchant ship and make his way home. Not one to bear a grudge, Krause returned to Fort Leonard Wood from his home in Germany for a POW reunion in 1993.

Fort Leonard Wood was deactivated in 1946, after the end of the war. A small contingent of Army officers and civilians remained on site to safeguard the post, but for the next four years, the post was largely abandoned. The buildings soon began to fall into a state of disrepair.

In 1950, though, thanks to military training demands brought about by the conflict in Korea, the fort came back to life. Once reactivated, it became a replacement training center for the 6th Armored Division, and in 1956, Fort Leonard Wood officially became the home of the U.S. Army Engineer Training Center. During the Vietnam War, the fort again buzzed with activity. Basic trainees from around the country arrived at the fort for Basic and One Station Unit Training, prior to shipping out to Southeast Asia.

Today, the tradition of training the finest enlisted soldiers in the U.S. Army continues at Fort Leonard Wood and it now serves as the headquarters for the Maneuver Support Center. Soldiers and officers from the Chemical, Engineer, Military Police, and Transportation Corps are taught combat and survival skills for the modern battlefield.

The post is also home to one of the country's best military history museums. The John B. Mahaffey Museum Complex, formerly known as the U.S. Army Engineer Museum, offers exhibits on the history of the fort, and a history of the Engineer, Chemical, and Military Police Corps. There is also a 25-acre section of the museum complex that is dedicated to life at Fort Leonard Wood during World War II. In 1981, a number of war-era buildings, including four barracks, two mess halls, three day rooms, tow orderly rooms, and a regimental commander's quarters were set aside as part of the fort's museum. The buildings have been completely restored and they serve today as the only interpretive World War II community in the army. In addition, several other buildings commemorate the life of Major General Wood and the prisoner of war camp that existed on the post between 1943 and 1946.

But this is not the only part of history that remains at Fort Leonard Wood. There are ghosts that remain behind there, as well.

One of the ghost stories of the post deals with the spectral residents of the former town of Bloodland. It is a little-known fact that the U.S. government used the right of eminent domain to acquire a very large part of the 71,000 acres needed for Fort Leonard Wood. The history of the post may have started with a celebratory groundbreaking event, but the fact remained that many of the residents of the small communities nearby were forced to move from their homes to make way for the new fort.

Construction of barracks at Fort Leonard Wood

Bloodland, Missouri, was a village of only about 100 residents. It was an old settlement, made up of hard-working men and women that were mainly of German descent. On the night of October 31, 1940, the townsfolk gathered for an annual community celebration. It was during this party that it was unceremoniously announced that the land on which the town rested was being taken over by the government so that a new military post could be constructed there. The residents were outraged by the news and it was later reported in a local newspaper that their anger towards the government, enhanced by a day of drinking, resulted in a small riot breaking out. However, based on the stories that were later told, it seems as though the people of Bloodland eventually had the last laugh.

According to local newspaper stories, a soldier named James Klown was court-martialed and imprisoned in 1942, after he was found intoxicated and unconscious while he was supposed to be on guard duty. Klown had been assigned to patrol the section of the post where the town of Bloodland had once stood. He stated that while on guard duty, he heard strange noises near his post. He claimed that he went to search for the source of the eerie sounds and was actually taken prisoner by "riotous ghosts" who were speaking a language that he didn't understand. The "ghosts," he said, forced him to drink hard cider through a straw until he passed out.

A year later, in 1943, it happened again. This time, a soldier named Randall Ellsworth suffered the same fate as James Klown. While on patrol, he was also attacked by a group of "ghosts" and hard cider was forced on him. This time, though, instead of court-martialing Ellsworth, commanders allegedly placed the part of the fort where Bloodland was located off-limits to all military personnel.

Many years later, in 1974, after the fort had been activated once again, the ghosts of Bloodland struck again. This time, the victims were three soldiers from the fort. Each man later claimed to have been taken hostage by a group of ghosts and forced to drink hard cider through a straw until they collapsed.

And there, it seems, the story ended. What became of Bloodland? The site of the former town became a small arms firing range on the post. By 1975, when a story about the "riotous ghosts" appeared in the local *Gateway Guide*, all that remained of the little town were the foundations of the old school and the boarded-up remnants of a Methodist Church. Today, two reminders of Bloodland can still be found along Iowa Avenue, within just a few miles of the main post. The Bloodland Cemetery is located near Range #11. It is a tiny burial ground that long predates the creation of the fort and the only remaining evidence of the little town that once thrived nearby. The only other reminder is that the fort's command and control building for the various ranges on post is called Bloodland Range in the former town's honor.

While some have suggested that the anger of the residents over the loss of their town may have caused some kind of supernatural energy to manifest and strike back at the very people who had displaced them, I think the solution for the "ghosts" is much simpler than that. I think the "attacks," that while frightening, were relatively harmless, were nothing more than practical jokes – a sort of passive aggressive revenge against the soldiers who had driven the residents of Bloodland from their homes. I can imagine a few of the young men from Bloodland, dressed in sheets, hoping to put a good scare into the soldiers that were out on sentry duty, walking a lonely and dark part of the post. Over time, the story of the "ghosts" took on a life of its own and became a true tale of the supernatural.

But this is not the only ghostly tale of Fort Leonard Wood. The other is more traditional in nature.

Located in the heart of the military post is the Partridge Preschool. According to stories that have been told on the post, a four-year-old girl died at the school a number of years ago and her spirit simply refuses to leave. Staff members and parents have seen a single swing moving back and forth by itself on the playground. The air has been reported as deathly still, and this is the only swing that moves. It is said that if someone rattles a doorknob inside of the school, and then sits back and waits, the little girl will rattle the doorknob in response. Workers who have been in the building late at night have heard the sound of music playing in the classroom that is the closest to the playground where the spirit's "favorite swing" is located. Sometimes the music stops abruptly. Other times, it plays very loudly. It all depends, witnesses say, on the little girl's mood. She is also very particular about where toys are placed. She likes them to be left in special spots when the school day ends, and if they are not, staff members will find them rearranged when they return the following morning.

The identity of this little girl remains unknown. It's possible that she could be just a story, a figment of fantasy created to explain the eerie things that happen in the building. But if it's not a little girl who haunts the school, then who does? Strange things do happen in the building, the staff members can assure you of that, but the name of the playful intruder remains a mystery.

The Remnants of "Gascozark"

After Waynesville, Route 66 scoots on toward Laquey and a short distance past it, travelers will spot a stone-faced building with a curved roof on the edge on the edge of the road. A few years ago, it would have been mostly hidden by the trees and brush that had grown up around it over time. Recently, though, a group of volunteers have cut away the weeds and bushes and have refurbished the Ozark stone veneer to preserve a bit of U.S. 66 history.

Route 66 through downtown Waynesville. The Fort Wood Theatre can be seen on the left side of the street.

This was the **Gascozark Café and Gas Station**, which was opened by Frank A. Jones in 1931. At the time, he already operated a popular tourist and fishing resort on the Gasconade River, and decided to open the café and service station above it on the hill. Jones had been the original settler in the area and had named the small community "Gascozark", a combination of "Gasconade" and "Ozark."

The building on the site started small. But as tourist traffic on Route 66 increased, so did business at the café, so Jones began adding on to the building. When he was finished, he had several stucco buildings that had been knitted together with an uneven roofline.

A few years later, in the middle 1930s, Rudy and Clara Schuermann took over the business, freeing Jones to focus on his fishing resort. In 1939, they

The Gascozark Café & Gas Station outside of Waynesville

hired a local rock man named Lilliard to give the place a brand new look. Lilliard wrapped a veneer of large, flat Ozark stones around the front and sides of the building, using small stones to fill the gaps between the big ones. To even out the roofline, he created an arch that spanned the façade and finished it with round stones that had been made smooth by the river. At the corners, he piled up columns of rubble and mounted lanterns on the top. It was painstaking work and amazing craftsmanship, which has endured both time and the elements. Even during its worst days of abandonment, the building has remained strong.

By the 1940s, the Gascozark Café became a regular stop on the Greyhound bus line, which provided a substantial boost for the business. In the 1950s, it transformed again into a local hot spot known as the Spinning Wheel Tavern, but it was not meant to last. After spending some time as a private residence, the once must-stop location on U.S. 66 had become forgotten and abandoned.

And yet, it refuses to surrender to the passing of history. Route 66 enthusiasts still make the site a popular stopping place and the recent refurbishments to the building have brought more attention to this relic of the golden age of the highway. Who knows what its future may still hold?

Walker Brothers Resort

As Route 66 twists and turns along, it passes through the small town of Hazelgreen, which was once home to the **Walker Brothers Resort**. Between Gascozark and Hazelgreen, the highway skirted the northern edge of the Mark Twain National Forest. Nearby, the Gasconade River cut through the hills,

The Walker Brother's Resort at Hazelgreen

providing a recreational area. In 1916, Elmer Lee and John Walker, along with Lee's wife, Alvia, built a hunting fishing resort with seven cabins. People from St. Louis and Kansas City often came to spend a week on the river and by the 1930s, tourists could come, rent a cabin, and enjoy home-cooked meals for $2 a day. Many had standing yearly reservations.

A few years after the resort was started, the office began serving U.S. 66 travelers with all of the basics of a roadside stop, including a gas station, café, and overnight cabins. It also served as the town post office. Alvia was the Hazelgreen postmaster for many years, until mail service in town stopped entirely in July 1958.

The building remained standing for many years, with short wooden columns set on tall bases of river stones. The false front of the building and the porch columns provided advertising spaces for travelers who could see what services the resort offered at a glance. The last time that I saw the place, the words "eats" and "groceries" were faded, but still legible, on the peeling wood.

A "Space Station" in Missouri

About four miles east of Lebanon, the largest town between Rolla and Springfield on U.S. 66, was once a place known as the **Satellite Café and Phillips 66 Space Station**, a popular roadside stop that came to be known simply as "the Space Station" by locals. Although the facility included both a café and service station, they were owned and operated separately. Norma

 and Loren Alloway owned the café and the gas station was owned by LeRoy Hawkins. The Satellite Café was a favorite stop for tourists and frequent highway travelers. Norma did the cooking and was well-known for her fried chicken, homemade pies, and oatmeal cake. As a convenience to travelers, a picnic area was located at the rear of the café. During the café's busiest years, a neon sign that was shaped like a rocket was placed on the roof to attract motorists. The Phillips 66 station also had a "space-age" theme, with a modern-looking rocket placed alongside the road, beckoning drivers to fill up their tanks and have their oil checked.

Although this wooded, tree-lined stretch of Route 66 was beautiful, it was also one of the most dangerous spots on the highway. While the interstate in this area was being developed, two-lane Route 66 became the eastbound lanes for Interstate 44, until the early 1970s, when construction on I-44 was complete. This caused many accidents as locals, accustomed to driving both directions on this part of Route 66, would head west to Lebanon, sometimes meeting eastbound traffic – with horrific results.

After the interstate was completed, both the Space Station and the Satellite Café eventually closed. The café, with a worn-out old sign marking its location, became a storage shed and then burned down in 1999. The site of the once busy café and service station was now an empty lot. Nothing was left the last time I traveled through the area, save for the sign and the canopy that once shielded Phillips 66 customers from the rain and weather.

Welcome to Lebanon

As travelers journeyed along on Route 66, they soon found themselves in Lebanon, a town that dated back to when U.S. 66 was an Indian trail and the old "Wire Road" that followed the same route. The first settler in the area was Jesse Ballew, who arrived in 1820 and built a log cabin on the east side of the Gasconade River. The early settlers to the area were mostly hunters and farmers from Tennessee, but when word spread about the rich farmland in the region, the rivers, springs, and plentiful game, people began migrating to what was soon a growing community. When Laclede County was formed in 1849, the settlement of Wyota, named for local Native Americans, became the county seat. Later, a highly respected minister requested that the name of the town be changed to "Lebanon," after his hometown of Lebanon, Tennessee. A courthouse was built on the town square and in the 1850s, the Academy was built. It offered a higher education to the area's students and became the center of the town's cultural activities.

At the start of the Civil War, Lebanon found itself embroiled in conflict. Though the state of Missouri had declared itself a neutral state, it did allow its citizens to own slaves. Its population was primarily from the south and therefore, sympathized with the Confederacy. It seemed that the farther away the population was from St. Louis, which was loyal to the Union, the more inclined they were to lean in favor of the South. During the 1860 election, Abraham Lincoln received exactly one vote in Lebanon. The town was occupied by troops during the entire length of the war. Except for about six months in late 1861, when Confederate forces were encamped nearby, the town was controlled by Union troops. After the war, the town worked together to rebuild the community and was officially incorporated in 1867.

More conflict was coming. When the railroad began its expansion west, short-sighted officials in Lebanon refused to provide land for a railroad depot. As a result, the railroad tracks were built one mile away from town, making it impossible for business owners to capitalize on the new access that the outside world had to the small town. Eventually, the commercial district in town moved closer to the railroad and the original site of Lebanon became known simply as "Old Town." Eventually, the original town square disappeared altogether.

The Lebanon Opera House opened in 1882 and, along with other buildings in town, helped to establish the community as a popular place to gather for meetings, events, and traveling shows. In 1889, a discovery was made that helped to draw even more visitors to town. As a new water well was being excavated in town, it was discovered that the water had an unusual taste and smell. The locals began drinking and bathing in the water and word spread that it had healing properties. The rumors of healing waters led to the building of the Gasconade Hotel, the grandest structure ever built in Lebanon. With the capacity to house up to 500 guests, the hotel also offered a ballroom, dining room, reception rooms, and a bathhouse next to the well where the mysterious waters came from. As this was an era in American history when people were flocking to mineral baths around the Midwest, the owners of the Gasconade Hotel rightfully assumed that the place would be successful. They turned out to be sorely disappointed. The hotel quickly failed, never making back the exorbitant amount of money that was spent on its construction. It later became a sanatorium, but that also failed. It was later used for community events and there was talk of turning the structure into a college, but it never happened. Then, just 10 years after it was built, the Gasconade Hotel was destroyed by fire in October 1899.

Lebanon continued to thrive as a community that catered to travelers along the edge of the Ozarks, but the town really changed when Route 66 came through town in the late 1920s. Lebanon became a major stop on U.S. 66,

Andy's Street Car Grill, serving the "finest foods in the Ozarks" in Lebanon in the 1940s

offering road services, food, and one of the first motels to ever open on the new highway in 1927.

Lebanon also offered travelers a number of interesting restaurants and perhaps the most unique among them was **Andy's Street Car Grill**. Located at the corner of Elm Street and Jackson Avenue, it was opened by Andy Liebel in 1946. Linking together two former street cars from Springfield, Missouri, Liebel created the grill and promoted it heavily with signs that advertised "Andy's Famous Fried Domestic Rabbit," and promised the "finest food in the Ozarks." Liebel liked to tell people that they had never eaten good fried chicken unless they had eaten at his place. The old streetcar was a classic diner, where patrons lined the stools, bantered with the waitresses, chowed down on great road food, and drank coffee as black as the night sky. Sadly, Andy's became just a memory in 1960.

Another spot was the **Bungalow Inn**, which was open from 1936 to 1946. Gail and Izola Henson served great food at this café and filling station, offering plate lunches for 35-cents each, and they rented out cabins out back for between $1 and $3 a night. Izola's specialty was her breaded pork chops, which became a favorite dish for travelers and locals alike. Over their 10 years in business, the Hensons made so much money that they could buy a farm and retire. Soon after, a new alignment wiped out the spot, leaving only memories of the place behind.

One of those great memories was when Izola served dinner to western movie star Tom Mix and his wife. Mrs. Mix had stopped by to fill up with gas at the pump out front. While she was in the Inn, her car caught on fire. Despite efforts to save it, the car burned up with her fur coat, diamond ring, and watch inside. She asked the Hensons to just leave it alone until the insurance man could get there, and Izola recalled seeing someone steal the fancy TM logos from its doors. When the insurance people went through what was left of the car, they sifted the ashes and found Mrs. Mix's diamond ring. Tom Mix gave the Hensons tickets to his performance in Lebanon when he and his group ate at the café a few nights later.

Another Route 66 landmark in Lebanon was **Wrink's Market**, which opened in June 1950 and continued to operate until the death of owner Glenn Wrinkle in 2005. It was a one-of-a-kind vintage market with groceries, collectibles, dry goods, and Route 66 souvenirs. But most who stopped said that the main attraction at the market was Glenn Wrinkle himself, who was always happy to spin tales of running his store on Route 66 for a half century. After he passed away in 2005, his family auctioned off the contents of the store. His son briefly resurrected the market as a convenience store for a time, but it also closed in 2009.

The market was revived again briefly as D.C. Decker's Cowboy Emporium and Chuck Wagon Museum a short time later. It was filled with Old West memorabilia, including an authentic 1896 chuck wagon. When travelers stopped in, they could get a taste of genuine Arbuckle coffee and have a fried pie. The owner was an expert on Old West and Native American history and offered "real" cowboy cooking demonstrations from his chuck wagon at special events. Unfortunately, the emporium turned out to be short-lived and, at the time of this writing, the building was empty once again.

Lebanon also boasted a large number of motels and tourist camps to serve travelers on U.S. 66. One of the first – in fact, one of the first to open anywhere on Route 66 – was **Camp Joy**. Almost as soon as the new highway had been designated, Ernis and Lois Spears, accompanied by Ernis's parents, left their home in Nebraska City, Nebraska, and began traveling back and forth, looking for the perfect place to open a new tourist camp. After arriving in each town, the two couples surveyed the area looking for possibilities, often spending days in one place, counting the passing cars. They found what they were looking for in Lebanon. They bought a chunk of land on the edge of town,

The main entrance to Camp Joy. What started as a simple campground for highway travelers later offered cabins, a café, and a service station.

opened a campground, built bath and cooking facilities, and started renting tents for 50-cents a night. Camp Joy became so successful that Ernis and his father, Charles, began building cabins.

They built a series of front-gable cabins of wood with a door and a window. They covered the small buildings in clapboard and painted them white. At first, they built no garages, even though offering shelter for automobiles, as well as their occupants, was sort of a staple for the early tourist camps. They later added lean-tos next to the cabins, which were later turned into garages, and then converted into more rooms. The progression from garage to cabin was typical in early motels. It was cheaper to turn garages into rooms than it was to buy more land.

As tourist travel increased, so did tourist demands, and indoor plumbing in each cabin replaced the communal bathhouse. A gas station and a café were also added, but they were eventually moved to accommodate even more cabins. By the end of 1935, Camp Joy offered 24 cabins that rented per night from $1 to $4, depending on the number of rooms.

At the entrance to the camp was a drive-through archway that read "Camp Joy" on the entrance side and "Teach your baby to say Camp Joy" on the exit side. Joy Spears Fishel, Ernis and Lois's daughter, after whom the camp was named, later recalled that the early customers seemed more like friends than customers. In the evenings, people would sit outside their cabins and visit.

But that was before television and air conditioning. After that, people started keeping to themselves.

The Spears owned and operated the camp until 1971. After the interstate came through and traffic began to drop off, they removed the café and service station altogether and renamed the place, Joy Motel. But it didn't last long after that. Today, a few of the old cabins remain at the site and are rented out on a monthly basis.

Another tourist camp opened in Lebanon in 1932 when William Otto August Lenz and his wife, Ethel, converted their three-story, 14-room house into a tourist home. Two large signs were located along the highway with the name **Lenz Homotel**, and promising "Better Sleep Here, by Nite or Week." This was no ordinary, bare-bones camp. They supplied linens and home-cooked meals when most places offered little more than tents and early cabin courts supplied bare mattresses and communal kitchens. As auto camps became upscale motels, tourist homes fell out of favor with the traveling public and it was eventually closed. The Lenz Homotel still stands today as a private residence, it's days of offering good food and comfortable beds to tourists long past.

The **4 Acre Court** was another popular rest stop in Lebanon. Built by Ray Coleman and Blackie Walters in 1939, the two men devised the place as a way to cash in on the ever-increasing traffic on Highway 66. To attract vacationing families, they built a collection of individual cabins with a fireplace in each one. The cabins were "rocked" using flat Ozark stones, which was so popular in the region during the 1930s and 1940s. For more adventurous travelers, a campground was located to the west of the main building. In time, the campground was turned into a children's playground. The two-story stone building in front served as the owner's residence and office and, at one time, also houses a service station and a small grocery store.

While it's no longer open to the traveling public, 4 Acre Court has managed to survive the passage of time. Today, the one- and two-room cottages make up an apartment complex known as Village Oaks. In 2003, one of the cottages was destroyed by fire, but the rest of them, along with the main building, remain standing today.

Munger Moss Motel: Still Keeping it like the '50's

There is no question, though, that the most famous motel in Lebanon is the popular **Munger Moss Motel**, a true survivor of the glory days of Route 66. The story of the motel will, of course, always be tied to the history of the famous Munger Moss Café, which began in Devil's Elbow. In 1946, it was relocated to Lebanon after the other community was bypassed by a new U.S. 66 alignment. A short time later, the owners of the café, Jessie and Pete Hudson, bought the Chicken Shanty Café and a piece of land that was located next to it. They changed the name to the Munger Moss Café, put in a barbeque, and built a motel.

The Munger Moss Café in 1946 and below, the original Munger Moss Motor Court

The Munger Moss Motor Court originally consisted of seven stucco cottages, with rooms on each end and a garage in the middle. They added a little gable over each door, ran neon tubing around it, and fixed a neon number in the center. They laid out the units along a semicircular drive in an open plan that was based on the design for Los Angeles bungalow

The Munger Moss Motel today is like stepping back in time to another era and truly defines the word "retro."

courts. They left a green space in the middle for garden and seating. They later added 11 more buildings around the drive. Like the Spears family had done at Camp Joy, they created more units by converting the garages into rooms, then filled in the gaps between the buildings. In time, they boasted 77 rooms. Rooms rented for $3 per night in the early days.

Pete Hudson turned out to have a genius for business. Everything that he did was designed to bring in more people. When the demand became apparent, they added air-conditioning, television, and a swimming pool. As architectural styles changed, they covered the stucco with brick and extended the roofline out to cover a walkway in the style of a suburban ranch house, which was gaining popularity at the time. The addition of small cupolas on the roof added respectability and a sort of colonial look. The motel took its final form in the late 1950s when Hudson added a fancy office and a giant sign with a yellow arrow that swept over the name of the motel.

In 1952, the Hudsons sold the Munger Moss Café to Jim Sponseller and he ran it until he retired in 1979. His mother, Iva, joined the business and became famous up and down the highway for her outstanding food, especially her Cherry Cream Pie. Many called Iva's pies "works of art." Sponseller's years in business left him with many stories of Route 66. He often fed people who were hungry and even "loaned out" money to travelers in need, never expecting to get it back. One man remembered the loan, though. His son returned to the café 10 years later and repaid Jim the $20 that his father had accepted as he struggled to get his family to California.

The café is empty today, but the Munger Moss Motel still operates next door. The vintage motel has been owned by Bob and Ramona Lehman since 1971, and they take pride in the fact that the immaculately clean and well-run business still brings in travelers, who always have the option of staying at high-priced hotels along the interstate. So, if you're looking for a great place to spend the night, which truly defines the word "retro," then the Munger Moss Morel is definitely the place for you.

"Nelsonville"

Of all of the Route 66 icons in Lebanon, though, none are remembered as fondly as the renowned **Nelson Hotel and Dream Village**, a tourist attraction that was conceived and built shortly after the creation of U.S. 66 by Arthur Truman Nelson, an outspoken proponent for good roads in Missouri. Dubbed "Nelsonville" by the locals, it included a filling station, restaurant, and guest cottages. Newspapers called it "the best known spot on Highway 66 between Chicago and Los Angeles," but it was a dream that would not last.

It probably started with apples. There was no question that Arthur Nelson had apples in his blood. Not only did the man who broke the ground for Route 66 in Missouri have the lushest apple orchard in the state, but he also won a gold medal for 75 barrels of fruit shipped to the Paris Exhibition, and had a standing order to provide fruit for the royal family of England. His life had taken an agricultural turn in 1882 when he moved with his parents from New York to Lebanon, Missouri. His father established an enormous apple orchard in Laclede County, which Arthur later made internationally known. He moved in the state's political circles and nine consecutive Missouri governors, from varying parties, appointed to posts on the State Fair Board and in the Marketing, Penal, and Highway Commissions. One governor gave him the honorary title of "Colonel" and he used it for the remainder of his life.

From childhood, Colonel Nelson had been fascinated with two things – apples and road travel. As early as 1913, he began using trucks to transport his harvest to market. After gaining the attention of political leaders in the state, he began lobbying for better Missouri roads. The state suggested Route 14 cut through his land and the Colonel allocated a 40-acre tract for this road, which would eventually become Route 66. Then, he noticed that the road crews were killing his apple trees.

Nelson was a member of the State Board of Agriculture and a lifetime member of the State Horticultural Society, but he knew that the time had come for him to get out of the orchard business. When his son, Frank, suggested that he build a service station and try his hand at a trade along the new highway, Nelson jumped at the chance. In July 1926, he opened the **Nelson Service Station and Rest Rooms** on Route 66.

But the Colonel would not be content to open just any sort of filling station. Long before "highway beautification" was heard of, Nelson opened a filling station that was more of a rock garden with gas pumps than it was a typical service station of the day. Quaint cobblestones formed the walls and ornate pillars marked the driveways. A huge flower bed was located out front and a hamburger stand was opened to take care of hungry travelers. For those early tourists who thought the service station was a good place to park for the night, Nelson put up a bathhouse with tents on each side. The tents rented for $1 a night. After he realized that the tents were going to be filled every night, he built cabins and gave the place a new name.

The entrance to Top O' the Ozarks Camp, which had 12 cabins, each named for a different state.

Below: Nelson's Tavern

Top O' the Ozarks Camp had 12 cabins, each named for a different state. The burger stand turned into a short order diner called the **Top O' the Ozarks Inn**. By 1930, the Colonel and Frank had torn down the diner and grafted the **Nelson Tavern** onto the end of the service station. The two-story stucco building opened in January and spent the next several years welcoming customers into a restaurant that could have passed for a greenhouse. Tables were covered in vegetables and vases were filled with rare flowers. Palm trees filled the corners and exotic birds sang from cages among the leaves. Upstairs, two communal bathrooms served 22 guest rooms that were fitted with velvet carpets and Beauty Rest mattresses. Guest windows looked out over the grounds, which was filled with trees, flowers, and a large pond that was swimming with goldfish.

The Colonel planted 40,000 gladiolus bulbs in and around the tavern, 165 varieties of which were imported from France, Germany, Australia, and New Zealand. The ocean of blooms prodded the Colonel into hiring a full-time gardener. Thanks to newspaper reports that claimed the place was the best-known spot on Route 66, there were reports of families traveling an extra 100 miles in a day just to spend the night at Nelson's place. One story even claimed that Oklahoma outlaw Charles "Pretty Boy" Floyd stopped in for a visit.

In 1933, Nelson attended Chicago's Century of Progress Exhibition. There he encountered a contraption that would haunt his dreams until he acquired one of his own – a musical fountain that was rigged to work with colored, synchronized lights. A year later, he went to bed one night and dreamed that he saw that same fountain spouting music in the center of a tourist court. He got out of bed in the morning and claimed that he had seen "Fairyland." He drew a sketch of his dream and it became the blueprint for **Nelson Dream Village**.

It would be the Colonel's greatest achievement – or so he told the newspapers before construction began. On the north side of Route 66, across the road from Nelson's Tavern, the cottages sprang up in a semi-circle. There would be 12 in all, each constructed of native stones with rock chimneys and surrounding a manicured courtyard. The fountain, located in the center, was excavated by the Colonel himself. A well was dug to keep the fountain filled and electricity was wired to provide the lights. A St. Louis company was contracted to provide maintenance for the mechanism, but other issues were not so easily solved. Modern-day musical fountains are computer synchronized, using bright lights and huge speakers. The Colonel had colored light bulbs, but he had no digital audio system and computers were the thing of science fiction. He had to find another way to fill the air with music.

In the central office of the Dream Village, a record player was installed and two of Nelson's daughters had the job of playing records all summer long. They took one record off and put another on, every evening, every single day. They played light classical and popular music and began their concert every evening at dusk. There was no formal announcement that the show was about to begin. The music began playing through a loudspeaker and the colored lights began to dance. The show wasn't actually synchronized but their guests weren't interested in counting the beats. Many locals and fans from neighboring towns watched the show from their car. Benches were placed on either side of the fountain, but they were seldom used. Guests staying overnight at the Dream Village typically sat on the chairs outside of their cabin doors.

The musical fountain at Nelson's Dream Village

Colonel Nelson died in 1936, and in 1944, Frank Nelson leased the Nelson Tavern – by then called the Nelson Hotel – to Mr. and Mrs. Lynn West. West became an active citizen of Lebanon, serving as mayor, city councilman, and president of the Highway 66 Association.

Lebanon became one of the first Missouri towns to be bypassed by the interstate. On July 29, 1958, the Nelsons sold the hotel property to a property development company in Springfield and the hotel and gas station were torn down. Dream Village survived into the 1970s, long after Route 66 had become nothing more than a city street. Frank Nelson passed away and his widow, Dorothy, did her best to keep Dream Village going. Overnight guests turned into weekly renters and Dorothy gave the motel to her children. They eventually sold it for there was little doubt that time had passed the place by.

Nelson Dream Village was demolished in the summer of 1977, bringing an end to the dream of a man who saw not only a "Fairyland" in his future, but had also seen the start of Route 66 in the Show Me State.

On to Conway

After Lebanon, U.S. 66 takes travelers away from the interstate and along a winding, up-and-down steep hills road that passes fading ghost towns, old barns, and vintage buildings. It's a beautiful stretch of highway and perhaps

Midway Camp in Phillipsburg, a now vanished relic of the past

almost forgotten because it had been bypassed long before Interstate 44, when a new four-lane alignment of Route 66 was built in 1957.

Along this quiet stretch of the highway, you can get a glimpse of yesterday, along with tumbled-down buildings, wandering cattle, and acres and acres of fields and trees. There are also a few towns that have survived, like **Phillipsburg**, which offers vintage buildings, including a former store and a long-abandoned school. The remaining population in town is small, but the historic structures that remain tell tales of better times.

Beyond Phillipsburg, the road through the rolling hills leads the traveler to **Conway**, which has fared much better, thanks to being closer to the interstate. Conway was first settled by farmers in the late 1860s and was named for a railroad contractor. The first store was started in town in 1869 and the settlement slowly began to grow. By 1880, it boasted a new two-story building that was used for the school, church, and area meetings. In 1913, a tomato canning factory was built in town and trainloads of tomatoes began to be shipped out of the area, marking the town's claim to fame.

By the time Route 66 came through, Conway was home to several businesses, including the Electric Theater, Stone Motor Company, and a bank.

One of the best-known places in town was the **Harris Café**. Opened by Marie and Barney Harris in 1929, the café's reputation spread up and down Route 66 as "The Home of the Little Round Pie." Marie had seen small meat pies on a trip to California and decided that she could copy the idea using fruit. She made meringue-topped cream pies with equal success. They sold for 10-cents each and made Marie a legend of the highway.

Years later, friends would recall the good times at the café and reminisce about the history that had passed through the place. All kinds of travelers dropped in, like repeat patrons who had gone to California, then came back again after an earthquake in 1933. There were unemployed men who rode the nearby railroad and stopped in search of food, and during World War II, soldiers who were being bussed across the country ate at the café. There were also the gypsies, with their colorful clothes and jewelry, who used to stop in Conway. Two just as colorful, and certainly more famous, customers were Bonnie and Clyde, who stopped at the Harris Café several times. Marie later recalled that they always ate by the window and that Bonnie had such bowed legs that she wore long dresses to hide them.

About six miles west of Conway is the long defunct **Abbylee Court**. Its surrounded by trees and overgrown bushes now, hiding the memories that were once made here, but a sharp-eyed traveler might just spot the sign as he passes by. The cabins now rent out by the month, but they have an interesting history here in the Ozarks region.

Built by a man named Haynes in the 1920s, the scenic auto court consisted of eight, spacious individual cabins that were situated around a semicircular gravel driveway. Billed as the Abbylee Court "Among the Trees," this auto court became known as one of the most secluded rest stops anywhere on U.S. 66. Considered quite large by the standards of the day, the cabins offered ample room for tourists to relax. Each was built with a private attached garage and, unlike most motor courts of the era with garages that were later turned into rooms, the ones at Abbylee Court can still be used today. There was also a café on site offering "meals and sandwiches" and it became popular all over the area for having simple, but delicious food. Sunday brunch was especially popular among the locals, offering the "best fried chicken in the county." The restaurant building also served as the court's rental office.

But all that was to change in 1950 when the café and one of the cabins were destroyed by a fire. Much to the disappointment of loyal customers, the popular restaurant was never rebuilt. In 2000, the Abbylee was purchased by a man from nearby Niangua and the entire property was renovated. It no longer serves the traveling public, but the cabins are rented by the month.

Tired Route 66 travelers may not get to take advantage of the secluded setting any longer, but at least the current residents can still relax a little "Among the Trees."

Heading Toward Springfield

A few more miles down the road is the town of **Niangua**, which still remains strong with its farming economy. The vintage buildings that line the streets of this tiny community also show evidence of a once booming time.

Soon, the road rolls into **Marshfield**, the seat of Webster County. The town was laid out in 1856 and was primarily home to the ranchers and farmers of the area. When the Civil War began, the town was the site of two Civil War skirmishes. The arrival of the railroad after the war made the economy boom and the town became known as a dairy, poultry, and livestock producer. Marshfield was once the home of Edwin P. Hubble and the community now proudly displays a replica of the Hubble Space Telescope on the town square.

The famed Garbage Can Café – it wasn't what it sounds like!

Marshfield is also the home to a now abandoned diner that shows no evidence of the fact that it was once a Route 66 icon called the **Garbage Can Café**. When Kermit and Letha Lowery decided to open a café on Highway 66 in 1952, a friend told them that no one would remember a name like Lowery's Café. So they started brainstorming and the same friend, as a joke, suggested that people would never forget them if the café was called the Garbage Can. The name stuck – and paid off in spades. Letha have been given the "Little Round Pie" recipe from the Harris Café in Conway and the Garbage Can became the second home of the famous pies. An employee later recalled that Letha made 300 to 400 of the little pies every day.

As travelers get closer to Springfield, the highway passes from steep hills to gently rolling hills and open plains toward the crossroads community of **Strafford**. The town is now home to the **Exotic Animal Farm**, a sort of drive-through zoo that lets tourists remain in the car and drive through acres of fields and trees, where the animals can roam at will. For anyone who longs for the Route 66 snake farms, coyote dens, and prairie dog towns of yesterday, this place is about as close as you can get.

The Ranch Hotel in Strafford

During the 1930s and 1940s, **Strafford's Ranch Hotel** made a comfortable stop for travelers between St. Louis and Oklahoma City. Located 16 miles east of Springfield, it dominated a county site at the highest elevation in the Missouri Ozarks. Practically everything that was served at the table came from the owner's farms and the hotel had one of the first electric dishwashers in the entire country.

Stop. Honk Loud for Information

Before following the remnants of Route 66 into Springfield, there is a side-trip worth taking, if the chance ever arises again. You see, in a state that is literally filled with caves – including scores of show caves that are open to the public – there are few as breath-taking as the wonders of **Crystal Cave**, located just north of the city. It has been attracting visitors for well over a century and visitors today can walk the same well-worn subterranean passages where motorists on old Route 66 once wandered about in awe.

The cave's first developer was a man named Alfred Mann, an Englishman who was born in Brighton and educated in France. He made his first trip to America at age 17 and spent three years roaming the country before returning to England to marry and father four children. In 1882, Mann moved his family to Salina, Kansas. Five years later, he started the Springfield Mattress, Bed Spring and Upholstery Works on Boonville Street in Springfield. He made a very comfortable living selling mattresses stuffed with hair, moss, cotton and wool, but Mann soon grew tired of the work. One day, he swapped the whole enterprise for 140 acres of land north of town – acres that rested over Crystal Cave.

Mann had seen how caves were used in France. After building a house for his family, he fashioned the cave into an underground nursery. He stacked

Two scenes from the early days of Crystal Cave

stones into planting beds and raised mushrooms and rhubarb in the cave's entrance chamber. For a time, his crops were sold throughout the state but then the mysteries of his beautiful cave got the better of him and he yearned to share it with the public. In 1893, he followed the lead of the Mark Twain Cave in Hannibal and opened Crystal Cave as the second show cave in Missouri.

In the early days, admission to the cave was 10-cents per person. Hand-cut stone steps led visitors through the cave's entrance room (the planting beds were now empty) and into fanciful chambers named by Mann and his family. One formation in the Rocky Mountain Chamber enjoyed such popularity that it got the attention of the Smithsonian Institute in Washington. The cave's most famous formation was first called the Twin Castles but was later changed to the Washington Monument because of the pool of water in front of it. When the cave first opened, it was one of the main attractions. Mann gave the Smithsonian permission to make a scale model of the formation for a display on caves at the famous museum.

At a Fourth of July celebration in Springfield, the Mann's nine-year-old son, Willie, was accidentally killed. The loss left Alfred Mann emotionally scarred and he never recovered from the loss. As his three daughters became adults, Mann was incapable of letting them free to live their own lives. When middle daughter, Ada, became engaged to neighbor William Funkhouser, Mann constructed a cottage on the Crystal Cave property so that the couple could live close to home. He stocked the house with furniture and believed that he had created the perfect living arrangement for them. The Mann sisters called it the "Honeymoon Cottage" but Funkhouser called it "impossible," broke off the engagement, and left the area. He eventually settled in Arkansas and married a woman whose father allowed her to leave home. Ada never married and neither did her sisters.

Alfred Mann died in 1926 and his wife passed away three years later. The care of Crystal Cave fell to the three sisters, Ada, Agnes, and Margaret. They had a lifetime of experience at the cave. In the early years of the business, it took three hours in a buggy to reach Springfield from the cave. The isolation of the farm encouraged independence among the family members and the Mann children were assigned duties in the cave in addition to their household chores. It was no different as adults. They divided up the chores between them with Agnes as the principal tour guide, Ada as business manager and automobile driver, and Margaret in charge of cooking and the upkeep of the grounds. Nervous about attracting too much business, the spinster sisters hung a few signs along the highway and called their advertising complete. If someone showed up at the house for a tour, they were instructed by a sign that was hanging on a tree to "Stop. Honk Loud for Information."

The Mann sisters told reporters that they preferred to conduct their cave tours at a leisurely pace and, true to their word, they never prodded visitors along. On one occasion, a gentleman from Kansas City spent the entire day in the cave, campaigning for senator. Years later, Margaret found his card among old cave papers and saw that his name was Harry S. Truman. Another time, a man spent an entire afternoon studying a living root that had worked its way into the cave from a mulberry tree 70-feet above. He introduced himself as Robert L. Ripley and he featured the root in his popular newspaper column.

In time, William Funkhouser's family moved back to his neighboring boyhood home. Ada Mann bore no animosity toward her former fiancée's family and she and his widow, Cora, became good friends. All three of the Mann sisters were especially fond of the Funkhouser's daughter, Estle, who had also never married. Estle adored the Mann sisters and took care of them as they got older.

Agnes died in 1960 and Margaret passed away in 1966. Only after Ada died in 1969 did Estle Funkhouser realize how much the sisters had treasured her friendship: the sisters had bequeathed the cave to Estle in their will. They left her the cave, 70-acres of land, the white frame farmhouse, and the Honeymoon Cottage.

Estle kept Crystal Cave for 13 years. She was third grade supervisor at a local school and split her time between her duties there and the upkeep of the cave. She built the cave's gift shop and restored the Honeymoon Cottage, installing a bathroom for the first time. Oddly, the cottage soon housed newlyweds – George Blower and his wife, Barbara, who came to work at the cave full-time. Barbara was Estle's niece and the granddaughter of William Funkhouser, for whom the cottage was originally built.

As Estle got older, the cave became too much for her and she wrote to her sister, Edith, and asked her and her husband, Loyd Richardson, to consider taking over the operation. Loyd had recently retired and was running an antique store in Wichita, Kansas, but when the opportunity to take over the cave came up, he bought it from Estle in 1982. They continued to operate the place just as the Mann family did for so many years – slow, quiet, personalized and friendly. At the age of 80, Loyd was still working to open new sections of the cave and replacing the old electrical wiring from 1932.

Crystal Cave continued to operate with Loyd and Edith still leading tours until just recently. As of this writing, the cave is closed to the public. Hopefully, the gates will be opened again someday. There are many caves in Missouri, but only a fraction of them are as wondrous – and the owners as welcoming – as Crystal Cave.

"Queen City of the Ozarks"

The town of Springfield was the last stop on the Old Wire Road that led west, but its history began somewhat before that with the removal of the Delaware, Kickapoo, and Osage Indians that had laid claim to the area before the white settlers first arrived in the 1820s. By 1830, the government had begun forcing the removal of the Native Americans to a reservation in Kansas and the region was opened for settlement. The county was established on January 2, 1833, and named for Revolutionary War hero Nathaniel Greene. Soon, small settlements like Brookline, Ash Grove, Republic, Willard, and Springfield were established throughout the county. Springfield was founded by a man named John Polk Campbell, who arrived there in 1829 and found a natural well of water flowing into a small stream at the bottom of a wooded hill. He carved his initials into a tree and claimed the spot for himself. He returned to Tennessee to fetch his family and came back to the region in March 1830. Soon, other settlers began to arrive, the first store was built in 1831, and other businesses, mills, a school, and a post office followed a short time later. In 1835, the town site was platted when Campbell deeded 50 acres of land for the county seat. In just two years, a two-story brick courthouse was completed in the middle of the public square, serving Springfield when it was officially incorporated in 1838.

In 1858, Springfield became a stop on the Butterfield Overland Mail stagecoach line, which ran from Tipton, Missouri, to San Francisco. The line brought even more people to the area and by this time, the town boasted over 1,200 residents, three hotels, two newspapers, three churches, five schools, a bank, and a wide assortment of businesses.

Within a few years, though, Springfield would be torn apart by the Civil War. Missouri was a state bitterly divided by sympathies for both the Union and the Confederacy. The first battle in the state, at Wilson's Creek, occurred on August 10, 1861, but it would not be the last. Less than two years later, in January 1863, a second conflict occurred when Confederates led by General John Marmaduke attempted to capture the city of Springfield itself. More than 100 men lost their lives in the fighting, but the attackers were driven back and Springfield avoided capture by Confederate troops. The city was nearly abandoned during the darkest days of the war, but those who left returned after the war was over and, with many new arrivals, rebuilt the city.

In 1865, Springfield earned a place in bloody history when James "Wild Bill" Hickok shot and killed a man named Dave Tutt over a gambling debt in the middle of the town square. The dispute occurred on July 21, one night after Tutt took Hickok's pocket watch in a poker game. Although he was arrested, he hired a future Missouri governor as his defense attorney and was acquitted at trial. Later on, he actually ran for the job of Springfield's town marshal, but came in second in the election. Just 11 years later, Hickok would be dead – gunned down during another poker game in Deadwood.

Like so many other cities heading southwest out of Missouri from Springfield, the railroad brought an economic boom to the area. In 1870, the St. Louis & San Francisco Railway built the line through town and within a few years, there were more than 150 businesses operating in Springfield. It had earned its nickname as "Queen City of the Ozarks."

The city continued to grow through the latter part of the nineteenth century. In 1880, a woolen mill began production, turning out 1,500 yards of cloth each day. Cotton mills converted 1,000 bales of cotton into fabrics each year, and mills were grinding over 200 barrels of flour overnight. In 1887, Springfield was one of the first cities in the entire country to get an electric trolley. The line soon traveled all over town and the streetcar became an everyday part of life until the last one ran in 1937.

By 1923, there were 148 miles of streets in the city, and 60 of those miles were paved. So, when John T. Woodruff of Springfield and Cyrus T. Avery of Tulsa, Oklahoma, began to suggest a transcontinental highway, Springfield was a logical choice for a city that would be on the new cross-country route. Both Woodruff and Avery worked tirelessly for a highway that would take Americans from Chicago to Los Angeles. Their persistence finally paid off in 1926 when U.S. 66 was born. Springfield became an important point on the road, which further added to the population and business growth.

Many knew that they had John Woodruff to thank for what the city had become. Woodruff was not only a Missouri promoter for Route 66, he was a hard-working businessman and a promoter of all types of transportation throughout the state. As an attorney for the Frisco Railroad in Springfield, he was largely responsible for the development of many businesses in the city, as well as the hospital, fairgrounds, and a public golf course. He also influenced the development of three dams and constructed the Woodruff business building, which still stands today. He built three hotels – the Sansone, Colonial, and Kentwood Arms – of which only the latter, built in 1926, remains today. It is now owned by Southwest Missouri State University and is a dormitory called Kentwood Hall.

In time, Springfield became the third largest city in Missouri and a favorite stopping point for those looking for fun in the Ozarks. Highway 66 brought carloads of tourists to spend the night, fill up with gas, and eat a few meals. The old road entered Springfield and gave birth to scores of diners, motor lodges, and filling stations. As was the case with several larger cities on the route, the course of Route 66 in Springfield changed several times as the city grew and new bypasses were created to ease congestion downtown. At various times, Kearney, Glenstone, and other city streets served as Route 66 in Springfield. St. Louis and College Streets continued as U.S. 66 Business Loop until 1960, when the Chestnut Street Trafficway was given that designation. In 1967, Interstate 44 was completed north of Springfield and a few years later, the old 66 markings were dropped altogether.

The city has changed a lot since the glory days of U.S. 66. Many of the old places are gone, vanished like the billboards and neon that once advertised them, but if you look close, a traveler can still find evidence that Route 66 once passed through town.

The Show Goes On...

For many tourists, a journey through Springfield would take them first past the long-abandoned **Sunset Drive-In Theater**. The drive-in has been gone for many years now, but the last time that I passed that way, the sign was still standing. The drive-in opened in 1950 with a single screen and closed down in 1985. It was later demolished and the property was turned into a trailer park.

But this was not the only theater in town. The **Gillioz Theatre**, located downtown, opened on October 12, 1926, just one day after Route 66 was named. It was completely renovated in 2006.

Also downtown is the historic **Lander's Theater**, which was built in 1909, and as the old adage goes about "every good theater," it has a ghost – or several of them. The four-story brick and terra cotta building has been in continuous use since it opened. Originally opened as a vaudeville house, it played host to performers like Lillian Russell, John Phillips Sousa, Fanny Brice, and scores of others. When the craze for movies came along, it converted to a motion picture house and was the first in the region to offer "talkies." In 1977, it was added to the National Register of Historic Places and in the 1980s was completely restored to its original grandeur. It continues to operate today, entertaining Springfield and the surrounding area with plays, musicals, and more.

The Landers Theater

Over the years, staff members, patrons, and visitors to the theater have reported that the Landers is home to a number of restless ghosts. The most often reported is that of a janitor who reportedly died in a fire at the theater on December 17, 1920. The fire swept through the building and only an asbestos curtain and other fireproofing precautions that had been put in place saved the building from destruction. The janitor suffered a tragic death, but luckily, no one else was killed. The theater was closed for a time in the wake of the fire, and after it opened, the janitor's ghost began to be reported, going about his daily work as if he was still tending to the place after death.

The ghostly sounds of a baby crying have also been reported in the otherwise empty building. The stories claim that a baby was once accidentally dropped over the upper balcony by her careless mother. Today, when actors are rehearsing on the stage, they claim to hear the baby crying as she repeats her terrible fall, over and over again.

Another ghostly figure, this one only seen from outside the theater, is said to peer out from a fourth floor window at people passing by on the street. There is never anyone living inside of the theater at the times when she is seen. She has been described as a blonde woman, wearing a costume that suggests she was in a performance set in the Elizabethan era, but she has never been seen by anyone inside of the theater.

And those figures don't seem to haunt the building alone. Other strange occurrences often take place, including unplugged spotlights that turn on by themselves, footsteps, disembodied voices, a sensation of being watched or followed, visitors being tapped or touched, and shadowy figures that are often glimpsed from the corner of the eye.

Who are the mysterious entities that linger at the Landers Theater? Likely they are simply memories of the past who have no reason to want to move on to the other side. For those who love the theater, what better afterlife can they ask for?

Chowing Down in Springfield

One of the main things that those who explore the past of Route 66 in Springfield will always complain about is the loss of the many vintage eating places and down-home-style chop houses that once graced the highway. There were many spots – from high-class eateries to greasy spoon diners – that bring back memories for those lucky enough to recall them. Coming into town, few could pass up **Pearl and Vern's Café**, which closed down in 1991. It had been built as part of **Carl's Truck Stop** in the 1940s and had first been operated by Carl Appleby and his wife.

Many of the old places are gone, but memories die hard in the Ozarks. One of the best spots was always **Gabriel's Waffle House**, where hungry diners found great food even before U.S. 66 arrived in town. Harry Gabriel, Sr., opened his first restaurant in 1918 and had three locations on Route 66 before closing down in 1966. For years, Gabriel's was the only eating place that was open 24-hours a day between St. Louis and Tulsa. Gabriel, Sr. opened the waffle house on the town square, moved to St. Louis Street in 1935, and then back to the square in 1948. His son, Bud, worked in the restaurant and later recalled that Harry Truman often stopped into Gabriel's when he was testing the political waters of southwestern Missouri. He felt the diner was a good place to see which direction that local politics was leaning.

There are many others that have disappeared over time. Among them are the **St. Louis Street Café, Cortez Coffee Shop, Corn Crib Café**, and the **Harvey House Restaurant** that was at the Frisco Station. There was also **K and K Hamburgers and Chili**, where the cook only had to open a window when business was slow and let the smell of the grill waft out across the campus of the nearby college. In the 1940s, **Davidson's Cafeteria** was a popular spot, known for its roast beef, baked ham, chicken, and acclaimed pecan pie.

After World War II ended, Red Chaney took his business degree and his new bride, Julia, and left Chicago by way of Route 66, looking to start over. He found Wayne Lillard's gas station and cabins on the western edge of Springfield and decided to turn the place into **Red Chaney's Giant Hamburg**. The original hand-painted sign was supposed to say "Hamburger," be he ran out of room, and the name stuck. He added a hamburger stand to the place, but when he found himself wearing too many hats, Red quit pumping gas and renting cabins. He converted the office and garage into a full-fledged restaurant and concentrated on the burgers. The place was an immediate success. He stayed open in the evenings as long as there was traffic, often spending the entire weekend at the café.

Red Chaney's Hamburg because a classic Route 66 icon — all because the painter ran out of room for "hamburger" on the sign!

Red and Julia loved doing things differently. Red would often place two-gallon water jugs on each table and two on the counter so that he didn't have to spend his time pouring water. It also gave the customers something to do while they waited for their food. Customers made their own change from a shoebox on the counter. During business hours, Red served the customers and turned the kitchen over to Julia.

They served root beer, giant "hamburgs," fish, chili, and shakes, all prepared using Red's unique recipes. He ground his own hamburger meat, using the best beef to insure the most flavor, and made his own root beer from licorice. The root beer was stored next to magnets to "take the nitrogen out of the water." Pinto beans started soaking at 5:00 a.m. every morning. He cooked the beans in crockpots that were scattered around the kitchen. He admitted to being a little bit crazy, but whatever he was doing, it worked. People flocked to the hamburger joint for over 40 years.

Red and Julia both retired in the 1980s and burgers in Springfield were never the same.

Located farther west on U.S. 66 was the **7 Gables Restaurant**. Built in the 1930s, it was a two-story affair with seven imposing gables out front. The café went through several owners over the years but was owned by the Hayden family in the late 1940s. Carl Hayden, Jr. later recalled that his father put up the biggest neon sign in the Springfield area during their time at the restaurant.

The Hayden family had a direct hookup with radio station KWTO and broadcast from the restaurant with Uncle Carl and the Hayden family playing folk music. They became an important part of the famous Ozark Jamboree Music that originated in Springfield. The Haydens had an apartment on the second floor, but when fire destroyed the restaurant in 1949, they sold out and moved to Nebraska.

The restaurant was rebuilt, without the gables and second floor, and was run for several years by Buel McCoy and his mother, Maude. A former employee named Ida Painter remembered her first job at the 7 Gables when she was just 15. She laughed about being shocked to find that many out-of-state customers expected Ozark waitresses to be barefoot hillbillies, right out of the "Lil' Abner" comics.

Truck drivers, tourists, and busloads of students heading for football games kept the 7 Gables in business for many years, but eventually time just passed it by. But all of the old favorite dishes are still available at the buildings latest incarnation, Alli's Family Restaurant, which still operates today at the place where the 7 Gables once called home.

A Bed for the Night

The Lone Star Cottages

During the years when U.S. 66 thrived, there were many tourist courts in Springfield, including the **Cordova, Black's Lone Star, Lone Pine, Snow White**, and **Otto's**.

The **Trail's End Motel** was built in 1938 and was one of the crowning achievements of rock man Ed Waddell. Waddell worked with a developer named "Mac" McCandless to build the Trail's End in 1938 and then the **Rock Village Court** and **Rock Fountain Court**, both in 1947. The area had already become well-known for using flat Ozark stones to create structures with a giraffe-like pattern, but Waddell took the art to a new level. He was the first of the Springfield craftsmen to use alternating courses of yellow and red brick to sharpen the edges around windows, doors, and corners. With these three motor courts, Waddell and McCandless built small front-gabled cabins with built-in porches and one or two bedrooms. The cabins were all laid out on a semi-circular drive. The motor courts managed to stand out from others in the area, largely thanks to Waddell's careful work.

Rock Fountain Court was the last of the two men's creations. Although the fountain that once stood in the middle of the tourist court is gone, visitors can still see the nine original stone cabins as Melinda Court, a rental property. It got its new name in 1961 when owner Sherman Nutt decided to rename it after his daughter, Melinda.

Another motor lodge was the **Wishing Well Motor Inn**, which opened with 17 units in 1947. A "Homelike Atmosphere You Will Always Remember" was promised at the motel, which continued operations until just a few years ago. Today, the motel has been turned into apartments.

One of the survivors of Route 66 in Springfield is the legendary **Rest Haven Motor Court**, with a brilliant lighted sign that still beckons travelers in off the highway. The motor court was built in 1947 by Hillary and Mary Brightwell and originally consisted of four rock cottages, with two rooms in each, and a Phillips 66

Top to Bottom: Snow White Lodge, Otto's Motor Courts, Rock Village Court, and the Wishing Well Motel.

Rest Haven Motor Court

service station out front. The service station had come before the motel. Brightwell had actually rented the place back in 1937, but seven years later, he and Mary bought it, remodeled it, and started building the Rest Haven. Many of the motels in Route 66 expanded at a furious pace after World War II and the Rest Haven was no exception. They added 10 more rooms in 1952, and another 10 in 1955. They added a swimming pool when the tourists demanded it, and finally, a huge sign with an arrow that was lit by 900 flickering bulbs. By that time, the motel offered "100% Refrigerated Air Conditioning," telephones, free radios, ice, a playground for the kids, and was recommended by Duncan Hines.

The service station was finally removed in 1955, and by the early 1960s, the gaps between the original four cottages were filled to add more rooms. Eventually, they added a porch and large cupolas and transformed the place into a ranch-style motel.

Hillary and Mary owned the motel and lived on site until 1979 when, after 32 years of greeting guests, they decided to retire. In 1980, the Rest Haven was purchased by the Pendya family, who have been the caretakers ever since.

The Rest Haven remains today as an example of a mom-and-pop motel that has managed to survive, outliving the official Highway 66 route by several decades.

While some of the motor lodges and diners of Springfield did manage to survive the arrival of the interstate and the demise of the Mother Road, most were lost over time, as virtually every American motel chain and franchise restaurant came to town.

But not all of the oddities visited by tourists, or sites that made the news, around Springfield during the Route 66 days have vanished. There are a few that remain in the vicinity, along with a site or two that no one – unless they were looking for ghosts – is brave enough to visit.

Spectral Soldiers at Wilson's Creek

The Battle of Wilson's Creek, also known as the Battle of Oak Hills, was fought on August 10, 1861, near Springfield, between Union troops and the Missouri State Guard. While considered by historians to be the first major battle of the Civil War that was fought west of the Mississippi – it's sometimes referred to as the "Bull Run of the West" – it's often forgotten by those who believe the war was fought only on the battlefields of the east.

The hours of bloody fighting that occurred at this lonely spot left an indelible impression on the landscape of Southwest Missouri and tales of hauntings still reverberate more than 150 years after the last shots were fired on the battlefield.

At the start of the Civil War, Missouri declared that it would be an "armed neutral" state in the conflict and would not send men nor materials to either side. However, that neutrality was quickly put to test on May 10, 1861, by Governor Claiborne F. Jackson, who leaned toward the Confederate cause. He had called out the state militia to drill on the edge of Pro-Union St. Louis and, after secretly obtaining artillery from the Confederacy, smuggled it into the militia camp at Lindell Grove that came to be known as "Camp Jackson." Federal Captain Nathaniel Lyon was aware of the guns and feared that the militia was planning to attack the St. Louis Arsenal. Thomas W. Sweeny was put in command of the Arsenal's defense, and Lyon surrounded the militia camp with Union troops and home guards, forcing the surrender of the militia. He blundered, though, when he marched the captured militia through the streets, attracting crowds, many of whom were angry and heckled the procession. Taunts turned to fighting and, eventually, to gunfire and many civilian and military deaths.

The following day, the violence in St. Louis led the Missouri General Assembly to create the Missouri State Guard, which was tasked with defending the state from attacks by perceived enemies, either from the North or the South. The governor appointed Sterling Price as the commander with the rank of Major General. The State Guard was divided into divisions, with each division consisting of units raised from a military district of Missouri and commanded by a brigadier general.

Fearing that Missouri would fall to the Confederacy, William S. Harney, Missouri's Federal commander, struck the Price-Harney Truce on May 12, 1861, which affirmed the state's neutrality. Governor Jackson then declared his support for the Union. However, Harney was replaced with Nathaniel Lyon, now promoted to Brigadier General, and Abraham Lincoln made a specific request for Missouri troops to enter into Federal service. With that, Jackson withdrew his support. On June 12, Lyon and Jackson met in St. Louis with hopes of resolving the matter, but things went badly. The meeting ended with Lyon's now iconic words, "This means war. In an hour, one of my officers will call for you and conduct you out of my lines."

Lyon sent a force under General Sweeney to Springfield while his own forces captured the state capital and pursued Jackson, Price, and the now-exiled state government across Missouri. Skirmishes occurred at Boonville and Carthage and in light of the crisis, the delegates of the Missouri Constitutional Convention that had rejected secession in February convened again. On July 27, the convention declared the governor's office vacant and then selected Hamilton Rowan Gamble to be the new provisional governor.

By July 13, Lyon's army of about 6,000 men was encamped at Springfield. His force was composed of the 1st, 2nd, 3rd, and 5th Missouri Infantry, the 1st Iowa Infantry, the 1st Kansas and 2nd Kansas Infantry, several companies of Regular Army infantry and cavalry, and three batteries of artillery. He divided the units into four brigades commanded by Major Samuel D. Sturgis, Colonel Franz Sigel, Lieutenant Colonel George Andrews, and Colonel George Dietzler.

By the end of July, the Missouri State Guard was encamped about 75 miles southwest of Springfield and had been reinforced by Confederate Brigadier General Benjamin McCulloch and Arkansas state militia Brigadier General N. Bart Pearce. The mixed Missouri and Confederate forces doubled the size of Lyon's Union force. They began making plans to attack Springfield but on August 1, Lyon marched out of the city in a bold move to try and surprise the Confederate forces. A short skirmish occurred at Dug Springs, with the Union emerging as the winner, but by then Lyon had learned that he was greatly outnumbered by the enemy and retreated back into Springfield. McCulloch went in pursuit and by August 6 was encamped at Wilson's Creek, about 10 miles southwest of the city.

The pursuit was slowed by bickering between Price and McCulloch. Price favored an immediate attack on Springfield but McCulloch, doubtful about the quality of the Missouri State Guard, preferred to remain in place. After Price threatened an attack without his support, McCulloch reluctantly agreed to attack on the morning of August 10, only to be stopped by a heavy rainstorm on the night of August 9. He cancelled his plans and ordered his men back to camp.

Meanwhile, Lyon knew that his smaller force was in great danger. He began making plans to withdraw northeast to Rolla where he could reinforce and resupply – but not before he launched a surprise attack on the Missouri camp to slow the enemy's pursuit. Colonel Franz Sigel developed a flawed strategy, with which Lyon unfortunately agreed, that split the already outnumbered Union force. Sigel proposed trapping McCulloch with a pincer movement. He would lead 1,200 men in flanking maneuver while the main body of troops under Lyon struck from the north. Going along with the ill-conceived plan, the Union troops marched out of Springfield on the dark, wet night of August 9, leaving behind about 1,000 men to protect the supplies and cover the retreat.

The Union force attacked at first light on August 10. The Confederates were indeed taken by surprise and Lyon's force overran their camps, taking the high ground at the crest of a ridge that came to be known as "Bloody Hill." But the Union's hopes for a quick victory were dashed when the artillery of the Pulaski Arkansas Battery opened up on their advance, which gave Price's infantry time to organize lines on the south side of the hill. Lyon attempted to counterattack from his position, but was unsuccessful. Price launched a series of frontal and flank attacks against Lyon, but they also failed. Eventually, a shortage of ammunition caused his attack to falter.

The two Union forces, commanded by Lyon and Sigel, lost contact with each other since they had no means of communicating and no way of supporting each other if anything went wrong. Sigel's attack was successful at first, with the brigade arriving in the Confederate rear just as the sun was coming up. Artillery fire routed the Confederate cavalry units that were encamped at Sharp's farm and Sigel started a pursuit that stopped along Skeeg's Branch. When he inexplicably stopped at this position, he failed to post skirmishers along his front and left his flank open for an attack. Meanwhile, McCulloch rallied several Confederate units, including the 3rd Louisiana Infantry and the 3rd Division from the Missouri State Guard, and launched a counterattack. Sigel's men mistook the 3rd Louisiana for the 3rd Iowa Infantry, who also wore gray uniforms, and withheld their fire until the Confederates were nearly upon them. His flank was consequently utterly devastated by the counterattack and his brigade was routed, losing four cannons. Sigel and his men fled the field and Lyon, Sweeny and Sturgis were left on the field alone.

After Sigel was driven from the battle, the momentum shifted in favor of the Confederacy. Nathaniel Lyon became the first Union general to be killed in the war. He was shot in the heart at Bloody Hill that morning, while leading the 2nd Kansas Infantry in a countercharge. General Sweeny was shot in the leg, and Major Samuel D. Sturgis, as the highest ranking Regular Army officer, assumed command of the troops. By this time, the Federal men were still in a defensible position atop the hill, but supplies were low and morale was worsening by the minute. By 11:00 a.m., the Union troops had repulsed three separate Confederate charges. Finally, fearing a fourth Confederate attack, Sturgis retreated and the Federals fled toward Rolla.

In the aftermath of the bloody battle, the causalities were nearly equal -- 1,317 Union and 1,230 from the Missouri, Arkansas and Confederate troops. Though the Confederates won the day, they failed to pursue the retreating Union forces. Once again, Price and McCulloch argued. Price wanted to start immediately in pursuit but McCulloch feared for the condition of the troops and didn't want to stretch the supply line to Arkansas any further than he had to. This Confederate victory buoyed southern sympathizers in Missouri and served as a springboard for a bold thrust north that carried Price and his Missouri State Guard as far as Lexington on September 20. The Confederate and Arkansas forces withdrew from the state.

After falling back to Springfield, Sturgis handed over command of the army to Sigel. At a council of war that evening, it was agreed that the Federal troops would fall back to Rolla. However, Sigel failed to get his brigade ready at that time, forcing a delay of several hours. Along the retreat route, Sigel's men took several lengthy delays in order to prepare meals and the other officers turned on Sigel and forced him to turn command back over to Sturgis. Throughout the rest of the war, Sigel largely failed to distinguish himself, often blaming poor health for bad decisions and defeats. He was soundly defeated by Major General John C. Breckenridge at the Battle of New Market, on May 15, 1864, which was particularly embarrassing due to the prominent role young cadets from the Virginia Military Institute played in his defeat. In July, he fought Lieutenant General Jubal A. Early at Harpers Ferry, but soon afterward was relieved of his command for "lack of aggression" and replaced by Maj. Gen. David Hunter. Sigel spent the rest of the war without an active command.

The Battle of Wilson's Creek was an important moment to the Confederate sympathizers in southwest Missouri. On October 30, 1861, the Missourians under Price and Jackson formally joined the Confederate cause in Neosho, Missouri. Officials passed the resolutions for Missouri secession and Jackson was named the Governor of Confederate Missouri. However, the new government never earned the favor of most of the population of Missouri, and the state remained in the Union throughout the war. To make matters worse, a series of defeats shattered what little control Jackson had and his Confederate state government was soon forced to leave the state.

War had shattered the peace of rural Missouri and it would be many years to come before the violence and bloodshed would come to an end.

More than a century after the last guns were silenced at Wilson's Creek, the battlefield was dedicated as a national park. Today, visitors, travelers, and history buffs visit this quiet park, which is filled with trees and prairie grass and

John Ray House

looks almost the same as it did in 1861. The stories of bravery and blood seem far in the distant past at this peaceful place, but they may not be as far in the past as one might think – there are ghosts that linger at Wilson's Creek.

One of the lingering haunts on the battlefield may not be linked directly to the battle. The John Ray house, which was in the midst of the fighting in 1861, was built in 1850 and was the Wilson's Creek post office for more than 10 years. It was home to Ray, his wife, Roxana, their nine children, and a mail carrier. The house was occupied by Confederate officers during the battle.

The Ray family has been gone for many years but at least one member of the family may have stayed behind. On several occasions, visitors have seen a young woman in a long period dress carrying water from the Ray springhouse, a small stone building that covered a nearby spring. The family stored perishables like milk, butter, and eggs there and used the water for drinking and cooking. Those who have seen the girl believed that she was part of a living history program at the battlefield but when they tried to speak to her, she didn't respond. Park rangers stated that there was no living history program going on at the time of the sightings.

But most of the ghostly occurrences at Wilson's Creek take place on the battlefield itself, where more than 2,000 young men bled and died in August 1861. Battlefields, with all of the trauma and death that occurred on them, are common places to find ghosts and hauntings. Wilson's Creek is no exception.

Stories of the resident ghosts date back as far as the 1940s, when a group of fisherman saw at least 15 Union soldiers, wearing dirty uniforms and carrying rifles, file past them and vanish. The same group of spectral soldiers have been seen several times near the creek. It was as if a supernatural recording imprinted itself on the location and now repeats itself over and over again.

Civil War re-enactor Steve Cottrell told of an incident that occurred in the spring of 1983 when the park sponsored a large encampment of re-enactors to present simulations of military drills, camp life, and battle recreations for visitors. During that weekend, a column of Union infantry re-enactors went on an early morning march. In the predawn light, the men became aware of a solitary horseman who was following them at a distance. Although his features were not clear, he was dressed in Civil War clothing. By the time the march was over, the lone figure on horseback had disappeared. The men assumed that the rider was a cavalry re-enactor out for an early morning ride. However, when the men in the cavalry unit (including Cottrell) heard about the incident, they were surprised because none of the men had been saddled at that time of the morning. As far as they were able to determine, no one – re-enactor, visitor, or park ranger – was on horseback in the park at the time the lone rider made his appearance.

But there is no place as haunted on the battlefield as "Bloody Hill," the site of numerous deaths during the fight. Union batteries on the hilltop dueled with Confederate artillery in the valley for more than six hours and the Federal men on high ground fought off three charges by the desperate Missouri and Arkansas men who threw themselves at the line over and over again. Hundreds of men died both attacking and defending the hill and, perhaps not surprisingly, some of them have apparently remained behind.

Over the years, many people who have visited "Bloody Hill" have spoken of feeling as if they are not alone on the hilltop. And while this could be merely imagination at work by those who know of the violent events on the hill, other incidents suggest that there is more here than meets the eye. Accounts have circulated of voices, cries, shouts, and screams that have been heard there, even when no living person is nearby. Some claim they have actually seen the mournful apparitions of torn and bloody soldiers on the hill, often sending those unlucky visitors hurrying back to their car.

There is little doubt to those who have encountered the unusual out in the trees and prairie grass of the park that something remains at Wilson's Creek.

Haunts of Pythian Castle

Hidden away outside of Springfield are the looming battlements of what has come to be called Pythian Castle over the years. Started in 1911, and requiring two years to build, the stone fortress was designed by a fraternal organization called the Knights of Pythias, who planned it as a home of the widows and orphans of its members.

As the years passed and the organization faded, the castle was taken over by the United States Army before finally being sold off as "surplus" and

The Pythian Castle outside of Springfield served as a home for orphans and later, as the O'Reilly Service Club during World War II — inviting lingering ghosts of several eras.

abandoned to time and the elements. Subsequent owners have managed to breathe life back into the place but have quickly found that not all of the buildings' past occupants have left. Stories abound there of scores of lingering ghosts.

    The Knights of Pythias was a fraternal order and secret society that was founded in Washington, D.C. in November 1864. It was the first fraternal organization to receive a charter under an act of the United States Congress. It was founded by Justin H. Rathbone, who had been inspired by a play by the Irish poet John Banim about the friendship between Damon and Pythias, figures from Greek mythology who symbolized trust and loyalty through true friendship. Rathbone used the merits of the legend as a basis for the order, building it around the ideals of loyalty, honor, and friendship.

    The Pythian order grew rapidly in the late 1800s and at one time, boasted over 700,000 members with more than 6,000 lodges across America. During the important years of the order, 22 homes were constructed across the country to provide shelter for the widows and orphans of the lodge members. Eventually, as members grew older and interest in many fraternal organizations faded, the Knights of Pythias reduced in size and began closing down the homes, which were expensive to operate. The order is still in existence today but membership is far less than what it was during glory days of the society.

The Pythian Home near Springfield was much like the others built during this same time period. The 27,000 square foot building, which was built to resemble a medieval castle, cost more than $150,000 to construct and was located on 53 acres outside of town. The foundation of the structure was made from Carthage stone, a strong variety of limestone that is quarried in the Ozarks. A steel framework was used to support the concrete floors, staircases, hallways, and ceilings. Pyrobar blocks (a gypsum-based material that was used to prevent fires and was developed in the early 1900s) made up all of the interior walls.

The castle was designed not only as a sort of glorified orphanage, but also as a place that would house and care for the widows of Knights of Pythias members. Because of this, it had an unusual design, which included a second floor theater with 355 seats, a ticket booth, projection room, and dressing rooms behind the stage. Funerals and church services were sometimes held there. The main floor had a foyer, meeting room, ballroom, dining room, and sitting parlors. The basement also had a gymnasium for the children and later, cells were installed there when the castle was used by the military.

Behind the theater on the second floor were dormitories for the orphans and bedrooms for the widows. The orphans were kept segregated by sex with boys on the right side of the building and girls on the left. There are many claims made that orphans at the Pythian Homes were not allowed to talk to one another or were abused in some way, but this is not the case. Most of those who grew up in Pythian Homes have looked back on the experience with happiness. The homes were well-funded and the children were well cared for. Most of the food served in the kitchen was grown on the property and the orphans were usually placed in charge of livestock feeding and other chores, in addition to their schoolwork. Being orphaned was undoubtedly a heartbreaking situation, but most residents look back in fondness at the days they spent at the Pythian Homes.

Around 1940, the U.S. Army's O'Reilly General Hospital Complex was erected next door to the Pythian Castle. Once completed, it contained over 200 buildings on 160 acres of land and was used for the treatment of servicemen. The complex expanded after the start of World War II and in 1942, the military took over the Pythian Castle, purchasing it for $29,500. The castle was turned into the O'Reilly Service Club for enlisted men and began to be used for both entertainment and the rehabilitation of soldiers wounded in battle.

The O'Reilly Service Club was said to be the best place of its kind in the country and featured not only Hollywood films in the theater but billiard rooms, a bowling alley, music listening rooms, a library, sitting lounges, and more.

Soldiers were able to attend USO dances and swing to sounds of entertainers like Cab Calloway, Benny Goodman, and Tommy Dorsey and laugh at the antics of performers like Bob Hope.

But not everything was happy and light at the old Castle. During this time, the castle was officially known as Building 501 and the former laundry room behind it was listed as Building 503, a military guardhouse. Located in the guardhouse and in the basement of the castle were cells that had been installed by the military to hold German prisoners of war. Little is known about the prisoners that were kept in those cells but it is said that they were used for labor duties throughout the complex. Rumors claim that some of these men were beaten and tortured and that at least one of them was killed in the steam tunnels under the castle, but whether or not these stories are true remains a mystery.

After the end of World War II, the castle became part of a Veteran's Administration tuberculosis hospital but this only lasted for five years. In early 1952, the VA moved out and the property went on the market. In the interim, the Department of Defense allowed the Southwestern Power Administration, a federal agency, to temporarily use some of the buildings for storage. The castle itself was used by the Army Reserves. In 1955, the property was divided and sold and the National Guard obtained the property around the castle, the General Council of the Assemblies of God obtained much of the remaining property for erection of the Evangel College of the Arts and Sciences, and several smaller groups bought various other sections of the grounds. In 1980, the Ozarks Area Community Action Corps leased the building and remained there until the end of 1993. In January 1994, the building was sold at auction to Gene and Rhonda Taylor, who owned it for the next six years. It was purchased by Linda and Frank Gray in 2000, who planned to use the building as a facility for the disabled, but their plans never materialized and the castle was sold again to current owner, Tamara Finocchiao, who offers murder mystery weekends, rentals, and tours. She has worked hard to restore the building and meet the city's requirements, finally landing the castle on the National Register of Historic Places.

The old Pythian Castle has seen a lot of history pass through its doors over the last century and has seen many changes occur within its walls. But during all of this, time has, in many ways, stood still – at least when it comes to the resident ghosts.

The stories of ghosts at the castle began to emerge in the last few years, about the time that a greater number of people began visiting the place for mystery events and tours. While these stories may not date back many years, if all combined together, then Pythian Castle is surely one of the most haunted locations in the region. Disembodied voices have frequently been heard within the walls, along with moaning and crying sounds that come from empty rooms and vacant corridors. Lights turn on and off by themselves and people frequently complain of batteries being drained in cameras and flashlights. Eerie cold spots come and go without warning, and objects, even heavy furniture, move about on their own. The castle seems to play host to a number of ghosts, but who are they?

Some have suggested that the resident spirits are orphans who lived there back in the days when the Pythian Home was in operation. Could this be the case? It does seem possible that some of the lonely little spirits who came to live in this new, strange place have lingered behind, even though in the official records, only two children ever died there during the days of the orphanage. But perhaps the sounds of laughter, running feet, slamming doors, and mysterious voices are impressions left behind on the atmosphere of the castle, repeating themselves over time as a haunting. This could certainly explain some of the strange events that occur with the building's stone walls.

Could the ghosts be those of soldiers who stayed there during the time that it was a rehabilitation hospital? Or could they simply be servicemen who so enjoyed their time at the O'Reilly Service Club that they never wanted to leave? There have been encounters with men in uniform in the castle, who often vanish when approached. The hard soles of shoes have been heard tapping on the stairs and down hallways, even when no one is there. Fire alarms sometimes go off, even though no one has pulled down the handle. Some claim they have been touched by unseen hands, usually comforting pressure on the shoulder or back when no one is standing nearby.

And what of the German prisoners who were once housed in the basement? There are those who blame much of the haunting activity on these luckless men, doomed to remain in their cells even after death. Many people become unnerved, or even violently ill, when they go down into the lower levels of the basement. Doors have been heard to slam in that part of the building, even when it's empty, and others have heard chains drop and the sounds of a man loudly screaming. One night, according to the current owner, her dog stood at the top of the basement stairs and barked at something down in the darkness. She turned on the lights, but there was nothing there.

Whatever the identity of these ghosts might be, they seem satisfied with their residence at the Pythian Castle. Whether trapped there or lingering by choice, it seems as though they will be within the walls of the castle for many years to come.

Ghosts of the "Brookline Massacre"

Driving west from Springfield, the Mother Road follows Missouri 266, and a few miles outside of town, it passes not far from the small community of

Brookline. Although most people don't realize it, the town holds a place of infamy in the history of not only Route 66, but the history of American crime. The early years of U.S. 66 marked the end of the Prohibition era and the start of the Great Depression. Over the course of the next few years, this era of national poverty gave birth to the days of bank robbers and so-called "public enemies," many of whom used Route 66 to flee from the law. Pretty Boy Floyd often used U.S. 66 to travel back and forth between his home state of Oklahoma and the Midwest. Bonnie and Clyde were nearly captured in Joplin, Missouri, leaving dead policemen behind. And the infamous Young Brothers carried out a massacre in Brookline, leaving a gruesome tale of blood, death, and ghosts in their wake.

During the Depression, many of the outlaws and bank robbers became folk heroes to the people who read about their exploits in the newspapers or heard their stories on the radio. There were few Americans in those grim days who didn't feel a twinge of jealousy when they saw these outlaws taking revenge on banks and politicians – institutions and people who had taken advantage of them. Stories were told that some of these outlaws actually stole from the rich and then gave back part of the money to those who really needed it. And in the 1930s, there were a lot of folks who needed it. Of course, those stories were more wishful thinking than reality, but this didn't stop some folks from giving a silent cheer each time that John Dillinger or Pretty Boy Floyd slipped away from a police roadblock – just as the people of western Missouri once offered assistance to another folk hero -- a bank robber named Jesse James.

But the story of the Young Brothers – and the deadly shootout in which they were involved in 1932 – was not a tale of folk heroes and bank robbers. It was a story of desperation, greed, and horror, but strangely, it is rarely mentioned in the chronicles of the "Public Enemy Era" of the 1930s and was never widely known outside of the Ozarks region. The tale is tragically overlooked, especially when we consider that, until September 11, 2011, the "Brookline Massacre," as it was called, turned into the worst loss of life in law enforcement history resulting from a single incident in which six police officers died in a single day.

The Young Brothers – Paul, Jennings and Harry – grew up on a small, 100-acre farm outside of Brookline, just southwest of Springfield. They were raised by a hard-working Christian couple, James David and Willie Florence Young, who undoubtedly hung their heads in shame as three of their 11 children turned to a life of a crime.

The three brothers, who dubbed themselves the "Young Triumvirate," seemed to be born under a bad sign. Juvenile delinquents who grew up to be petty criminals, they flaunted their disrespect for the law and despite a string of robberies and assaults, law enforcement seemed unable to pin anything solid on them. That changed in 1919 when Paul and Jennings broke into a

The Young brothers – little-known desperadoes of Depression-era Missouri

small-town store outside Springfield and were quickly arrested with stolen merchandise. In light of the overwhelming evidence, they confessed to the theft and were sent to the state penitentiary in Jefferson City.

The pair was indifferent to the pain and humiliation they caused their family. James Young was inconsolable over the actions of his sons. It seemed that this burden was too much for him to bear and he grew sick and died while they were in prison. Only Mrs. Young continued to defend them, claiming that they were framed for the crime and didn't deserve to be in prison. This continued for years. At one point, Mrs. Young was nearly arrested after police officers found stolen merchandise in her home. She claimed she knew nothing of the items (tires and rugs) stored in the farm house and Jennings stepped up and admitted to the crime so that his mother wouldn't be charged with possession of stolen merchandise. While he was in prison, Paul and Harry committed numerous robberies and burglaries. Harry was back in the penitentiary in 1927, but soon all three were free again.

On June 2, 1929, Harry was driving recklessly through the town of Republic and was pulled over by City Marshal Mark Noe for drunk driving. Marshal Noe's body was found outside of town in a ditch the following day – and one of the Young brothers graduated from small-time robberies to the murder of a police officer. Harry's name and face were put out over the wire and he was hunted for over a year by officials throughout the United States and Canada. Somehow, though, he managed to elude capture, even though he returned to Missouri and went back to law-breaking with his brothers.

By Thanksgiving 1931, Paul and Jennings had joined their brother on the wanted list for stealing cars and taking them over state lines. Federal warrants were issued, along with state warrants for theft, and there was still Harry's outstanding warrant for the murder of Mark Noe. Greene County Sheriff Marcell Hendrix made sure that word got back to the Young farm that he was tired of looking for Harry and believed that he had left the country for Mexico. Sheriff's deputies and police officers from Springfield began staking out the Young family farm, believing that the brothers were occasionally returning home to see their mother. They were careful not to tip off Mrs. Young, who they were convinced would tip off the boys that the police were watching.

In the meantime, the investigation into the Youngs' activities continued. Federal and state officers in Oklahoma and Texas had linked the Youngs to stolen cars in Missouri, Kansas, Arkansas, Iowa, and Illinois, making up a car theft ring that was more elaborate than the authorities had ever seen up until that time. This information caused the manhunt to heat up and more pressure was put on the stake-out at the Young farm. A few days after Thanksgiving, officers narrowly missed a visit by Jennings. He stopped in to see his mother and soon left, probably on his way to Texas with an automobile that had been stolen in Illinois. He allegedly stopped at the farm again on the way back from Texas, but the authorities missed him again.

On Saturday, January 2, 1932, evidence indicated that Jennings -- and probably Paul and Harry -- were at the family farm. Since the farm was outside Springfield city limits, Chief of Police Ed Waddle handed the matter off to county authorities. Sheriff Hendrix organized the raid, gathering ammunition, as well as deputies and detectives. A total of 11 police officers went to Brookline and the Young family farm that day. Hendrix had been a friend and neighbor of the Young family for many years and did not believe the boys would hurt him, which is likely why no one contacted federal agents to assist in the arrests.

When the officers arrived at the farmhouse, they milled about for a few minutes, banging on doors and yelling for the brothers to come out. They thought they heard noises inside, but no one answered their calls. It was soon agreed that the men would fan out in front of the house, fire a gas canister into one of the upstairs windows and, after the gas had time to saturate the upper floor, the sheriff and a few others would force their way into the back door and flush the brothers out the front, where officers would be waiting. A detective fired a gas canister into an upstairs window while the other officers waited a few minutes before taking their assigned positions.

Sheriff Hendrix and Deputy Wiley Mashburn, accompanied by Detective Virgil Johnson, left the southeast corner of the house and walked to the kitchen door in the rear. In order to cover them, Chief of Detectives Tony Oliver waited out of sight behind a tree on the outside of a small lawn fence.

Lawmen at the Young family home. The photo was taken after the massacre left six police officers dead.

Patrolman Charles Houser stood unprotected by the lawn gate. Detective Sid Meadows waited behind a tree outside of the lawn fence on the north side so that he could see anyone exiting on the northwest side of the house. Detective Ben Bilyeu stood in the open, near Tony Oliver. Detective Frank Pike and a civilian who came along for assistance, R.G. Wegman, were assigned to remain behind the officer's cars so that they could cover the barn and shed. Detective Owen Brown and Deputy Ollie Crosswhite were at the northeast corner of the house so that Crosswhite could see into the downstairs windows. Essentially, the lawmen had the house surrounded, but they were unprepared for what happened next.

Sheriff Hendrix banged loudly on the kitchen door. He, along with Deputy Mashburn, called out several times for the Young brothers to come out, unarmed and with their hands raised. There was no response from the house so the officers decided to kick the door open. Johnson forced the door from the center, with Hendrix and Mashburn on either side of him. The door creaked when the three men slammed into it and it crashed partway open. Mashburn raised his revolver and took one step inside. Suddenly, a shotgun roared in the kitchen and a blast of bird shot hot Mashburn in the face, ripping his skin apart and blowing both of his eyes out of their sockets.

Hendrix yelled and shoved into the opening left by Mashburn, just as the mortally wounded deputy was staggering backward onto the concrete sidewalk in back of the house. Another blast came from the shotgun inside, hitting Hendrix in the upper part of the right shoulder, just under his collarbone. The shot tore a ragged hole between his first and second ribs and tore open his chest. Hendrix fell to his knees, but did not collapse.

Deputy Mashburn, who was somehow still standing, continued to stagger backward. He swayed and stumbled and then fell down, cracking his head on the concrete. His body convulsed with pain as his hands fumbled over the bloody ruin of his face.

Sheriff Hendrix must have seen his killer as he fell to his knees in the kitchen because he raised his gun to fire. But his torn muscles refused to function and the gun slipped from his fingers. He did not retreat. Instead, without saying a word, he crawled forward on the linoleum floor, inching his way forward in a growing puddle of his own blood, until he died at the feet of his murderer. Hendrix had come as a neighbor and friend to peacefully arrest the law-breaking sons of an honest and upright man, only to be gunned down by those sons for his generous efforts.

Detective Johnson, who had taken cover after the first shots, ran for the front of the house as Chief Oliver yelled to the others that Hendrix and Mashburn has been shot. Johnson turned at the gate and prepared to fire another gas canister into the house. He aimed and pulled the trigger, but it refused to fire. In his haste, he realized that the chamber had not been closed. He slammed it shut and raised the gun, but before he could fire it, it went off unexpectedly and sent the canister wide of its mark. It hit the outside of the house, bounced off, and fell onto the front porch roof, where it started to burn. Johnson turned to Oliver and shouted that he had no more gas canisters.

Oliver instructed Johnson, along with the other officers, to take cover, have their guns loaded and extra ammunition at hand. He feared that a long and bloody siege was at hand. Deputy Crosswhite suggested that Oliver send someone to get long guns – rifles and shotguns – and to bring more gas and bullets. Oliver sent Johnson for ammunition and reinforcements and the detective made his way behind some trees to his car.

Just as he was backing up to turn around, Detective Bilyeu and the only civilian on the scene, R.G. Wegman, scrambled into the backseat. The gunmen inside of the house had come to the front room, likely wearing bullet-proof vests, and when they saw the three men starting to drive away, they opened fire on the car. Two bullets shattered the windshield, narrowing missing Johnson's head, and exited through an open window. Three or four shotgun blasts from the house blew out the rest of the glass in the car and wounded Johnson. In spite of his injuries, he sped away toward Springfield to get more help.

When the men inside of the house opened fire on the automobile, Chief Oliver yelled for his men to fire into every downstairs window. In between shots, Patrolman Houser looked around for better cover and spotting a large tree across the yard, he made a run for it. As he slowed to peer around the front of the house to see if it was safe, a bullet that was fired from a south window hit him in the forehead. His head blew apart as the bullet plowed through his skull. "My God!" he shouted and fell to the ground with his legs and arms outstretched. He was likely dead before he completed his fall.

The killers returned to the kitchen to try and escape the house. One of them peered out the back window and was spotted by Crosswhite, who opened fire until his gun was empty. One of the Young brothers, firing with a rifle, went to the dining room window and standing on a chair, fired at Crosswhite to keep him pinned down as one of his brothers slipped out the back door, crept up behind the deputy with a shotgun, and blasted him point-blank in the back of the head. Crosswhite was killed instantly.

Chief Oliver, while continuing to fire at the house, looked over and saw that Detective Sid Meadows was dangerously exposed. He ordered him to fall back. Meadows replied that he was out of ammunition, putting his hands in his pockets, hoping to find a stray bullet or two. Moments later, shots were fired at Meadows, splintering the tree he was hiding behind. Again Oliver ordered Meadows to fall back, trying to cover him by firing round after round with his pistol toward the house. Meadows started to move, leaning cautiously around the trunk of the tree, looking for his break. As he stuck his head out, a bullet from the house hit him just above his right eye. His head snapped back and he fell to the ground. He also died instantly.

Detective Pike leaned out from behind his tree and sent a steady roar of bullets into the house. He was answered by several shotgun blasts from a north window. Most of the shots went wild, but several pellets struck Pike in the left arm. Fearing that they were all going to be killed, Chief Oliver ordered Pike and Brown to make a run for the barn.

Before he could move, Oliver became the target for the shots from the house. The tree where he hid was ripped apart by shotgun blasts and he took a step backward to keep splinters from spraying into his eyes and he was hit hard by another blast, which ripped apart his heavy overcoat and clothing and tore into his flesh. In pain, he forgot his perilous position and stepped to the right, exposing that side of his body. He was struck by a rifle bullet, but did not fall. Bleeding badly, and struggling to stay upright, he ran for the cover of a nearby automobile. A second bullet hit him in the back, entering just below his left shoulder and bursting outward from his chest. Oliver pitched forward, sprawling in the dust next to the patrol car. He died painfully, slowly bleeding out as his chest cavity filled with blood.

Only two officers remained alive: Detectives Owen Brown and Frank Pike. They heard a yell from the house: "Lay down your guns and come up! We've killed the others!"

Both men refused to answer the killer's demands but knew that they were now hopelessly outnumbered and outgunned. They had no choice but to run for their lives.

With all of the lawmen either dead, dying, or running away, the killers – suspected to be Jennings and Harry – came out into the yard. They yanked the spark-plug wires from the sheriff's car, grabbed what guns they could easily find, and went back into the house. They searched the sheriff's body, which was lying in the kitchen, and found his wallet, which had several hundred dollars in it. They hurriedly packed some clothes, along with five stolen revolvers, a rifle, a shotgun, and dozens of rounds of ammunition and shotgun shells, into two traveling bags and began running. Investigators later believed that they fled through cornfields and orchards on foot, escaping in a northwest direction.

When Johnson returned with additional officers, weapons, and ammunition, he could scarcely believe the horrific scene. Dead and dying men were strewn about the farm and the killers had escaped. Detectives Brown and Pike were soon located and Pike's wounds were treated. Despite the seriousness of his wounds, Deputy Mashburn was still alive when Johnson returned, but he died later that evening.

This brought the death toll to six – a record number of lawmen killed during one incident.

Many would find it hard to believe that just two men had held off the raid and killed six lawmen, but both were vicious and were expert marksmen. They also had the high ground from the second floor of the house and considering that the police officers, armed only with pistols, were poorly prepared for a shootout and had little cover in the yard outside of the house, it was feasible that two men could carry out the massacre.

A full-scale investigation was launched into the shootout, as was a nationwide manhunt for the perpetrators. Another of the Young brothers, Oscar, confirmed to lawmen that Harry and Jennings were the only two family members at the house that fateful day. Despite rumors that famous bank robber "Pretty Boy" Floyd was at the Young farm that day, it was later determined that he was in Texas at the time of the massacre. The hunt was on for the Young brothers, but with no solid leads, the authorities had to wait for them to resurface.

The first break came for Greene County Prosecutor Dan M. Nee, who was in charge of the case, from Streetman, Texas. The Young brothers were driving at a high rate of speed on U.S. Highway 75 and ran their Ford coupe

Farmer D.H. Carroll unknowingly helped the Young brothers after a car accident. They fled the scene and he called the police to recover the car, stolen license plates, and several guns.

into a ditch about 80 miles south of Dallas. Battered and bruised, the pair climbed out of the wreck, waving away motorists who tried to stop and offer aid. Shortly, a farmer named D. H. Carroll came onto the scene with his daughter and asked the men if they needed help. The brothers convinced them that they were not seriously hurt and asked for a telephone to call a wrecker. Carroll replied that he had a phone at his house, which was nearby. He did tell them, though, that there weren't many wreckers in the area and it would take a while for one to arrive. The brothers, claiming now that they actually had been hurt and might need a doctor soon, didn't want to wait for the wrecker, even though they needed to get the car out of the ditch. This led to an offer from Carroll to pull the car out of the ditch and store it in a shed until the brothers could get a ride into town, see a doctor, and return to Carroll's farm with a mechanic.

As promised, Carroll used a team of horses to pull the car back onto the road and tow it to his yard. When he looked inside, he was surprised to see a shotgun and a rifle sitting in plain sight. He thought the two men might be hunters. He snooped around and saw a checkbook from a bank in Parsons, Kansas, and other things that seemed appropriate, so his fears were somewhat allayed. The only thing that really bothered him still was the fact that the license plates were missing from the car. When he mentioned this, his daughter informed him that she had seen one of the men remove something from the car and toss it into a field. Carroll returned to the accident scene and after a few minutes, found two Missouri license plates numbered 363-662.

He brought the plates back to the car and waited nervously for the Youngs to return. When they didn't come back, he called the Navarro County Sheriff's department to tell them about what had happened and to tell them that the Missouri car was at his farm. They agreed to look into the matter and several officers were sent to the Carroll farm, where they examined the car and took an inventory of the contents, including the guns.

But the real break in the case came about because of a nosy telephone operator.

Mrs. A.E. Gaddy, the local operator, overhead Carroll's conversation with the sheriff's department, but she said nothing about it to her family. Later that evening, her son was listening to a radio broadcast on station KMOX out of St. Louis and heard a story about the massacre in Brookline. The story included descriptions of Jennings and Harry Young. When he mentioned it to his mother, she instantly remembered the overheard conversation between Carroll and the sheriff's department. She told her son about it and out of curiosity, the young man called Carroll about the details of the wreck and to get descriptions of the two men. After talking with the farmer, he became convinced that the occupants of the wrecked car were Jennings and Harry. He immediately contacted Prosecutor Dan Nee in Springfield and explained the situation.

At the time of Gaddy's call, which was just 24 hours after the massacre, Nee, his assistant Horn Bostel, Federal agents Burger and DeMoss, and three Frisco Railway detectives, Wilson, Nolan and Arndt, were questioning Mrs. Young and her two daughters, Lorna and Vinita, about the events at the farm. The three women said that they had been away visiting relatives when the massacre took place.

Nee gladly took Gaddy's call and was convinced that the possible lead was worth checking out. He phoned the Navarro County officials and from them, he obtained the serial numbers on the guns. Nee knew that the brothers had connections in Houston and other Texas cities, where they operated their auto theft ring. Even though it was late, he and the other investigators began wiring and calling law enforcement agencies in south Texas to be on the lookout for Harry and Jennings Young.

Early the next morning, Nee and his men learned that the two occupants of the wrecked car had stopped E. C. Hogan, a Fort Worth drug salesman, near the scene of the accident and had asked for a ride to the town of Fairfield, where they planned to see a doctor. On the way there, a bearing on Hogan's car burned out near Caney Creek Bridge. The hitchhikers thanked Hogan for the ride and flagged down the next traveler, Isaac Levy, who was also on his way to Fairfield. He was not suspicious when he picked them up, but grew worried when they asked him to drive them all the way to Houston for any amount of money that he wanted. As they neared Fairfield, the obviously injured men changed their mind about seeing a doctor and said they were anxious to get to Houston as soon as they could. Levy left the men at a filling station on the outskirts of town, glad to be rid of his questionable passengers. The Young brothers apparently walked for a short distance before being picked up by another, unidentified motorist. None of the people who had contact with the brothers in Texas remembered seeing them with handguns on their persons or in their bags.

Meanwhile, Nee was still working to establish the identities of the two men. He found that by tracing the license plates that had been dumped in Texas, he could connect them to a Ford coupe that had been reported stolen in Springfield on the night of the massacre. In addition, the serial numbers on the rifle and shotgun found in the car were traced to Oscar Young, the outlaws' brother, who admitted when questioned that he had loaned the guns to Harry and Jennings a day or two prior to the massacre so that they could go hunting. Armed with this information, the lawmen felt certain that they were on the trail of the Young brothers. The prosecutor pushed Texas officials even harder in his efforts to get them to use every possible resource to apprehend the murderers.

By Sunday night, the Youngs had arrived in Houston and managed to stay hidden, despite the local police pulling out all stops to find them. Lawmen raided the known hangouts of the Young brothers and questioned their friends and associates, but no one seemed to know where they were. Despite the heat that was placed upon them, Harry and Jennings managed to stay one step ahead of detectives and elude capture. Additionally, the bags of clothing and stolen guns, which they had packed and then left behind at their mother's house, somehow found their way to Houston and were retrieved by the brothers at some point on Monday. It was later suspected that their brother Paul may have gotten the bags from Missouri to Texas without being detected. Detectives quickly learned that it was not just Mrs. Young who was trying to keep the brothers out of prison.

On Monday afternoon, a Houston police officer believed that he spotted Harry Young, but lost him in a crowd. Early on Tuesday morning, January 5, a carpenter named J.F. Tomlinson called the police to report that he had seen pictures of the Youngs in the morning newspaper and that they resembled the men he had rented a room to the previous afternoon – and they were sleeping in his house at that moment.

Police officials quickly put men into action and gathered there near Tomlinson's home. They made hurried plans to raid the carpenter's small bungalow and capture the Youngs, dead or alive. They moved in on the house shortly after 9:00 a.m., surrounding the place with lawmen armed with every conceivable type of weapon, including handguns, rifles, gas grenades, smoke bombs, and Thompson machine-guns.

Lieutenant Claude Beverly of the Magnolia Park substation was placed in charge of the raid. He led the way to the front door, grabbed the doorknob and pushed into the house, followed closely by Officers Peyton and Bradshaw. Tear gas canisters were hurled through a rear window into the bedroom where the outlaws were believed to be sleeping and then tossed into the front room of the house. Allowing time for the gas to spread through the rooms, Beverly walked down the hall and found another visitor to the house, who was handcuffed and taken outside. Beverly and Peyton continued to the rear bedroom door, threw it open and stormed inside – to find it empty. The Youngs were not in bed, or hiding beneath it. The closet was empty. One of the officers then stepped toward the bathroom door, turned the knob, and started to open it, just as three blasts hit the other side of the door, barely missing the lawmen. They retreated to the kitchen and positioned themselves so that they could see the bathroom door. Things were eerily still for a moment and then the bathroom door opened slightly and one of the Youngs peeked out.

Beverly fired point blank at the face with a sawed-off shotgun. The door slammed shut and from inside the bathroom, several shots rang out. Someone behind the door shouted, "We're dead – come and get us!" Suspecting a trap, Beverly kept his men back until another gas canister could be tossed inside. Then, they unlatched the door and pushed. It stuck before it could be opened all of the way, but once they pushed on it, the barricade moved inside. A body had been blocking the door. When they got into the bathroom, they found Jennings Young lying dead in a pool of blood. Harry Young was bleeding badly, but he was still breathing. The two of them had shot each other so that they could never be taken alive.

Harry Young was placed in an ambulance and rushed to St. Joseph's Infirmary, where he died soon after arriving. He did not regain consciousness on the way to the hospital so the detectives that accompanied him were unable to get a deathbed statement from him. It's unlikely that he would have made one anyway. The Youngs were merciless killers and never regretted the crimes they had committed or the destruction they caused to their family.

The two men were laid out on cold slabs in the Houston morgue, 700 miles from Springfield, where widows and fatherless children were mourning the loss of their husbands and fathers at the hands of the now deceased outlaws. There was no rejoicing in the Ozarks over the bloody end of Harry and Jennings Young, but the final act was over and the Youngs had come to a rather inglorious end.

The story of the Young brothers became little more than a forgotten footnote in the annals of Depression-era crime. Outside of the Ozarks, few people ever heard of the infamous brothers and the deadly massacre that claimed the lives of six policemen in 1932. Strangely, though, reports from what was once the Young family farm seemed determined to make sure that the bloody day was not entirely forgotten.

According to subsequent owners of the farm house, strange happenings began taking place not long after the Young family moved out of the house.

After the massacre, the house was repaired and the damage from countless bullet holes was covered over and hidden away, just like local memories of that horrible afternoon. The house was eventually sold and new families moved in over the years, almost every one of them encountering what seemed to be echoes of the house's past.

Bizarre temperature drops were common in the house, as were knocking and banging sounds on the walls, thudding footsteps in empty rooms, voices and music that seemed to come from nowhere, and feelings as if the residents were being watched. On several occasions, a woman who lived in the house complained of seeing faces looking in the window. When investigated, no one was ever there – including one winter's night when there was snow on the ground. She knew that a man in an old-fashioned, fedora-type hat had been looking in the window, but when her husband went outside to look, he found no man – and no footprints on the snowy ground. Could this be a supernatural recreation of police detectives looking into the windows, trying to find out where the Young brothers were?

All of the odd happenings in the house seemed to be memories of the past, replaying themselves over and over again, except for one report, which told of something a little more frightening. On several occasions, a woman who once lived in the house stated that she had awakened on several occasions to find a dark figure standing at the end of her bed. When she tried to move, the figure grabbed hold of her legs and wouldn't allow her to move. Then, he vanished and she was free. She later said that she would have believed that she dreamed the entire incident, if not for the fact that she woke the next morning to find dark bruises on her legs that looked exactly like handprints.

What haunted the old Young family farmhouse? Was it merely a bit of bad energy left behind at a place where men fought, killed and died? Or was it something else? Had the ghosts of the Youngs returned to prey on the living, just as they had when alive, or were they returning in despair to the one place where they had felt safe in life? A place where their mother always protected them?

That troubling question remains unanswered.

"Las Vegas" in Halltown

Driving west from Springfield, and from the area where the grim history of the Young Brothers Massacre left its mark, a few lonely miles brought travelers into what was once the town of **Plano**. Although little remains of the community today, there is at least one crumbling stone building that dates back to the days of the Wire Road. The old general store remains across the street today from a former Tydol Station and Garage, which now serves as a private home.

This stretch of old U.S. 66, between Springfield and Carthage, is about 70 miles of original road, completely free of the interstate. Remnants of motor courts and old gas stations can be found motoring west over small hills and through acres of forest. Remains of the tiny communities that sprang up along Route 66 still linger there. When the residents moved on, empty buildings were left behind to harbor the ghosts of the past. Along this stretch of the road, travelers find it easier to imagine what it must have been like when Highway 66 was in its heyday and it was the road that kept the towns live.

From Plano, Highway 66 continues to roll over gently sloping hills to the small community of Halltown, once home to **Sylvia's Halltown Café.** Sylvia Rogers opened the café on Route 66 in the early 1930s and served thousands of hungry customers before the place was reduced to ashes in a fire in the mid-1950s. But memories linger. Sylvia and her daughter-in-law, Wilma, were known as excellent cooks and were particularly famous for their pies and their mouth-watering chili, which became up and down the Mother Road.

Next door to Sylvia's was the **Las Vegas Hotel and Café**, which was built after Halltown barber Charlie Dameron took a trip out west to the famous desert city and returned home with his winnings. Those who knew him would tell the story for years that Charlie won so much money that his wife had to help him carry his suitcase home from the Greyhound Bus stop. Charlie built the hotel and café and dubbed it "Las Vegas." It had six rooms upstairs and a ground floor café with a big circular counter. He moved his barber shop into the small metal building next door to the café.

Just west of Halltown, in a beautiful rural setting, was the **White City Motor Court**, which was built around 1935. The 12-unit court was laid out in a wide semi-circle with an office and a café located in the front. All of the

The White City Motor Court in Halltown

units, along with the office, were painted a stark white color. The café had air conditioning, but this amenity was never available in the cabins.

When the interstate bypassed this section of Route 66 in the mid-1960s, the motor court closed a few years later. Today, the building that housed the office and café is used as a residence, while many of the cabins, mostly without roofs, appear to be used for rough storage. There is little about the site now that hearkens back to its glory days. This is truly a forgotten spot on the Mother Road.

The Gay Parita Station first opened for U.S. 66 travelers in 1930

One spot, just a little west of Halltown, that has not been forgotten, though, is the **Gay Parita** Sinclair gas station. Known as a Route 66 landmark, the service station operated from 1930 to 1955, offering gas, snacks, and cold drinks to travelers. It remained abandoned for many years until Gary Turner re-opened it in the early 2000s and began treating modern-day U.S. 66 travelers to a homespun version of yesteryear. Gary and his wife, Lena, made the restored station a memorable stop for thousands of people over the next decade or so. Gary was known for chatting with people from sunrise to sunset and many Route 66 travelers who planned just a quick stop at the station would find their 15-minute stop had turned into two hours.

Sadly, Gary passed away in 2015, but this prompted his daughter, Barbara, to move home from Charleston, South Carolina, to keep the Gay Parita alive. But, not long after Gary died, Lena also passed away, leaving Barbara the sole owner of the old station. It was an easy decision for her to make that she wanted to keep the station going, so it's thriving once more on the old highway out of Halltown. And should you fear that your experience at the station won't be the same with Gary gone, Barbara is happy to say, "they always called me 'Little Gary' because I talked all the time, just like my dad."

Make the Gay Parita station a must-stop on your list of Route 66 Missouri locations.

"Cottages with Convenience"

Between Halltown and the site of old Log City Camp, outside of Avilla, a scattering of lost communities and ghost towns can be found along Highway 66. Towns with names like **Heatonville, Paris Springs, Albatross, Phelps, Rescue, Plew, Log City**, and **Stone City** lived and died with the highway.

The town of Avila is a small survivor. Years ago, Floyd Melugin operated the **Friendly Café and Tavern** in town and there was a choice of filling stations and eating places. A sign for the old **Avila Dew Drop Inn** survives and it reads: "Sandwiches – Cold Drinks – Ice Cream – Smokes – Candies – Coffees – Homemade Pies – 6:30 a.m. to 10:00 p.m."

Just east of Avila, a war of sorts raged during the 1920s and 1930s as Carl Stansbury and his competitors, Whitson and Hammond, competed for the dollars of overnight travelers along this isolated stretch of Highway 66. In 1926, Carl Stansbury began clearing trees from the site of what became **Log City Camp** and he used them to build 14 log cabins. In front of the camp, he also built a café made of stone, a gas station, and a store. The cabins were advertised as "modern cottages with conveniences" and he began renting them out to a steady stream of tourists for $1 per night.

Log City Camp opened in 1926.

Below: Forest City Camp opened – right across the road – in 1928. The two motor courts battled for U.S. 66 customers for years.

Two years later, in 1928, Whitson and Hammond bought their own property, directly across the highway. They went to work on what became **Forest Park Camp** and built 10 rock cabins the size of small suburban homes with front porches. Stansbury promptly added four more cabins at his camp. Whitson and Hammond added a café, so Stansbury added a coffee shop. Stansbury added a dining room, and Whitson and Hammond built a tavern and a dance hall. Stansbury's dining room was advertised as having "washed air, serving excellent food at popular prices. You Name it, We've Got it!"

The "friendly" competition went on for years; as one topped the other, the other undercut and undersold the first. Eventually, the new interstate beat both camps and when it bypassed Avila, both places went out of the business. Today, only a single rock cabin remains at what used to be Log City Camp.

"Crossroads of America"

Past **Forest Mills** and **Maxville**, Route 66 drifts into **Carthage**, the hometown of Belle Starr, the notorious outlaw and "Bandit Queen" of the Wild West. During the Civil War, the Battle of Carthage was fought on July 5, 1861, and was a clash between Union troops from St. Louis and Confederate troops led by pro-Southern Missouri Governor Claiborne Jackson. The "Second Battle of Carthage" occurred in October 1863, when Union troops confronted Confederate troops north of town and forced them to return to Arkansas. The town experienced minor skirmishes and attacks throughout the war, with the worst being in September 1864, when Confederate guerrillas burned most of the town, including the courthouse.

Jasper County, where Carthage was located, was purchased by the federal government from the Osage Indians for $1,200 in cash and $1,500 in merchandise in 1808. They were then moved out west to the Osage Nation reservation, a removal that took several tries. It finally stuck in 1837. Jasper County was formed four years later and Carthage eventually became the county seat.

In 1856, John Shirley, father of "Bandit Queen" Belle Starr, moved his family from a nearby farm into Carthage. Once in town, they built an inn, tavern, livery stable, and blacksmith shop on the north side of the town square. Their businesses took up almost an entire city block and Shirley became a respected member of the community. Although his daughter was raised as a wealthy young woman, her life would change when the Kansas-Missouri Border War broke out.

In 1854, the Kansas-Nebraska Act opened up the new state of Kansas, and residents there were allowed to decide for themselves about the question of slavery. Having strong southern sympathies, the state of Missouri quickly became embroiled in a bitter fight with newly settled anti-slavery groups in nearby Kansas. Border towns in both states, including Carthage, became scenes of fierce guerila warfare. Bloodshed continued during the Civil War that followed a few years later. On July 5, 1861, a battle took place in Carthage when 6,000 poorly equipped Missouri State Guardsmen held off 1,100 Federal soldiers. Both sides declared victory and met up again a month later at Wilson's Creek. Both armies would pass through the region during the war, forcing residents to take sides. After the burning of a large part of the town in 1864, the community was forced to rebuild.

It did so without prominent businessman John Shirley, however. When his son, Bud, joined up with Quantrill's Raiders, the notorious band of Confederate sympathizers who frequently skirmished with Union troops and boasted members like Frank and Jesse James and the Younger brothers, Shirley was proud of his son. But in June 1864, Bud was killed in Sarcoxie, Missouri, and took the fight out of John Shirley. The war had already wreaked havoc on his business and after his son was killed, he packed up the family and moved to Texas. It was in Texas where Belle began her outlaw career.

Carthage slowly recovered from the war. By 1868, the population had rebounded to over 1,200 people and now boasted a school, four churches, three doctors, two hotels, five boarding houses, six dry goods stores, several grocery stores, and many other thriving businesses. The city continued to grow and was, by 1873, home to 6,000 residents, as well as new industries like a woolen mill, two foundries, three wagon and carriage makers, furniture factory, and more. In the late 1880s, rich deposits of limestone, lead, and zinc were discovered beneath the town and it became one of the most prosperous towns in the state.

By the end of the nineteenth century, Carthage had more millionaires per capita than any other city in the United States. The primary source of wealth was the rich deposits of lead and zinc. The mine owners, of course, built grand homes in the city, often using material taken from the newly discovered deposits of gray marble that were found north of town. The Missouri State Capitol, the U.S. Capitol, and the White House were all faced with marble that came from Carthage. More mills and factories arrived in town and by 1900, Carthage had over 12,000 residents and over 100 business and industrial operations.

When Highway 66 passed through Carthage, it brought another era of prosperity to the city. In no time, all kinds of services sprang up to serve the travelers who were pouring through town each day.

Driving into Carthage on the old alignment of Route 66, motorists can only imagine the nightly activities that went on at the **Riverside Inn**, which was built in the 1930s. It was off-limits to the younger generation because the roaring nightclub served alcohol, but the stories abounded. Little information remains about its operations, but the club mysteriously burned down one night in the late 1960s.

Nearby was the **White Court Motel**, built in 1927 with a café and gas station. It later became the **Red Rock Motel** and then the **Red Rock Apartments**. Directly across the street was the **Buster Brown Inn**, which was owned by E.J. Brown. During the years when U.S. 66 brought thousands of cars past its doors, the inn earned a shady reputation as a rumored brothel.

The White Court Motel later became the Red Rock Motel and then the Red Rock Apartments.

Below: The Kel-Lake Motel, which remains in business today.

The building still stands today. In the 1950s, Route 66 was realigned to follow what is now Missouri Route 96, effectively turning the motels, diners, and taverns in this part of town into distant memories.

The **Kel-Lake Motel** was built along the new road alignment in 1954. The motel catered to travelers, as well as hunters and vacationing fisherman, who appreciated the close proximity to Kellogg Lake. The Kel-Lake had eight guest units in a single line with parking in front of each unit. The motel was AAA recommended at the time and offered tile baths, air-conditioning, steam heat, and 7-foot beds. Ernest J. Jackson ran the motel from 1955 to 1965 and became well-known for helping out less-fortunate travelers. After Interstate 44 was constructed, Jackson sold the place, but the Kel-Lake has hung on and remains in business today.

Also nearby was the **Lake Shore Motel**, which advertised excellent fishing in Lake Kellogg. Owner J.K. Bunk's motto was "Wonderful Rest in Cleanliness." The motel still stands today as the Best Budget Inn.

Boots Motel at the "Crossroads of America"

Carthage was a town of great distinction for highway travelers during the glory days of Route 66. One of the things that made it special was that it was situated at what was called the "Crossroads of America." It was at this spot where Route 66, running from Chicago to Los Angeles, and Highway 71, which ran from New Orleans to Canada, intersected with one another.

At the corner of this intersection was the legendary **Boots' Court**, a tourist cabins court that was built by Arthur Boots in 1939. He built the first section of his modern, streamlined motel in stucco and it consisted of four units with two rooms in each. The sleek, white buildings, with rounded corners, had a covered driveway next to each room. Boots defined the roofline of the office with black glass tile and bright green neon, which became one of the motor lodge's most distinct features. He added new rooms in the back section in 1945, bringing the total to 14. Early advertising bragged of a "a radio in every room" and offered all the modern amenities – tile showers, radiant heat in the floor, and air conditioning. Clark Gable was rumored to have once stayed at the lodge, in Room 6, and signed the guest book "Clark Gable and party."

In 1948, Boots sold the motel to Ruben and Rachel Asplin, who left the cold winters of Minnesota for the warmer climate of southwestern Missouri. When the Streamline Moderne style fell out of favor in the 1960s, the Asplins plunked down a gabled roof over the office, but the neon continued to glow in the night, beckoning motorists who were traveling in every direction of the compass.

After Ruben passed away, Rachel continued to run the place by herself until her own death in 1991, at the age of 91. The motor lodge fell on hard times after that. Owner John Ferguson kept turning on the neon at night, but the rooms began to be rented only on a weekly basis. His hope was to find a buyer who might restore the place to its former glory. While he waited, the motel slowly decayed. In time, the green neon lights became a thing of the past.

In 2011, though, Boots' Court was purchased by sisters Deborah Harvey and Priscilla Bledsaw, who were intent on bringing the old motor court back

Boots' Court, one of the surviving icons on the Missouri stretch of Route 66.

to life. They went to work, first bringing back the original style of roof on the office, then opening up some of the rooms again for nightly rentals. Trying to keep it as close to the way that it was in the late 1930s and early 1940s, none of the rooms have televisions. They have been furnished with period décor, old radio, and even chenille spreads on the beds. The motel offers board games to help guests pass the time and many of them often gather in the courtyard at night to talk and tell stories, often about their travels on Route 66.

While the two sisters are currently at work on restoring more of the rooms, there was one part of the motel's history that had not been revived – the green neon light. Then, in April 2016, artist David Hutson from St. Charles, Missouri, repaired and installed the iconic lights around the motel office, finally bringing one of Route 66's most enduring locations into the modern era.

Boots' Drive-in: "Good Food"

Across the highway from the motor court was the **Boots' Drive-in**. Seven years after opening the motor lodge, Arthur Boots expanded his enterprise and built the diner. Boots gave travelers a comfortable place to spend the night and the drive-in on the east side of Route 66 offered them a good place to eat. The two businesses not only shared the same sleek lines and curved corners, but the same green neon that lit up Boots' Court each night also blazed from the exterior of the drive-in. The location of the drive-in at the "Crossroad of America" prompted such hoopla that a national radio program was broadcast from the diner each day. "Breakfast at the Crossroads" was heard each morning by hundreds of thousands of people across the country.

Throughout the 1950s, tourist traffic through the "Crossroads" was steady and business was great. In fact, things were so good that the drive-in added novelty items and souvenirs to its menu. Unfortunately, though, the good times didn't last. When the interstate finally arrived, business took a turn for the worse and even the addition of the gift shop couldn't prevent the inevitable. Boots Drive-in sold its last burger basket and chicken dinner in 1970. The building that played host to hundreds of thousands of tourists and a national radio show now serves as a branch for the local bank.

Motoring to Webb City

As the highway scoots out of Carthage, it passes through **Brooklyn Heights** and a dead end alignment of Route 66, before heading on toward Joplin. Just before reaching **Webb City**, travelers now pass through the small town of **Carterville**, another lead mining town in the region. Once prosperous, the town declined following World War I and never recovered like Webb City and Joplin did.

Webb City, which now blends almost smoothly into the city of Joplin, was once nothing more than a large corn and wheat farm that belonged to John Cornwall Webb. He had come to Missouri from Tennessee in 1856, acquiring a large section of farmland that would later become the community that was named in his honor.

In 1873, Webb discovered lead deposits in his corn fields. After taking on a partner, W.A. Daughtery, he started a mining operation. His inexperience soon got the better of him. When the mine continually filled with water, a discouraged Webb sold his interest and leased his land to Daughtery and another mining expert, G.P. Ashcroft. Webb decided to plat the town of Webb City on his land in July 1875. The following year, the Center Creek Mining Company began operations on Webb's land and the area was soon overrun with miners, most of whom made their homes in Joplin, which, at that time, was filled with gambling halls, saloons, and brothels.

In the meantime, the owners of the mine built luxurious homes in prosperous Webb City. The town was incorporated a year later, in 1876. Webb's younger brother, Benjamin C. Webb, became the town mayor. Before long, a business district was started with Webb leading the development. He provided land for a school and the First Methodist Episcopal Church and built the first brick home in town, the first brick business building, and the first hotel. Other businesses soon followed, as well as a school and hospital.

In 1879, the St. Louis & San Francisco Railroad ran a line into Webb City, followed by the Missouri Pacific Railroad two years later. By 1880, Webb City was home to nearly 1,600 people. In January 1882, John Webb and his son, Elijah, established the Webb City Bank. After his father died in 1883, Elijah continued to run the bank for many years, and it still exists today. Elijah also managed the family's land and mineral interests, which were leased to various operators. Having become very wealthy, he built a magnificent Queen Anne-style home with two floors, 12-foot ceilings, inlaid wood floors, three fireplaces, oak trim, and refinements found nowhere else in the city. It is one of several historic homes that still stand in Webb City today.

Downtown Webb City in the late 1800s

Webb City continued to grow. Most of the wooden buildings in town were replaced by brick, the handsome Newland Hotel was opened with 100 rooms, there were 18 churches, an opera house, two railroad depots, and many other businesses. The city also boasted a fire department, paved streets, electric lights, water works, sewer system, and two telephone companies. By this time, there were 700 mines located near Webb City, which produced $23 million in lead and zinc between the years of 1894 and 1904. They went on to reach their peak in 1918.

One of the innovations of historic Webb City still has a presence in town today. In 1889, A.H. Rogers established a horse-drawn street car line from Carterville to Webb City. Four years later, the horses were replaced by the Southwest Missouri Electric Railway, which used the same line and now extended into Joplin. It was one of the pioneer interurban railways in the country, and over the next few years, it expanded to Carthage and on to Galena, Kansas. In 1903, the company expanded again, building a loop line through Duenweg and, in 1906, north to Alba. It then became known as the Webb City Northern. With Webb City as its hub, numerous company buildings were constructed, including offices, power house, and car barns, all located on Madison Street between Broadway and Daughtery Streets. In 1901, a clubhouse was added for employees to pass the time between shifts. It was equipped with showers, beds, card, and pool tables. Adjacent to the company buildings was a small business district with several restaurants and retail businesses. Today, a fully-restored streetcar still operates on special occasions and the old depot now houses the local chamber of commerce. The power house and clubhouse are also still used today as a skating rink and the home of the Webb City Historical Society.

The start of World War I became another boom time for the city. The mines were busy producing for the war effort and the population rose to more than 15,000 people. The railroad expanded again, now reaching as far as Picher, Oklahoma, and workers flocked to the town to take advantage of the labor demand. But the boom days were nearing an end. By 1918 and the end of the war, demand for lead and zinc dropped off considerably and mine stocks plummeted. More mineral deposits were discovered in Oklahoma that were cheaper and easier to retrieve and workers began drifting out of Webb City.

But unlike towns such as Carterville, which dried up after the war, Webb City diversified by attracting more industry and going back to what had put it on the map in the first place: agriculture. A number of factories were enticed into locating in town, offering leather goods, clothing, shoes, cigars, boxes, caskets, and other products. So many new factories opened in town that in 1920, the city attained the distinction of increasing local industry more than any other city in America. There was also an expansion in the gravel industry and countless tons of gravel and sand began shipping out to all parts of the country. In the 1930s, and during World War II, explosives were manufactured by several plants around Webb City. Mining would cease in the area entirely after World War II.

When U.S. 66 was established in 1926, the route ran through the center of Webb City's downtown area. After World War II, when people began to travel like never before, all kinds of businesses sprang up to serve the tourists who were traveling on the popular highway. Today, the old alignment continues to run through downtown and is prominently marked. Several historic buildings can be seen and the **Route 66 Center**, located in a renovated service station, offers information and Route 66 displays. There is also an amazing mural by Mayor John Briggs that depicts 1940s travelers on old Route 66. Visitors can also see movies at the **Route 66 Theater**, one block off of Route 66. The theater is situated in the historic Newland Hotel building.

From Webb City, Route 55 continues south on U.S. 71 Business Route into Joplin, the self-proclaimed lead mining capital of the world.

Wicked City of the Ozarks

"Joplin, Missouri..." sang Bobby Troup in his hit song "Route 66", making the city one of only 14 to be listed in the legendary lyrics. Joplin is basically the last stop on Route 66 in Missouri, and located in the southwest corner of the state, it was once touted for its lead mining and has long called itself the "Gateway to the Ozarks."

Founded in 1840, the city is located near the center of a region that was considered the greatest zinc-producing area of the world. Once lined with saloons, dance halls and gambling rooms (the Lord Hotel advertised "fine cuisine, gambling and soiled doves") Main Street was part of the path Route 66 took through the heart of the city. None of the scores of downtown hotels or theaters survive today, since the chain motels and restaurant franchises east of the city have stolen the business away. Only a few taverns, café's, and eateries still serve the downtown area. Like Route 66, their glory days have faded into the rearview mirror.

But Joplin's history is one that is steeped in sin.

The town that would someday be Joplin was (ironically, as it turned out) first settled by Reverend Harris G. Joplin, who held church services in his home for other local pioneers. Before the Civil War, lead deposits were discovered in the Joplin Creek Valley, but the mining operations were interrupted by the war. By the beginning of 1871, though, mines were flocking to the region. In July of that year, John C. Cox laid out the town of Joplin City, named in honor of the minister who arrived first in the area. Meanwhile, a Carthage man named Patrick Murphy organized his own town, which he humbly called Murphysburg. The two mining camps were mostly made up of tents and rough wood shacks, all filled with miners who were becoming quite wealthy at $40 to $50 a day hauling lead out of the ground. As the two towns both grew, an intense rivalry developed between them.

Neither Joplin City nor Murphysburg had any local government or law enforcement, and with the miners left to police themselves, virtually anything could – and did – happen. The winter of 1871 – 1872 became known as the "Reign of Terror." Street fighters were common and, occasionally, "excitement was heightened" by a gunfight in one of the many saloons that opened for business. Considering the lawless conditions, though, there were few murders, and most of the rowdiness was dismissed at "good-natured revelry."

Initially, the majority of the men who came to Joplin and Murphysburg were single men or married men unaccompanied by their families who hoped to strike it rich in the mines, but businessmen, gamblers, prostitutes, and assorted riff-raff soon followed. By the end of 1871, as the place started to take on some semblance of permanency, some of the miners started to fetch their families to live with them. Citizens soon began to see a need for a local government and officers to enforce the law. By February, it was clear that the two towns needed to join together as one. The two towns were briefly incorporated as one, but the old rivalry reared its ugly head and a court order dissolved the merger. Finally, in December 1871, Patrick Murphy, founder of Murphysburg, suggested the name of simply "Joplin" and early in 1873, the

Main Street in Joplin when Route 66 was still America's Highway to the West

two towns were permanently incorporated as one city. Murphy would go on to become a huge success with the founding of the first local bank. He lost a town, but gained a fortune.

The merging of the two towns brought structure to the area, but very little peace. The town was still filled with saloons, dance halls, gambling parlors, and brothels, and the next two decades brought plenty of lawless deeds and rowdy behavior from the miners in the town's midst.

Lead had built the town, but the railroads made it boom. The simple mining town of tents and shacks was soon filled with lead smelters, mines, large homes, businesses, and the ever-present saloons and sporting houses. One of the buildings that housed the most famous tavern in the city still stands today. The House of Lords opened as a saloon at 319 Main Street in Joplin in 1891, and its owner, William B. Patton, gave it an aristocratic name a few months later. Legend has it that he invited all of his customers to write down a possible name for the place on a piece of paper and all the suggestions were tossed into a fish bowl. When he drew out "House of Lords," which had been placed in the bowl by an Englishman who was staying at the nearby Keystone Hotel, Patton liked the name and had a royal crest inscribed in the floor of the saloon's entryway. He later expanded the place to add a billiard room, cigar stand, and café. On the second floor was a gambling hall, and for those who wanted to climb to the third floor, they would find a well-stocked brothel on the premises. The café developed a reputation for not only fine food, but as a place where power brokers met and hashed out deals and other transactions over a meal and a drink or two. The House of Lords saw a number of owners, as well as a number of fights, stabbings, and gunshots, through the early 1900s. By World War I, though, the local police had cracked down on gambling and prostitutes, and when Prohibition came into effect in 1920, the saloon was closed, leaving the café in operation. It closed down for good in 1922.

By the turn of the century, soaring prices and continued demand for lead and zinc brought large profits for the mines in the Joplin area. These profits attracted the attention of wealthy investors from the east, and in 1899, a group of Boston capitalists formed a corporation called the American Zinc, Lead, and Smelting Company. American Zinc, as it was commonly known, became one of the major operations in the Tri-State Mining District of Missouri, Kansas, and Oklahoma. Joplin became the center of the mining activity with a population of over 26,000 people. With its many homes, businesses, hotels, street cars, and railroad lines, it became the most important city in the entire region and was dubbed the "lead and zinc capital of the world." Those products created and sustained Joplin's economy for more than 70 years.

During World War I, the mines thrived, providing product for the war effort. But when it ended in 1918, the mining industry declined due to the low price of ore and the newly discovered deposits in Oklahoma. By 1920, the population had declined, but not as much as it would after World War II, when most of the mines were closed down for good. As Joplin tried to reinvent itself, nearly 40 acres of the city's downtown area was destroyed in the name of progress, destroying some of the old hotels, and many of Route 66's landmarks in town.

However, there are still brick and mortar memories that remain. When Route 66 made its way through Joplin in 1926, dozens of new businesses appeared to serve highway travelers. A few of them have left both stories and their metal and stone skeletons behind. There are many tourists who still recall **Law's Silver Castle** on Highway 66 in Joplin. During the late 1940s, the restaurant's varied menu included their famous "ring-cooked" steaks.

Another spot, **Daniel's Grill**, became an original "Chicken in the Rough" franchise in 1937. Although scarcely remembered today, **Chicken in the Rough**, was a fried chicken restaurant chain and one of the earliest chain franchises in the country. It was founded by Beverly and Rubye Osborne in Oklahoma City, and its specialty was a fried half-chicken, shoestring French fries, and a biscuit with honey. The chain's logo was an image of a rooster smoking a cigar and carrying a golf club. The name had been devised during a cancelled 1936 road trip to California, in which Beverly spilled a picnic basket of chicken after Rubye hit a bump on an Oklahoma road. Rubye remarked something to the effect of "this is really chicken in the rough." Others have claimed that the name came from eating chicken on a picnic, without silverware and using one's hands, which made it "eating chicken in the rough." Regardless of where it came from, it soon became an overnight success. The "home base" for Chicken in the Rough was Beverly's Pancake House in Oklahoma City, but the idea soon spread. The first standalone restaurant location was on U.S. 66 in Oklahoma City and it was a drive-in with nine stools and four booths. In time, the place was expanded to seat 1,100 people and was visited by tourists, politicians, and film stars like Bob Hope and Gene Autry. Chicken in the Rough became the first nationally franchised restaurant chain in the United States. By 1937, there were locations on Route 66 in Arizona, Oklahoma, Missouri, and Illinois. During its heyday, there were more than 300 stores, including franchises in South Africa. But in the 1960s, the franchise was sold to an investors group, who began whittling down the number of stores to just 68. Today, only three remain: two in Ontario, Canada, and one in Port Huron, Michigan. The rest of them, like Daniel's Grill in Joplin, have vanished with time.

Matchbook cover from one of the original Chicken in the Rough Restaurants

But those restaurants were not alone. There were others that served U.S. 66 in Joplin, like **Bob Miller's Restaurant**, which was famous for "steaks, fried chicken salads, and the best pastries." The Art Deco-inspired building was faced with ultramodern, pigmented, structural glass and was built on the site of the former Heidelberg Inn after World War II. It

Top to Bottom: The Top Hat Diner with its revolving bar

The State Line Mercantile Co.

The Oasis Night Club, the top spot for country acts passing through Joplin

remained in business until the 1990s, when it was torn down and replaced by an office building.

And there were others, like **Dolly's Chili House**, **Bill's Hamburgers**, and the **Top Hat Diner**. **Dana's Bo Peep** – no one knows where the name came from – opened in 1948, moved in 1953, and moved again three years later to Tyler Avenue, where the Bo Pee operated for almost 50 years. **Dixie Lee's Dine and Dance** was a fixture in town for many years. The building still stands, but the sign is gone, erasing another remembrance of a bygone era. It's now a "Route 66 Pit Stop" and the relic of yesterday has been replaced by a plastic, backlit sign.

When Kansas was a dry state, Joplin was a last-chance watering hole for travelers going west and many of them stopped at the **State Line Mercantile Company** in Joplin. The first building to occupy the location was a filling station that opened in 1925, but it was replaced a few years later by a larger structure, which liquor made profitable. In 1933, after Prohibition was repealed, liquor laws in Kansas continued to be fraught with complicated restrictions. The hard-line stand on alcohol turned the Kansas-Missouri border into a hotbed of activity. Music blared from the nightclubs and liquor flowed into every glass on the Missouri side of the state line. For many Kansas residents, Route 66 was their link to a place where you could enter a restaurant or bar and purchase liquor by the glass. Established in 1925, the **State Line Bar and Grill**, just west of the mercantile, was the first alcohol available to Kansans who crossed the state line.

Directly across Route 66 from the mercantile was a very popular nightclub called the **Oasis**. Major country music acts of the day made the Oasis a regular stop on their tour schedules. The addition of the **Shady Rest Motel**, **Gillead's Barbeque**, and several other similar businesses made the state-line area seem more like its own disreputable little town than a part of the west side of Joplin.

In 1979, the Paddoc family purchased the mercantile business and it continues to operate as **Paddoc State Line Liquor**. Today, the state line area is quiet and pretty peaceful, a ghost of its storied past. The Oasis burned down years ago and the Shady Rest and others are nothing more than distant memories of a time when Joplin was still the "wicked city of the Ozarks."

Joplin had plenty of places where a traveler could lay his weary head, too. There was the **East Seventh Street Motel**, which was owned by Mr. and Mrs. A.C. Jergens in the 1950s. The motel had started

East Seventh Street Motel

with 17 units and expanded to 22, with steam heat and free television by 1957. Kitchenettes and baby beds were available. It's now the site of an auto parts store. The **Castle Motel**, originally **Castle Kourt**, was also located on Seventh Street and has been replaced by a clothing store. Tourist cabins were available for $2 a night and each included a private garage.

The **Plaza Motel** advertised "twenty-one luxuriously furnished units, carpeting, tubs, or showers, tile baths, refrigerated air-panel ray heat, free

TV, free coffee bar, and cubed ice" in the 1940s. It remains in business today, but is not recommended for anyone but the most adventurous traveler.

The **Kornado Hotel Kourts** on U.S. 66 were owned by Harry Bennett and offered a number of small gabled cabins with 60 units and a private garage with each. They were advertised as the "finest and most up-to-date tourist kourts in the entire Southwest on U.S. 66 Highway." It's now the site of a Wal-Mart store.

According to its advertising, the **Twin Oaks Court** was "the place to sleep" and it also offered "just good food." And while its ad slogans were certainly low-key, AAA said the place was "a very good court on spacious shaded grounds." Each of the individual cabins was southwest adobe-inspired with stucco walls, wooden beams at the roofline, and flat tops. There is now a

Top to Bottom:

Castle Kourt Motel
Kornado Kourts
Twin Oaks Courts

No, I have never seen an explanation for the "K" in Joplin motels of the era.

sandwich shop where the court once greeted sleepy motorists.

The **Elm's Motel** called itself "Joplin's Finest," with 25 "beautifully furnished fireproof cottages on spacious grounds." The chalet-style cottages offered "wall-to-wall carpeting, tile showers, free radios, vented wall heaters, and individual telephones." The motor court closed down in 1964 and a toy store is now located at the site.

As it was in too many other towns, the bright and shining years of Route 66 came to an end. Joplin has done what it could to keep memories of the road alive, but these days, old Route 66 is a four-lane highway into Kansas, lined with used car dealerships, automobile graveyards, crumbling buildings, and mountains of weed-infested leftovers from the mines that once flourished in the region.

Hiding Out with Bonnie and Clyde

For years, the city of Joplin had enjoyed a notorious reputation as a "wide-open town" and a rowdy spot for hard-drinking miners. But in 1933, crime in Joplin made headlines when it was revealed that it had been a temporary hideout for notorious bank robbers Bonnie Parker and Clyde Barrow.

Bonnie and Clyde were not the first gangsters to take advantage of the wide-open reputation of Joplin. The Barker brothers – Dock, Herman, and Fred – had lived in Webb City during their youth and repeatedly returned to the area to lie low after joining up with Alvin Karpis and becoming infamous for bank robbery and kidnapping. In the early 1930s, Joplin was a place where the law didn't ask too many questions and its location near several state lines made it an ideal hideout. If things got hot, Oklahoma and Kansas were both a few miles away.

Clyde Barrow and Bonnie Parker

Before arriving in Joplin, Clyde Barrow, Bonnie Parker, and Clyde's childhood friend, W.D. Jones, had already engaged in a number of robberies and at least five murders. Although they were from Texas, Bonnie and Clyde had made several trips to the Ozarks and had become familiar with the area. In late November 1932, they had holed up in a Carthage motel and robbed the Farmers and Miners Bank of Oronogo, about 15 miles from Joplin. Eight weeks later, on January 26, 1933, Bonnie and Clyde, along with W.D. Jones, kidnapped Springfield motorcycle policeman Thomas Persell and took him on a wild trip across southwest Missouri, including a drive through north Joplin. They let him out near Stone's Corner north of town.

On March 22, 1933, Clyde's brother, Buck, was released from prison. Within days, he and his wife, Blanche, set up housekeeping with Clyde, Bonnie, and Jones in Joplin. Using the name "Callahan," Clyde rented an apartment from Paul Freeman in the Freeman Addition of south Joplin at 3347 ½ Oak Ridge Drive. The apartment was located over a two-car garage that faced Thirty-Fourth Street. For the gang's purposes, it was ideally situated on the edge of town, just a couple of blocks from Main Street. They used one of the spaces in the garage to park their stolen Ford V-8 sedan. The other space was reserved for Harold Hill, a tenant in a nearby house. Because of this, Buck rented a small garage from another neighbor, Sam Langford, to park the car that he had bought after he was released from prison. The car, a Marmon, was the vehicle that the outlaws mainly used during their stay in Joplin.

The gang members mostly kept to themselves and didn't arouse much suspicion at first. Neighbors noted, though, that they always kept their blinds drawn and stayed up very late at night. Also, they always backed their cars into the garage so that they would always be ready to leave in a hurry. Mostly, the men idled away the days playing cards, while the women cooked and served the meals. Bonnie used part of her spare time to compose poetry, and Blanche played solitaire and worked crossword puzzles. When the group ran short of money, Clyde and W.D. pulled off a few burglaries, including one at the Neosho Milling Company. The pair also stole another vehicle, a Ford roadster, and Buck talked Harold Hill into letting the gang park it in the second space below the apartment.

As would often happen with Bonnie and Clyde, their brush with the law in Joplin occurred because of their obnoxious behavior and not because their identities had been discovered. Beer had just been legalized after Prohibition and the group held loud, alcohol-fueled card games late into the night in an otherwise quiet neighborhood. They went through nearly a case of beer each day, coming and going noisily from the house, and once, a BAR (Browning Automatic Rifle) discharged in the apartment while Clyde was cleaning it. The loud blast didn't bring the neighbors directly to the house, but at least one complained to the Joplin branch of the Missouri Highway Patrol. The informer said that the strangers in the apartment, who came and went at all hours of the night, had switched license plates from one vehicle to another and had

Bonnie and Clyde's hideout in Joplin

driven one of the cars without a license plate. It turned out that one of the vehicles matched the publicized description of an automobile that was linked to the Neosho burglary. State troopers investigated and learned that the Marmon had been licensed by a man named "Barrow," even though the apartment had been rented under the name of "Callahan."

Suspecting that the gang in the apartment were either bootleggers or burglars (the name "Barrow" meant nothing to them because, at that time, Bonnie and Clyde had not yet achieved the notoriety that was still to come), the lawmen decided to raid the apartment on April 13. Since the apartment was located in Newton County, state troopers G.B. Kahler and W.E. Grammar enlisted the help of Newton County constable J.W. "Wes" Harryman in obtaining a liquor search warrant, and they drove to nearby Neosho to get the warrant. Back in Joplin, they were joined by Joplin police detectives Harry McGinnis and Tom DeGraff, and the five lawmen drove toward the apartment around 4:00 p.m. The two troopers were in one car, with Kahler driving, while the other three men were in the second car with DeGraff behind the wheel. Harryman was in the passenger seat and McGinnis was in back. The two police cars turned off Main and approached the apartment from the east.

Clyde and W.D. had just returned home when the police cars pulled up. The lawmen saw the two of them standing just inside the garage with the door partly open. Kahler pulled to a stop on Thirty-Fourth Street, but DeGraff whipped into the driveway and screeched to a halt just as the man standing next to the garage door slammed it shut. Harryman sprang out of the passenger's seat while the car was still moving and lunged toward the garage door to prevent it from closing. He was too slow. Worse, from inside of the garage, Clyde opened fire with a sawed-off shotgun and W.D. opened up with a Browning Automatic Rifle. The guns punched holes into the wood of the door. Although taken by surprise, Clyde, known for keeping his cool under fire, had a lot more experience with gun battles than the small town policemen did. Harryman collapsed on the other side of the garage doorway and was dead before he hit the ground.

As DeGraff came to a stop, Detective McGinnis had jumped out of the backseat with a revolver in his hand. DeGraff exited the driver's side door. McGinnis opened fire at the smashed-up garage door and one is his bullets winged W.D. Jones. Clyde's shotgun roared again and the detective was hit with a load of buckshot and stumbled backwards. Crouching next to the police car, DeGraff fired several shots, making his way around to the rear of the vehicle, just as McGinnis staggered past him and collapsed, mortally wounded.

The shooting had already started by the time that Officer Grammar jumped out of the trooper's car and ran toward the back of the garage. Kahler quickly followed him, taking up a position at the corner of a nearby house, where he opened fire on the men he could see inside of the garage. Meanwhile, DeGraff made his way around the east side of the garage, and when he saw Grammar at the rear of the building, he shouted at the trooper to call for backup. Grammar hurried to Harold Hill's home to telephone for reinforcements.

The situation inside of the apartment was as chaotic as the scene outside. When the shooting started, Buck, who had opened the garage door for Clyde and Jones when they returned, ran upstairs and shouted to Bonnie and Blanche that they had to get out – the police were there. Buck then ran downstairs and took Jones's weapon from him so that he could back up Clyde. Jones stumbled up the stairs, clutching his wounded side and yelling for the women to hurry up and get to the car. Once downstairs, Bonnie jumped into the passenger's seat of the Ford, while Blanche and the wounded Jones helped Clyde open up the garage door.

Kahler, now the only lawman in front of the garage who was not already dead or dying, continued to fire at the bandits with his pistol. A ricocheting bullet lodged just beneath Clyde's skin, and Buck was grazed by a separate shot. Inside, the gang now fired back at him. Clyde quickly stepped out of the garage and fired the shotgun. Kahler quickly retreated and, as he did, tripped over a wire on the ground. Clyde, thinking that the officer had been hit, turned around and started back inside. As he did. Kahler fired his last shot at him, but missed.

With the engine of the Ford raced, Clyde, Blanche, and Jones tried to roll DeGraff's car out of their path, but were unable to release the parking break. Clyde then decided to use the Ford to push the car out of the way and ordered

Two of the photos found on the roll of film in the abandoned apartment. Bonnie and Clyde were fooling around with guns and cigars. When they photos were published, Bonnie was appalled and sent letters to newspapers, insisting that she did not smoke cigars.

everyone into the getaway vehicle. Jones climbed into the backseat as Buck pulled Harryman's body clear of the path between the two vehicles. Clyde knocked up against the police car with the bumper of the Ford and managed to roll it out of the way. The police car, now loose from its brake, went careening down the sloped driveway toward the street. Blanche's little dog, Snow Ball, darted into the street at about the same time the police car rolled away. Blanche, already hysterical over the gunshots and the sight of the dead police officers, chased after the dog. Clyde hit the gas and the auto only slowed down enough for Buck to pull Blanche off the street and into the car. The bandits sped away as Officers Kahler and DeGraff frantically reloaded their guns. Grammar raced over from the Hill home to belatedly rejoin the battle.

The gangsters were already long gone. They were driving so fast by the time they reached Redings Mill, according to an attendant at a service station in the area, that they almost lost control rounding a curve approaching a bridge over Shoal Creek. A few minutes later, the gang sped through Seneca on their way back to Texas.

Ambulances and additional police cars quickly began arriving at the apartment. Only minutes had passed but Harryman was already dead. McGinnis was rushed to a local hospital but he died a few hours later.

The gang escaped from Joplin, but left most of their possessions behind at the apartment, including Buck and Blanche's marriage license; Buck's three-week old parole papers; a badge from the Police and Sheriff's Association of North America, believed used as a decoy during robberies; jewelry from the Neosho Milling Company heist; a guitar; bags of clothing; some of Bonnie's poetry; a large arsenal of weapons that included an automatic rifle, four high-powered rifles, a shotgun, a revolver; and a camera with several rolls of undeveloped film. The film was developed at the *Joplin Globe* and yielded the now famous photos of Bonnie, Clyde, and Jones clowning around and pointing guns at one another. When the photos, including one of Bonnie clenching a cigar in her teeth and clutching a pistol in her hand, went out on the newly-installed newswire, the obscure gang from Texas became front-page news across America – and almost instant folk heroes.

The death of Bonnie and Clyde in a police ambush just a little over a year after the Joplin shootout sent them out in the proverbial "blaze of glory," but their legend began with the discovery of those photos in the Joplin apartment. Without them, the Barrow gang would have likely continued their criminal careers as the little-known hoodlums that they were before April 13, 1933.

Today, public enemies-era enthusiasts can get a glimpse of the apartment where Bonnie and Clyde stayed by renting it out for a night, a weekend, or a week. Called the "Joplin Hideout," it has been restored and decorated just like it was in the 1930s, before Bonnie and Clyde became household names – and when Route 66 was still America's favorite highway.

Billy Cook's Unmarked Grave

The Route 66 town of Joplin certainly has its ghosts.

The old **Freeman Hospital**, which began operating on land donated by John W. Freeman in 1922, was said to be haunted long before it became abandoned. Phantom footsteps were said to roam the hallways and workers refused to stay alone on the unoccupied fourth floor. There were cries, moans, and whispers that simply should not have been there. Many died at Freeman Hospital when it was still in operation. It seems many of those patients have never left.

Prosperity School, which served the children of miners in the Prosperity Township on the outskirts of Joplin from 1907 to 1962, is believed to still harbor the spirits of former students, or perhaps staff members, or perhaps the victim of a murder that may (or may not) have happened there in the 1950s. After being left vacant for more than 30 years, it has since been restored and is now used as a bed and breakfast. Guests who have stayed there have reported voices, footsteps, lights that turn on and off, the tapping of high-heeled shoes, and the dark figure of a man who is often spotted walking between the kitchen and the front door.

And while such places are undoubtedly unsettling, there is nowhere in the Joplin area that is regarded with the kind of dread that so many people afford to Peace Church Cemetery, an old, ramshackle, 1850s-era burial ground outside of town. Over the years, reports have circulated about strange sounds, voices, and eerie lights that have been heard and seen in the cemetery. There are also reports of a ghostly figure that has been seen lurking in the trees, peering out at passersby and then vanishing when approached. It

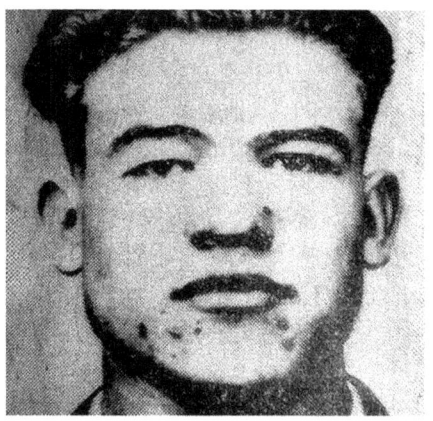

Spree killer Billy Cook

would be safe to assume that one of the restless souls buried here does not rest in peace. And when those who visit this place learn just who is buried in this cemetery, in a forsaken, unmarked grave – a likely culprit for this restless spirit emerges.

Few mass murderers have ever gone on a worse killing spree than the one 21-year-old Billy Cook started on December 30, 1950. On that day, Cook, posing as a hitchhiker, forced a motorist at gunpoint to get into the trunk of his own car and then drove away. Over the next two weeks, Cook went on a senseless rampage. He kidnapped nearly a dozen people, including a deputy sheriff, and murdered six of them in cold blood, including three children. He also attempted other killings and terrorized the southwestern border states.

Cook was born in 1929 and grew up near Joplin. His early life was hard and he had to make do with what he could between seven brothers and sisters. His father was an uneducated mine worker and after the death of Cook's mother, he raised the children in an abandoned mine shaft. One night, after drinking in a local tavern, he hopped a freight train and left the children to survive alone. Authorities found them huddled in the old mine, living like animals. Welfare workers were able to find foster homes for all of the children, except for Billy. His attitude caused people to stay away from him and he had a sinister-looking affliction of the right eye that would not allow the lid to close all the way. He was finally taken in by a woman who did it purely for the money paid to her by the government, and she and the boy never got along.

As he got older, Billy stayed out at night, getting in trouble, and he ended up spending most of his formative years in reform school. He told a judge that he would prefer it to foster care and he got his wish. He was simply born bad, most believed, and when he was young, he had the words "Hard Luck" tattooed across the knuckles of both of his hands. After being released, Cook immediately robbed a cab driver of $11 and stole a car. He was soon caught and sent back to reform school for five years. He became one of the most dangerous inmates in the institution and was sent to the Missouri Penitentiary to finish his sentence. While there, he beat another inmate so badly with a baseball bat that the man almost died. He had made the mistake of laughing at Cook's drooping eyelid.

In 1950, Cook was released and returned to Joplin to look for his father. The reunion was short-lived and Billy left town and started hitching rides through the southwest, ending up in Blythe, California. The only job that he ever held was there, washing dishes in a diner, and he soon grew bored and began to roam again, this time heading for Texas. Somewhere along the way, he picked up a snub-nosed .32- caliber pistol and he kept it tucked away in his pocket. Cook had little use for anyone and, frankly, hated people – all people – and he decided to put those feelings into action when he kidnapped his first victim, a motorist, near Lubbock, Texas. Cook locked him in the trunk of his own car, but the driver managed to use a jack handle to open the trunk from the inside. He held it down until Cook turned off the highway and onto a secondary road. Convinced that the young man planned to kill him, he jumped out when the car slowed down and escaped by running across the flatland.

Cook drove the lonely stretch of highway between Claremore and Tulsa, Oklahoma, before the stolen car ran out of gas. He left the vehicle on the side of the road and walked on. A few minutes later, he saw a 1949 Chevrolet coming toward him. Cook waved frantically, as if he had encountered car problems, in an effort to get the car to slow down.

The driver, Carl Mosser, came to a stop. Mosser, his wife Thelma, and their three small children were on vacation from Decatur, Illinois, on their way to New Mexico, when they picked up Cook alongside the road. Many wonder today why they would have picked up a hitchhiker with small children in the car, but those were different times and Americans had not yet been bombarded with the gruesome images of death and murder that were to come in the media and in entertainment. They had nothing to fear, they believed, and simply wanted to help out a young man who was down on his luck. Cook repaid the family's kindness by pulling a gun and forcing Mosser to drive into Oklahoma and then to Texas. Carl Mosser, frantically worried for his family, hoped that his twin brother, Chris, who lived in Albuquerque and was expecting the family for a visit, would start to worry and alert the authorities.

Cook forced him to drive to Wichita Falls, Texas, and Mosser desperately kept thinking of ways to try and get rid of the maniac. He thought he saw a chance in Wichita Falls when the car started to run low on gas. He urged Cook into a filling station for some fuel and food. Mosser pulled into the station and told the elderly attendant to fill the tank. When he asked, at Cook's orders, that some lunch meat be brought to the car, the attendant told him that he would have to get that himself. Mosser went inside, followed by Cook, and it was then that Mosser grabbed Cook and tried to pin him from behind. Frightened, the old attendant pulled an old revolver and waved it nervously at the two struggling men. He ordered Mosser to let loose of Cook and Carl tried to explain what was happening. Too scared to help, the old man ordered them out of the station. The two continued to fight until Cook broke away and pushed Mosser through a plate glass window.

The old man, now terrified, locked himself inside as Cook ordered Mosser back to the car. As the automobile drove off, the old man now jumped into his truck and gave chase. Cook saw him coming and fired several shots at him. With that, the attendant's bravery vanished and he stopped the truck.

Cook was now seething with anger and he forced Mosser to drive to Carlsbad, New Mexico, and then on to El Paso, Texas. From there, the terrifying journey continued to Houston and then on to Winthrop, Arkansas. Cook then had Mosser turn the car toward his old stomping grounds in Joplin. Finally, after more than 72 hours since the family had been kidnapped, Thelma Mosser became hysterical and started to cry. The children also began to wail and Cook gagged all of them except for Carl. Soon, after Cook spotted a police officer that seemed to be paying too much attention to the Mosser car, Cook grew tired of his game and turned his pistol on the family. He shot and killed all of them and for good measure, shot the family dog, too. He dumped their bodies in a place he knew well: an abandoned mine shaft near Joplin.

Eventually, the Mossers' car was found abandoned near Tulsa, Oklahoma. It looked like a slaughter pen, with the upholstery ripped by bullets and blood splashed everywhere. The victims' bodies were soon discovered, but Cook left something behind in the car: the receipt for the handgun that he had bought. His identity was soon learned and a massive manhunt was launched.

Cook headed for California and there, he kidnapped a deputy sheriff who almost captured him. He forced the deputy to drive him around while he bragged about executing the Mosser family. After more than 40 miles, Cook ordered the lawman to stop and forced him to lie down in a ditch with his hands tied behind his back. He told the man that he was going to put a bullet in his head and then, for some reason, climbed into the car and drove away. The officer waited for the bullet but it never came. He would never know why he was spared. A short time later, Cook flagged down another motorist, Robert Dewey, and wounded him. The two men struggled and the car left the road and careened out into the desert. Cook ended the fight with a bullet to Dewey's head and he threw the body into a ditch.

Cook was arrested in Mexico and turned over to American authorities.

By this time, an alarm had been raised all over the southwest and so Cook decided to head into Mexico. He kidnapped two men and brought them along to Santa Rosalia, a number of miles across the border. Amazingly, though, Cook was recognized by the local police chief, Francisco Morales. He simply walked up to Cook, snatched the gun from the man's belt and placed him under arrest. Cook was then rushed to the border and turned over to FBI agents.

Despite the slaying of the Mosser family, the Justice Department turned Cook over to the California courts and he was tried for the murder of Robert Dewey. Cook displayed as much regret about this murder as he had the others – in other words, none – and he was sentenced to death. On December 12, 1952, he died in the gas chamber at San Quentin.

And then things took a curious turn. Glen Boydstrun, an undertaker in Comanche, Oklahoma, had been around long enough to remember the crowds that had turned out to see the bullet-riddled bodies of some of the slain gangsters of the public enemies-era, like Pretty Boy Floyd. So, Boydstrun decided to try his luck at putting Cook's body on display in Comanche, despite the fact that the town had nothing to do with Cook or his crimes.

Boydstrun contacted Cook's father, Will Cook, in Joplin and made a deal with him. He would pay for a proper burial for Cook's son, if the man would allow Boydstrun to claim the body at San Quentin. The undertaker immediately drove to California and three days after his execution, Cook's corpse, outfitted in a suit and tie, was placed on public display in Comanche. Boydstrun was disappointed with the first day's turnout so he added loudspeakers and, like a sideshow barker, urged people to see the "last American desperado." Thousands came on the second day, including busloads of schoolchildren. In all, as many as 12,000 curiosity-seekers turned out, before Cook's siblings hired a lawyer, got the body away from Boydstrun, and returned it to Joplin.

Cook was buried in the dark of night at Peace Church Cemetery. According to a 1952 *Joplin Globe* article, a brief service was held with flashlights and lanterns with about 15 people in attendance. Just as the grave service ended, a reporter wrote, "the cry of a small child could be heard in the chill of the night air." As news spread, the public objected to the now infamous killer being buried in the cemetery, so the family quietly had his grave moved just outside of the original grounds.

Peace Church Cemetery

Over time, Billy Cook has proven to be a dark inspiration to several films, books, and even a song. He was cited as the inspiration for the film, *The Hitch-Hiker*, which was directed by noted actress Ida Lupino. In the film, two men on a fishing trip pick up a hitchhiker who turns out to be a psychopath who has committed multiple murders on the road. Lupino interviewed two men who were held hostage by Cook, as well as Cook's father, so that she could integrate parts of Cook's life story into the film. When the film was released in 1953, it was marketed with the line, "When was the last time you invited death into your car?"

There is also the legend that Billy Cook was the inspiration for the Doors classic song "Riders on the Storm." It's been said that some of Jim Morrison's lyrics were inspired by Cook's exploits: "There's a killer on the road; his brain is squirming like a toad; Take a long holiday; Let you children play; If you give this man a ride, a sweet memory will die; Killer on the road..."

And that's not the only kind of mayhem that Cook has inspired. It is common to go to the cemetery and find piles of items – like flowers, notes, and candles – left in various spots that people believe Cook's unmarked grave lies. It has been rumored that local teenagers have congregated at times to try and contact the spirit of Cook. In 1987, three 17-year-old boys from nearby Carl Junction were discovered to have been killing animals and then murdered a 19-year-old acquaintance by beating him to death with a baseball bat. At trial, their defense claimed they had been engaging in satanic rituals and had been influenced to commit the murder by the spirit of Billy Cook. The jury wasn't buying it and they were convicted of murder.

Despite what the jury believed, though, there are quite a number of people who believe that Billy Cook does not rest quietly at the edge of this old graveyard. Throughout the years, stories have circulated about the shadowy figure that has been seen lurking about on the grounds and wandering among the nearby trees. Whoever this man is, he seems lost and confused and some have remarked that he appears to be angry about something.

If this lingering spirit is that of Billy Cook, then his anger becomes clear. As in life, Cook hated everyone and everything, and it's likely that his hatred with simply being born hasn't gone away, even in death.

In Search of the Hornet Spook Light

Located about 10 miles or so southwest of Joplin, is an old paved road where one of America's favorite spook light puts in a regular appearance. This remote and otherwise forgotten track runs across the Oklahoma border, but is only about four miles long. Nearby is the border village of Hornet, and close to that is the site of what once was a spook light museum. The place is secluded and far from civilization, so why do so many people come here?

They are searching for an unexplained enigma, a puzzle that many of them actually find. But even when they find it, they can't really explain it. It has been seen along this road since 1866 and has created such a mystery that even the Army Corps of Engineers officially concluded that it was a "mysterious light of unknown origin." It has been called by many names since it started appearing near what is called the Devil's Promenade, but it's most commonly known as the Hornet Spook Light.

This light has appeared, looking like a ball of fire, for a century and a half, varying in size from that of a softball to larger. It spins down the center of this gravel road at great speed, rises up high, and bobs and weaves to the right and left. It appears to be a large lantern, but there is no one carrying it. The light has appeared inside vehicles, seems to retreat when it is pursued, and never allows anyone to get too close to it. Does it have some sort of intelligence? This remains just one of the many mysteries connected to this light.

No one has ever been injured by the light, but many claim to have been frightened by it while walking or driving down this road at night. Sometimes it seems to come from nowhere and a few witnesses claim they have felt the heat from it as it passed close to them. Occasionally, some observer will even take a shot or two at the light, like Franklin Rossman, who lived near the Devil's Promenade for years. He twice attempted to shoot the light with a hunting rifle but the shots had no effect on it whatsoever. He told a spook light investigator that he was unable to judge the distance to the light because it had such an odd look to it. When asked what he meant by this, Rossman was unable to explain. It just looked "sort of blurry," he said. There have been

A popular Joplin area postcard for Route 66 travelers about the nearby Hornet Spook Light

many theorists who have attempted to explain why this mysterious light appears along the old road. Originally, a number of legends sprung up around the place. One of them claimed the light was connected to the spirit of two young Quapaw Indians who died in the area many years ago. Another claimed the light was the spirit of an Osage Indian chief who had been beheaded on the Devil's Promenade and the light was said to be his torch as he searched for his missing head. Another legend tells of a farmer whose children were kidnapped by Indians and he set off looking for them with only a lantern to light his way. The light is said to be that very lantern, as the farmer's ghost continues looking for the children that he will never find.

Locals claim that the stories of the Hornet Light originated back in the 1800s, but most printed accounts are of a much more recent vintage. As far as is known, the first account of it appeared in the *Kansas City Star* in 1936, and then in the 1947 book *Ozark Superstitions* by Vance Randolph, the famed Missouri folklorist. Randolph was the first to write down the legends of the light's supposed origins, from beheaded Indians to lost children.

In 1958, a writer for the *Ford Times* investigated the light and described it as a diffused, orange glow that floated and weaved along the roadway. He also noted that it seemed to change size as he watched it, varying between the size of an apple to that of a bushel basket. He also saw the light split off into three different lights and then merge into a single light, as it settled down upon the branch of a tree and changed colors from orange to blue.

Over the years, the light has been studied, researched, chased, photographed and shot at ---- but what is it? While legends give one reason for the light, its genuine origins seem to present a formidable problem. Many suggestions have been offered as to what could cause the light to appear, and for many years the most popular theory was that it was merely a will-o'-the-wisp, the name given to a biological phenomenon that is caused by the decay of wood and organic materials. The emission of light that comes from the decay often glows brightly and can be seen on occasion in wooded areas and damp regions. As fascinating as this is, it really doesn't explain the Hornet Light. Instances of will-o'-the-wisp simply do not give off the intensity of light – or behave in the manner of the light that has been reported along the Devil's Promenade.

Another suggestion has been the ever-popular "marsh gas." Unfortunately, while an abundance of marsh gas in a marsh or swamp would certainly be flammable, it cannot spontaneously light itself. Even if it did, wind and rain would soon extinguish any flame that appeared. Strong winds that have been reported during sightings of the Hornet Light do not seem to disturb the light and they don't keep it from moving in whatever direction it pleases.

There have also been suggestions that the light might be a glow coming from minerals in the area. This seems doubtful too, as the light does not always appear in the same place. One plausible suggestion theorizes that the light might be formed by electrical fields in areas where earthquakes and ground shifts take place. This is a possibility since there are fault lines in the region. Four large earthquakes took place in the area in the early 1800s that had a devastating effect on this part of the state. It is possible that the lights started appearing around the time of the earthquakes, but were not reported until the population in the area started to grow around the time of the Civil War.

Other "experts" claim they have the mystery solved and that it's not unexplainable at all. They claim the light is caused by automobiles driving on the highway about five miles east of what's known as "Spook Light Road." They say the highway is on a direct line with it but at a slightly lower elevation. When it is pointed out that a high ridge separates the area from the highway, the experts explain how refraction causes light to bend and creates the eerie effect that so many people have reported as the spook light.

Believe it or not, several investigations that have been conducted at the site have shown that some of the sightings may be attributed to this. Dr. George W. Ward, formerly of the Bureau of Standards in Washington, D.C., and later with the Midwest Research Institute, investigated the light in 1945. He said that shortly after arriving at the site, he saw a diffused glow appear over some low hills. A few moments later, a sphere of light appeared that looked to be four to six feet in diameter. Ward humorously added that the

Publicity Director of the Midwest Institute remarked to the others assembled that he had seen all that he cared to and as the light approached the group, he quickly locked himself inside their car.

But Ward was critical about the source of the light. During his study, he decided that the light must originate to the west of the viewing site and over the range of hills in the distance. He surmised

A group of teenagers looking for (and finding) the Spook Light in the 1950s

that the refraction of auto headlights from a road that was in line with the country lane could create an illusion of a traveling light. Dr. Ward checked his maps and found that such a road did exist, a section of Highway 66 that ran east and west between Commerce and Quapaw, Oklahoma. He suggested that an airplane might be used to spot cars on the highway and relay the information to observers at the Spook Light site. If the lights could be shown to correspond with the Hornet light, the mystery would be solved.

Captain Bob E. Loftin followed these speculations with his own experiments a few years later. He discovered that colored test lights that were placed on the suspected areas of Route 66 could be seen from Spook Light Road. He further reasoned that the presence of moving cars along the highway would appear as spheres of light, closely grouped together. He also added that changing humidity and temperature would cause the lights that were created to behave strangely. This, they reasoned, would explain the number of unusual stories told about the way the light acted.

And while this would admittedly explain some of the sightings of the Hornet Light, it is impossible that it could explain them all. The most important point to remember is that the light was being seen before the invention of automobiles.

These were far from the only investigations conducted at the site. Author Raymond Bayless embarked on an extensive study of the spook light in October 1963. Around dusk on the evening of October 17, he and several assistants spotted the light for the first time, as it appeared as a bright light some distance along the roadway. He reported that the light fluctuated in intensity and at times became two separate lights, hovering one above the other. The light returned again about an hour later, and according to Bayless, was so bright that it caused a reflection on the dirt surface of the road. A few minutes after the light appeared, the investigation group began moving westward along the road in pursuit of it. The light receded backward (or appeared to) as they got closer to it. The group began navigating the hills and ravines of the road and the light vanished. It did not reappear until they reached a point near the old spook light museum, which was still in operation at that time.

The "Spooksville Museum," then operated by Leslie W. Robertson, offered not only photographs and a collection of accounts about the light, but also a viewing platform for people to observe the light with the naked eye or through telescopes and cameras. A member of Bayless' group set up a small refracting telescope on the platform and they were able to learn that what appeared to be a single light was actually composed of a number of smaller lights. Bayless stated that they moved very close together, weaving slightly, expanding and contracting back and forth. It was amber and gold in color and sometimes gained a reddish tint for a few moments at a time. Through the telescope, the edges of the light were observed to be like a "flame" in that they were not uniform and constantly changed.

Bayless was fascinated with the many explanations given for the light and was able to rule out almost all of the ones that had been proposed, including the theory that all of the sightings could be explained away as the refraction of auto headlights. In fact, Mr. Arthur Holbrook, a resident of the area and a man who had investigated the light many times, told Bayless that he had first seen the light in 1905. At that time, Holbrook explained, there were only about a dozen automobiles in Joplin, the closest large town. He also added that there had been no highways at that period, and because of this, headlights could not have explained his sightings of the light. The few cars that were in existence in the area at that time did not travel about on remote, dirt lanes that were best suited for horses, and any autos that would have traveled around the region were only fitted with oil and carbide lamps, which would not have been capable of creating the long, intense beams of modern headlights. To add even more credibility to his account, Holbrook was in the automotive profession and would have been very aware of the number of autos in the region in those days and the state of the roads and highways.

But did the light actually exist before automobiles came to southwest Missouri or was this merely a part of the local legend? Many skeptics claimed that the enigma's longevity was merely a part of the light's folklore, but Bayless did not agree. After conducting a number of interviews in the area, he believed that it had been seen in the 1800s. He did not feel that his own sighting of the light was comparable to auto headlights, but as it had been shown that some lights would appear on the road as refraction from the highway, he needed to gather as much evidence as possible to show the light pre-dated automobiles. Holbrook had experienced his first sighting of the light in 1905, and had heard of the light for several years before that. After that first sighting, he rode out in a buggy to see the light many times and told Bayless that the light was the same in the 1960s as it had been in 1905.

Bayless also interviewed Leslie Robertson, the curator of the Spooksville Museum, who first saw the light in 1916. He was only 14-years-old at the time and, during his lifetime, he had seen the light literally "thousands of times."

John Muening of Joplin first saw the light around 1928, and had heard stories about it for a number of years before that. He told Bayless that, "We have watched it all night... Highway 66 has nothing to do with the light. It couldn't have, as it didn't exist when the light was first seen, of that I am sure."

Bayless also collected testimony from Rene Waller of Joplin, who also said that she had seen the Hornet Light before Route 66 was put in through Quapaw, Oklahoma. She stated that the original highway was a dirt road that was traveled infrequently. She had first seen the light in the early 1920s, when auto headlights would have been too seldom on the road to have created the effect of the spook light.

Mr. and Mrs. L.C. Ferguson of Joplin also stated that they had been familiar with the Hornet Light since 1910, and at the time they first saw it, they were told that the light had been seen along the road for many years already.

These claims of the light's longevity were substantiated in the early 1960s by J. Leonard, a member of the Miami Indian tribe. He told Bayless that his parents had spoken of the light many times when he was a boy. He could personally remember seeing it for as long as he had been alive (he had been born in 1896) and according to stories at that time, the light had been in existence for several generations or at least 100 years. Another Native American from the area, Guy Jennison, recalled hearing about the light when he was a boy attending the Quapaw Mission School in 1892. By that time, it was a local topic of conversation, implying that reports of the light had been around for at least a few years. Jennison, like Leonard, believed that the light might have appeared several generations before, based on the Indian legends that had been suggested to explain its origin. Unfortunately, during the time of the Bayless investigation, there were few Native Americans left who had knowledge of when the stories originated.

Even without the earlier dates, Bayless was able to show that the Hornet Light existed prior to the use of automobiles in the area. He did not dispute the idea that some sightings could be caused by headlights, but he did debunk the idea that headlights could be the *only* cause. Others have suggested that perhaps lights from Quapaw or from mining camps in the area could have caused a refraction of light, thus creating the Spook Light, but there is little evidence to suggest this or to suggest that these stationary lights could manage to create a light that moves about and comes and goes as the Hornet Light does.

With that in mind, Raymond Bayless' investigations of the light should be considered groundbreaking. Although he certainly did not solve the mystery of the Hornet Light, he did manage to present some compelling evidence for its early existence. The only problem to come out of his investigations was that he managed, by showing how long the light had been around and by showing that not all of the sightings could be dismissed, to make the mystery even more perplexing.

*Garland "Spooky" Middleton, who operated the Spooksville Museum in later years.
(Courtesy of Crystal Lovell)*

Bayless was not the first, nor would he be the last, to investigate the Hornet Spook Light. Literally thousands of curiosity-seekers visit the Devil's Promenade each year and many of those are serious researchers of the unknown. The old "Spook Light Museum" is gone now but long after Leslie Robertson came Garland "Spooky" Middleton, who also operated the place for a time. Along with displaying photographs and newspaper articles about the light, Middleton sold soda to tourists and entertained them with anecdotes about his own encounters with the mysterious light, like the time he saw it in a field near the museum. He said that the light appeared one night on the road, just after sunset, and began to roll like a ball, giving off sparks as it traveled along the gravel road. It entered a field where several cattle grazed and managed to move among the animals, not disturbing them at all.

On three different occasions, starting in the late 1990s, I visited Spook Light Road, each time hoping to get a glimpse of the elusive light. My diligence was never rewarded, but I didn't give up on the hope that I might be at the right place at the right time at some point. Eventually, my persistence paid off. In December 2005, I returned to the site with a group of friends and after a near case of frostbite, I finally got a look at this mysterious wonder. We had several false alarms during the night, with several of us thinking we saw the light, but each time it turned out to be headlights approaching along the lonely road. When the light did show up, there was no mistaking it for anything else. One member of the group spotted it first and her response got the attention of several of the others who were standing together and we saw the light appear at the crest of a small hill about 50 yards away.

The spook light was directly west of where we had parked along Spook Light Road and it did not seem to have come up the hill, it just appeared there. Then it shot sideways to our right about seven or eight feet. The light was yellowish-orange in color and it left a faint "trail" behind it as it moved. The trail streaked out in a jagged motion, moving slightly up and down, and then blinked out into darkness. It was almost like a fireworks display on a summer night, shooting outward and then burning itself out as quickly as it had appeared. The sighting lasted no longer than 10-15 seconds, but it's not something that I will soon forget.

What is the Hornet Spook Light? No one knows, but I think that it's still described best in the words of the Army Corps of Engineers as a "mysterious light of unknown origin." Regardless of what it may be, one thing is certain: it's something that has to be seen, if possible. There are those who believe that the Hornet Light is slowly burning itself out, that sightings of the light are going to become more and more infrequent in the years to come. I hope that this is not the case, and not only for my own selfish desire to see the light again, but also for all of those who have not had the chance to experience this wonder first hand.

The Hornet Spook Light is one of America's greatest unsolved mysteries and since no one has managed to puzzle out the answers to this enigma just yet, we need the spook light to be around for future generations to ponder for themselves.

Weird Highway: Kansas

Cutting off the Corner of the Sunflower State

If you travel across Missouri on Interstate 44 with the intention of reaching Oklahoma, you won't pass through Kansas at all. Motoring west, and passing through the corner of Kansas is a thing of the past, like Route 66 itself. However, just west of Joplin, straddling the border of Missouri and Kansas, is an almost hidden right turn that takes a traveler along an old strip of unimproved highway. The center stripes faded away years ago, but the road, which passes by the remains of zinc smelters and ugly piles of mine waste is a bit of the original Route 66. The highway goes through the middle of Galena, turns west for a couple of miles and crosses the Spring River, heads nine miles south to Baxter Springs, and then, after just two more short miles, crosses into Oklahoma.

The short Kansas stretch of Route 66, just like the long route through Illinois, was completely paved by 1929. At that time, Missouri was only halfway covered, Oklahoma was a quarter concreted, the Texas Panhandle hadn't even considered paving the road, and only about 64 miles of the remaining miles of Route 66 through New Mexico, Arizona and California were paved.

Kansas may have only had a little more than 13 miles of Route 66 – a short section that sliced the corner of the state – but the highway was a source of pride to the farmers, miners, and small town merchants who lived and worked along the route. The highway gave the rest of the nation the chance to see their small part of the country, from the raw mineral mines to the thriving farmland.

Valuable minerals had been discovered in the region where Missouri, Kansas, and Oklahoma came together in the late 1800s and mining operations sprang into being soon after. Several boom towns appeared in the region offering places for the miners to live, sleep, drink, and spend their money. During the years of two world wars, the area became a major producer of zinc and lead ores, but in time, like the highway that cut through the area, they faded into history.

By the early 1960s, Kansas, with just its short piece of the highway, had the dubious distinction of being the only Route 66 state to be completely bypassed. A few miles to the south, on the Missouri-Oklahoma border, Interstate 44 was connected to the Will Rogers Turnpike, a much faster route for travelers heading west. The detour of Kansas received little attention. The name 66 was retained as a state highway and life moved quietly on in the area.

In fact, things were much quieter after Route 66 officially left Kansas than they had been both before and after the heyday of the Mother Road.

"Bloody" Galena

Along the faded highway in Kansas, a traveler will find none of the violence that plagued the areas back in the turbulent 1930s, when mine strikes and labor problems brought bloodshed to the region. In fact, aside from the scarred remnants of the mine operations (once referred to as "Hell's Half Acre") outside of the town of Galena, there is little to suggest that this was anything other than a peaceful community.

Galena got its start before the nearby lead deposits were discovered in 1877, but the inhabitants in those days were mostly just farmers trying to eke a living out of the soil. The existence of lead in the area had been known to the earlier Native American inhabitants and, in fact, was so plentiful that lumps of pure lead were often found right out on open ground. It was melted down and turned into bullets around campfires. In the spring of 1877, though, two white men found heavy stones that were filled with lead on land that belonged to a German farmer named Egidimus Moll. He soon made a deal with a mining company in Joplin, and before long, other rich deposits of lead began turning up in the area. By June, two rival mining companies were bidding against each other for the lease and sale of mining lots. The two companies also formed their own town sites – Empire City, which was north of Short Creek, and Galena, which was south of the creek.

Galena was immediately laid out and soon saw a huge crush of new arrivals. In the space of just two months, the town boasted more than 3,000 people. New businesses were hastily established, buildings were quickly constructed, and miner's shanties and tents lined the muddy streets. A post office was opened and a newspaper, the *Galena Miner*, was established. More

The Eagle-Picher ore smelter in Galena

wagons, tents, and miners continued to arrive, and by May 1877, the town swelled to 10,000 citizens.

For a time, the heated rivalry between the two mining companies was carried out between Galena and Empire City, each boomtown seeking to outdo the other. Because Empire City was closer to the mining area, the majority of new settlers first camped there. However, the natural advantage went to Galena, since the largest and richest lead field was near – and beneath – the town. Once this was discovered, Galena began to overshadow her rival camp. This change soon began to cause serious problems for the leaders of Empire City and they worked hard to try and turn the tide and keep their camp from being swallowed up by Galena.

As the rivalry became heated and thousands of additional miners rushed into both camps, the problem of keeping order in the two towns became a difficult one. Things became more serious when Empire City decided to stop their population from moving to Galena by building a wall between the two towns – virtually making the residents of Empire City prisoners and cutting off all contact with Galena. The wall was to enclose the south end of Columbus Street and close the bridge over Short Creek. The wall would be eight feet high and one-half mile in length. A resolution for the construction of the wall was passed by the Empire City Council on July 25, 1877.

As the wall began to be built, it created such havoc in town that the workmen had to be given police protection in order to finish it. Galena residents protested in vain, petitioning the city, which, in turn, appeared to the U.S. government because Empire City was closing a public highway and interfering with mail delivery. The government acted too slowly for the people of Galena, however, and they decided to take matters into their own hands. The Galena mayor and city council organized a group of 50 men to prevent the completion of the wall, and on August 15, they tore it down and set fire to the remains. Empire City, which had not anticipated the attack, was unprepared, and this resulted in only a few shots being fired in retaliation and very little bloodshed.

The destruction of the wall did not end the feud between the two towns. Violence escalated to the point that the road that connected Empire City and Galena became known as "Red Hot Street." Doctors and undertakers began working nights and sleeping during the day since their services were most in need after the miners had ended their daytime shifts. Frequent fights and gun battles occurred between the miners, but the violence was made worse by the transients and outlaws that preyed on both towns. The saloons and gambling halls that sprang up were a welcome distraction for the hard-working miners, but made them easy targets for the thieves and killers in their midst.

Over time, the population of Galena began to change. Many of the mining men and entrepreneurs who came to town became wealthy and built fine homes and buildings in town. Others, whose luck was not so favorable, soon left to pursue other endeavors. In the fall of 1877, a building was constructed to serve several church denominations, and that winter, the first school was opened in a downtown building. Two new school buildings were finally constructed in 1879 and 1880. Also in 1879, the Kansas City, Fort Scott and Gulf Railroad extended its line to Galena, and before long, the St. Louis and San Francisco Railroad followed suit. By the late 1890s, Galena had 265 producing mines, two banks, 36 grocery and mercantile stores, and nearly 50 other stores of all kinds. Galena was no longer just a mining camp; it had turned into a real town.

During this time, the dispute between Galena and Empire City had continued to boil. By the early 1900s, it had made its way into the courts, and after a long period of litigation, a truce was finally declared between the settlements. When Empire City became a suburb of Galena in July 1907, a celebration was held and the towns made a declaration to work together as one great community. Empire City was eventually annexed into Galena as its Fifth Ward in 1910. By that time, Galena was home to three banks, three newspapers, and an opera house. Although its primary industry was lead and zinc mining, there were also foundries, grain elevators, a novelty company, and a broom factory. The population in 1910 had settled to just over 6,000 souls.

In 1926, when Route 66 came through Kansas, Galena, like other towns along the new highway, responded quickly with diners, motor lodges, and

Labor unrest in Galena became so bad that sheriff's deputies had to detour traffic on U.S. 66 to keep travelers out of harm's way

filling stations, bringing additional prosperity to the town. However, just a few years later, terrible labor strikes between the miners and the mining companies would result in hundreds of unemployed miners and bloodshed along Route 66.

In 1935, John L. Lewis, the powerful union chief of the United Mine Workers, called a labor strike and the members of the Mine, Mills and Smelter Workers International Union went on strike in the region. The mining companies quickly replaced the strikers with non-union workers who were organized into a company union, commonly called the Blue Card Union. The union miners simply called them "scabs."

Angry union men, who were now out of work, blocked Route 66 and began throwing rocks and firing guns at any passing vehicles that failed to follow their commands. They were looking for cars that were being used to transport the scabs from the Blue Card Union. Sheriff's deputies were forced to detour traffic on Route 66 to keep innocent travelers out of harm's way. Finally, Kansas Governor Alf Landon declared martial law in Galena. Landon dispatched National Guard troops, armed with machine guns, to Galena to quell the rioting miners.

Things remained on edge and labor unrest continued for the next few years, before finally exploding into violence again in April 1937. At that time, the Committee for Industrial Organization (CIO) began offering aid to the still-unemployed workers of the Mine, Mill and Smelter Worker's Union. While the unemployed miners were distributing leaflets for the CIO at a smelter in Joplin, they were attacked by a number of Blue Card Unionists and badly beaten. On April 11, about 5,000 Blue Card unionists met in Picher, Oklahoma, and armed with clubs and pick handles, scattered a meeting of CIO organizers and wrecked the local union hall. Leaving the destruction in their wake, they

Main Street in Galena, Kansas

traveled to Treece, Kansas, where they demolished another union hall and then continued on to Galena.

Union members in Galena were warned about what was coming and they barricaded their meeting hall. When the Blue Card mob arrived, waving clubs and firearms, gunfire broke out and nine men were shot, one of them fatally. In the end, the blockade was all for nothing. The union hall was wrecked and records were stolen and destroyed. There were 25 Blue Card men and 10 members of the CIO that were later arrested.

Mining continued in the area until the 1970s, but it was never the same. The mines were eventually exhausted and the population dwindled to a fraction of what it was when Galena was in its glory. There is little left to remind travelers of those early days. And there is no marker on the road outside of town to commemorate the blood that was once shed on the highway. Today, the old highway is quiet except for a few passing cars and trucks. It flows over a bridge and enters town as Front Street, then makes a sharp turn to become Main Street. After several blocks, it goes right and continues on as Kansas 66.

Along Main Street, there are only a handful of businesses still thriving among the many empty brick buildings. In what was once a rip-roaring mining town, there is no sign of the miners, gamblers, killers, and thieves that once haunted the place. They vanished long ago, taking the saloons and gambling halls with them. They left a ghost town in their wake.

And then Galena bounced back – all thanks to a Disney cartoon. A team from Pixar came through town and stumbled upon a 1951 International

Harvester boom truck whose crane had been used to lift gear from nearby mine shafts. This truck became the inspiration for the character Tow Mater in the 2006 animated movie "Cars." The popularity of the movie brought people back to this quiet town in search of the original Tow Mater, whose name was changed to "Tow Tater" to prevent any issues with Disney. With the tourists came their pocketbooks and Galena's economy began to bounce back. Travelers today can see "Tow Tater" and a few of his friends at **Cars on the Route**, which is a restored Kan-O-Tex service station that was built in 1934.

There are also murals, a mining history museum, a historic old jail, and even Galena's **Murder Bordello,** a stark black and gray building with a flock of ravens carved into a tree trunk out front. This is a former sporting house where an infamous madam and her sons allegedly killed numerous patrons and then buried their bodies in nearby mine shafts.

A deli that is now found on Main Street in Galena was once home to **Vi-D's Café**. The café had been located all that remained of the old Miner's State Bank, which was once located on the first floor of the New Century Hotel. The hotel and bank were razed many years ago, leaving the annex where the deli now stands. The huge walk-in vault was too large to move, so the original locking pins were removed and the vault became the most secure pantry on Route 66.

Across the street from the Galena Mining and Historical Museum was once the site of **Brown's Café**, which stayed open 24 hours-a-day. **Brown's** served folks from the highway and anyone in the area who wanted a late-night dining spot. Before Brown's, the café was called **Rosie's** and served thousands of travelers heading east and west on U.S. 66.

Motoring Across the Corner of Kansas

Leaving Galena, the Kansas state highway signs point the way on toward Riverton – or what used to be Riverton. There's not much of the town left these days but during the years of Route 66, all three of the towns on the Kansas leg served travelers well. Their main streets were full of tourists filling their automobiles with gas or catching a quick bite at the local café. Many drivers, too tired to drive another few miles to Oklahoma, spent the night at the **Jayhawk Court** or the **Spring River Inn** in Riverton or at the Baxter Modern Cabins in Baxter Springs.

Travelers who once drove out of Galena had to cross the **Spring River Bridge** before they made it to Riverton. Built in 1922 by the Marsh Bridge Company, the bridge was an elegant three-span structure designed by James B. Marsh, who began his career as a bridge designer in Cleveland in 1883. By 1889, Marsh had become general western agent and contracting engineer for the Kind Bridge Company and was placed in charge of the western office in Des Moines. In the spring of 1896, he formed his own company, the Marsh

The Spring River Bridge

Bridge Company, and at the turn of the century began to design bridges using a steel skeleton structure encased in concrete, which gave his bridges a unique and graceful look.

In 1912, Marsh received a patent for the Marsh Rainbow Arch Bridge, a design that became a favorite with state engineers and county commissioners. The bridge could be built using inexpensive materials and it was durable, aesthetically pleasing, and almost maintenance free. A standard Marsh bridge consisted of one to three arches, although some were built with as many as 11 arches. The earliest known Marsh bridge was built in Kansas in 1917, and the last was erected in 1934. Construction of arch bridges peaked in the 1920s.

The Spring River Bridge was built during the busiest times of the Marsh bridges, although in 1986, it was deemed too narrow to handle modern traffic flow and became obsolete. Soon after, the bridge was dismantled.

However, there is one other Marsh bridge remaining on Route 66 – just a few miles down the road, west of Riverton over Brush Creek. Built in 1923, it was listed on the National Register of Historic Places in 1983, but was still scheduled for demolition in the 1990s. Thanks to the Kansas Route 66 Association, the Cherokee County Commission, and Route 66 buffs from around the country, the bridge was saved and was fully restored. Today, it stands as a tribute to its designer, a man who helped millions of Route 66 motorists get from one side of the river to another in as safe a manner as possible.

Gas, Food and Lodging in Kansas

Along Highway 66 in Kansas, there were a number of motels and tourist camps that sprang up to offer travelers a safe and comfortable place to lay their head. They included the **Sunbeam Tourist Court, Satterlee's Tourist Cabins**, and **Camp Joy**, which was a popular motor court and gas station located between Galena and Riverton. Even before Interstate 44 came along in the 1960s, bypassing Kansas, Camp Joy had already disappeared. All that remains today is a tiny unincorporated community on the banks of the Spring River that locals refer to as "Rest Awhile Hill" or "Rock-a-Bye Hill."

The town of Riverton was never a metropolis, even in the best of times, however, it did offer several services to travelers during Route 66's busiest years. Just after crossing the river, the **Spring River Inn** offered wonderful meals to travelers for many years. The Inn began its history as a private home that was built by B.F. Steward in 1902. Three years later, he sold the house to the Country Club of Joplin, Missouri. Catering to wealthy patrons from all over the area, it became the social center of the region. When the Depression hit in the 1930s, the club fell on hard times. In 1932, club president J.W. Grantham bought the building and used it for several years as a summer home with his wife, Cora Pearl. They regularly entertained theater celebrities there as the actors made their way through the area on tour. After only a few years, though, the house was abandoned and stood vacant along the highway, lonely and forgotten.

In 1952, the Spring River Inn was purchased and saved by Gates and June Harrold. They fully converted it into a large restaurant with six private dining areas, including a room that seated up to 350 guests. The inn became a favorite stopping spot for regular travelers on Highway 66. It became widely known for its 35-foot buffet table that was loaded with home-cooked food, cinnamon pull-apart rolls, and squaw bread. The inn changed owners a couple of times over the next 40 years, but was purchased by partners David and Kay Graham and Dewayne and Lavern Treece in 1994. It only survived two more years. The Spring River Inn closed in 1996 and was destroyed by fire in October 1998.

The old sign for the inn, a neon sign mounted on a pillar of stacked stones, still stands next to Kansas 66 near Riverton. Route 66 buffs have made plans to restore the sign, but as of this writing, plans are still in the works. But as long as we remember the place, the history of it is not lost altogether.

The Eisler Brothers Market, with the "Y Not Eat Williams Barbeque" sign.

A don't-miss attraction in Riverton is the **Eisler Brothers Market**. On March 20, 1925, Leo Williams and his wife, Lora, opened a Standard service station and a small roadside grocery store on what was to become Highway 66. It was a typical "general" store of the era, offering almost everything, including clothing, shoes, milk, eggs, dry goods, and fresh meat. In 1932, they also added the "Y Not Eat Barbecue," which offered chili and beef, cooked on a grill out back. A regulation croquet court was built on a lot next to the store and even had lights so that people could play at night. Local residents often held long-running tournaments on the court, but as traffic on the new highway started to grow, business flourished, and the court was dismantled to accommodate a parking lot for the store.

In 1945, Leo leased the store to Lloyd Paxton and purchased a roller skating rink in Galena. When Paxton's lease expired, Lora, then a widow, returned to manage the store for a time as the AG Food Market. In 1971, she turned the place over to her daughter and two years later, Joe and Isabelle Eisler bought the place and the family continues to operate it today as a store and deli. Although the interstate bypassed the store in 1961, it survives, thanks to the loyalty of local customers and the continued support of Route 66 explorers.

Baxter Springs: "The Toughest Town on Earth"

Just north of what would someday be the Oklahoma border, the town site of Baxter Springs already existed on the Black Dog Trail, which was started in 1803 by Chief Black Dog and his band of Osage Indians. Years later, John Baxter and his family settled there in 1849. The nearby mineral springs were said to have miraculous healing powers by the local Native American populace, and as white settlers began arriving, their popularity exploded. To accommodate visitors, Baxter opened an inn and tavern, but he was brutally murdered in a land dispute in 1859, and didn't live to see the town that was named for him.

Four years later, in 1863, the Baxter Springs Massacre took place, earning the town a place in notorious Civil War history.

During the war, Baxter Springs was located along an old military road that made its way from Fort Smith, Arkansas, through Fort Scott, Kansas, and southwest to Fort Gibson in the Indian Territory. Initially, Baxter Springs was mostly used as a rest stop for the wagon trains that supplied the troops and for the soldiers who were assigned to protect them from hostile Indian attacks along their journey. However, once the Civil War began, the region found itself the target of both regular Confederate forces and guerilla fighters.

In the spring of 1862, a field camp that was first called Camp Baxter Springs, was built by Colonel Charles Doubleday's 2nd Ohio Brigade and Colonel William Weer's 2nd Kansas Brigade to garrison about 6,000 troops. Several more field camps were also established along the old military road, including Camp Five Mile, built by Colonel John Ritchie's Indian Home Guards in June 1862, which was just to the southeast and across the Spring River. Two more field camps were also built nearby in the summer of 1863 – Camp Joe Hooker and Camp Ben Butler, both constructed by Colonel James Williams' 1st Kansas Colored Troops.

During those days of the war, camp life on what was then the frontier, far from the most heated battles of the war, was easy and fairly dull. The men had little to do until July 1863, when the decision to build a permanent post was made. Colonel Charles Blair placed Lieutenant John Crites, with Companies C and D of the 3rd Wisconsin Cavalry, in charge of the construction and he arrived in the area in August. Although the new post was officially called Fort Blair, it was commonly referred to as Fort Baxter. When completed, it consisted of a block house and a few cabins, which were surrounded by a breastworks made of logs, rocks, and mounds of dirt. Crites was soon reinforced by a detachment of the Kansas Colored Infantry, under command of Lieutenant R. E. Cook. Early in October, further reinforcements were added under Lieutenant James B. Pond of the Third Wisconsin Cavalry, which provided a 12-pound howitzer.

The men settled back into the slow, dull monotony of the post, but that would all change in October 1863. On October 4, Lieutenant James B. Pond arrived from Fort Scott to take command of the fort, which was then a post for 155 men. Pond set up camp about 200 yards west of the fort and after looking things over, decided that the structure needed to be enlarged. The following day, he ordered the west wall of the fort to be removed for the expansion. A number of the men set to work, while others were chosen for a foraging party to go out into the countryside and look for food and supplies for the post. The party, made up of about 60 soldiers, departed the next morning, leaving Pond with about 90 men to defend the fort.

What Pond had no way of knowing was that Confederate renegade William Quantrill and about 400 guerilla fighters were making their way south, passing through the area as they headed to Texas for the winter. As bad luck would have it, Quantrill had captured and killed two Union teamsters who had recently left Fort Blair and decided to attack the post. Even though he was outnumbered and outgunned, Pond fought off the guerilla attack with the howitzer. The Union soldiers suffered a number of casualties but repulsed the Confederate charge. Quantrill went away, licking his wounds, but soon found another opportunity for bloodshed.

On October 4 – the same day that Pond had arrived at Fort Blair – General James G. Blunt left Fort Scott with an escort of 100 men of the Third Wisconsin and Fourteenth Kansas Cavalry, headed for Fort Smith, Arkansas. By noon on October 6, they were nearing Fort Blair and saw a group of mounted men advancing from trees along the Spring River. Since they were dressed in Federal uniforms, Blunt assumed they were Pond's men and sent his chief of scouts, Captain Tough, out to meet them. Tough quickly returned with frantic news – the men were not Union soldiers, they were Confederates and a battle was taking place at Fort Blair.

Quantrill's guerillas, driven away from the fort, attacked Blunt's troops. The Union forces tried to organize a battle line, but they were heavily outnumbered and were soon scattered about the field. One of Blunt's officers slipped through Quantrill's men and made it to Fort Blair and told Pond about the turn of events, but it was too late. The troops were nearly annihilated. Only General Blunt and a handful of his men escaped and eventually reached Fort Scott.

According to their account, they were massacred in the open fields by the guerillas. The Federal troops were ordered to surrender, they said, but once they did, and were disarmed, the Confederates gunned them down where they stood. They slaughtered 85 of Blunt's men and left eight men behind to die from their wounds.

After destroying the Union force, the guerillas plundered the supply wagons, seizing weapons, food, and whiskey. Although two of Quantrill's leaders, George Todd and William "Bloody Bill" Anderson, wanted to attack Fort Blair again, Quantrill was more concerned about carrying away the guerillas that had been wounded in the skirmish. Any plans for another attack were abandoned and the Confederates continued their march to the south.

The casualties from the fights at the fort and near the river – including six men who died in the initial attack on the fort – were all buried near the post. General Blunt was temporarily dismissed from his command, but was later reinstated. In 1885, Congress appropriated funds for a national plot about a mile west of Baxter Springs, where many of the bodies from the fort were re-interred, bringing an end to a bloody, but largely unknown, chapter in Civil War history.

After the war, Fort Blair was abandoned but the town of Baxter Springs grew up around its former site. It was incorporated in 1868 and after becoming an outlet for the Texas cattle trade, came to be called "the first cow town in Texas." It was the terminus of the famed Shawnee Trail, so Texas cattlemen drove large herds of longhorn northeast across the Red River and up through Indian Territory to reach it. To do so, they had to cross the Arkansas River and then continue on the old military road to reach this border town.

At Baxter Springs, large corrals and collecting pens were built so the cattle could be fattened before they were driven or shipped to Kansas City. The influx of Texas cowboys created a need for food, drink, women, and entertainment, and soon there was a saloon or a sporting house on every corner in Baxter Springs. Public hangings, gunfights, and brawls over prostitutes and card games became common occurrences. The town quickly earned the notorious moniker of "the toughest town on earth."

After the completion of the Missouri River, Fort Scott and Gulf Railroad through Baxter Springs, even more people flooded into town. Fortunately, in addition to the outlaws, gamblers, thieves, and whores, came plenty of merchants, traders, ranchers, and honest settlers. They turned Baxter Springs into a real town, but after the longhorn cattle drives shifted westward, the community fell on hard times.

But the town had more to offer than just cattle and gunfights. Residents fell back on what got the place started in the first place – the mineral springs. For some years, Baxter Springs built on its reputation as a resort when claims again began to be made that the springs had curative powers. A park was laid out on Military Avenue near the new bathhouses and it became a relaxing place for the town's young couples and for the visitors who came from all over the country to take in the healing waters.

Downtown Baxter Springs

The discovery of rich deposits of lead and zinc along the Missouri border also helped Baxter Springs to thrive and attract more residents. The mining operations grew and reached into southeast Kansas and the northeast corner of Oklahoma. In its day, Baxter Springs was one of the most prominent cities in the region, but once the lucrative mining operations started up, the dependence on the mineral springs disappeared. The bathers stopped coming and this local anomaly was all but forgotten.

As time went on, Baxter Springs settled down into a respectable city, although it managed to draw national attention for a time through "Soldier Reunion Week," when Union veterans of the Civil War gathered in town from all over the nation. But as the old soldiers began dying off, the reunions came to an end in the early 1900s.

During the 1940s, when Route 66 was still running through town, a young kid from down the highway in Commerce, Oklahoma, began playing baseball for the Baxter Springs Whiz Kids. He played for three years before signing on with the New York Yankees. The young kid's name was Mickey Mantle.

These days, it seems that Baxter Springs has changed very little since the time when Mickey Mantle was still playing baseball there. The streets are still lined with trees and Route 66 still runs right along Military Avenue, just as it did when it was started back in the 1920s. There may not be as many cars passing through town as there were back then, but you can still stop at the

Mickey Mantle and the Baxter Springs Whiz Kids

local Phillips 66 station, although it's now a Route 66 Visitors Center. There are no Texas cowboys raising hell in the streets, but there are still places where you can get a drink and a bite to eat.

"Gasoline Alley" and Beyond

Route 66 rolls into Baxter Springs in the part of town known as Gasoline Alley. After that, it curves left on Third Street and turns right onto Military Avenue. As travelers entered town, they found places to fill up their tanks, like the **Phillips 66** station that opened in 1930. The cottage-style station was first offering only Independent-brand products but after the stock market crash of 1929, Phillips Petroleum, in an attempt to increase holdings and maintain stockholder interest, merged with Independent Oil and Gas. Within weeks, the new station was only offering Phillips products. To keep the place competitive, an L-shaped garage with a grease rack and repair bays was added in the late 1930s. Phillips owned and operated the station until 1958, when it was sold to J.R. Parsons. They were the first of several owners over the next 20 years or so, before the station closed and the building was converted to a dog grooming service. In 2005, the old station was purchased by the Baxter Springs Historical Society, which restored it to its original look and turned it into the Route 66 Visitor's Center and Information Bureau.

And this was not the only station that operated along the town's Gasoline Alley. A.T. Spencer ran several gas stations and eating places along Highway 66 in town. Years later, his daughter, Dorothy Spencer Waddell, recalled her memories of the time when the highway came through town. She remembered that where the Frisco and Kansas City Southern Railroad crossed Route 66 as it curved into Third Street, a hobo camp grew up next to the highway in the 1930s. Her mother found that she couldn't hang laundry out on the line without losing a few items, so her dad began keeping old clothes and suitcases in a back room to help those who needed it. He fed folks when they were hungry and loaned them money when they had run out. He often received letters from California repaying the loans that he made to those who were heading west.

Dorothy said that Pretty Boy Floyd gassed up regularly at **Spencer's Shell Station** in the mid-1930s. She remembered him pacing in front of the window and talking to her while her father serviced Floyd's car.

In 1944, the Spencers opened an authentic diner car café after Mr. Spencer found an old KATY passenger coach in Chetopa City, Kansas. He bought the car for $250, but had a terrible time getting it back to Baxter Springs. The heavy railroad car broke the axle on the mover's truck so it took a great deal of time and maneuvering to get it into place. The family served hamburgers, hot dogs, and chili from **Spencer's Diner** until they retired in 1962. The diner car was sold to a new owner, who moved it again, this time to a graveyard location on Highway 66, just over the Oklahoma line.

Another popular stop in Baxter Springs was **Bill Murphey's Restaurant**, a vintage café that once served the town as a bank, which had some notorious visitors in May 1876. One spring afternoon, Jesse James and Cole Younger rode into town, tied up their horses and walked into the bank. They asked the cashier to change a $5 bill and when the cashier turned his back, James and Younger pulled their guns and made a withdrawal of $2,900. The outlaws jumped on their horses and made a run for Indian Territory to the south. A posse was quickly organized and set off in hot pursuit. About seven miles south of town, the bandits, apparently not realizing they were being chased, stopped at a blacksmith shop to get their horses shod. Suddenly, the posse came riding by and Jesse and Cole stopped them in their tracks. They disarmed the men and then sent them back to Kansas. Not a single shot was fired during the entire incident.

Bill and Wanda Murphey moved into the historic location in December 1941. The old bank had housed a sandwich shop in the 1930s, but didn't last long. Murphey's, though, fed U.S. 66 travelers for decades. Today, the restaurant is closed, but memories remain of the Slip Slide Custard Pie that really put the place on the map.

Byrd's Drive In

Many other eateries from the heyday of Route 66 in Baxter Springs are gone today, victims of the economy, Interstate 44, declining population, and time. Some travelers remember the **Merry Bales Hotel, Byrd's Drive In, Anna and Goldies, Ranch House, Gene Young's Luncheonette, Ma and Pa Lewis's Café**, and the **Blue Castle Cafe**.

Ralph and Frances Adams bought the Blue Castle Café shortly after they were married and opened for business in January 1947. The tiny place only seated 32 people and Ralph and Frances had an apartment in the back. Business was so good that they purchased the old Ritz Theater building next door, remodeled it, and opened up 82 more seats for hungry diners. Ralph, who loved to experiment, came up with a tremendously popular deep-fried boneless turkey bites. He knew it was a winner, but never marketed the idea. Years later, McDonald's introduced the world to their Chicken McNuggets, which were very similar, and they became an instant hit. Ralph and Frances's three children worked at the restaurant, but didn't want to go into the business, so the Blue Castle became only a memory when they retired in 1980.

Baxter Springs also offered places to sleep for highway travelers. The **Capistrano Courts** were built on the south side of town between 1948 and 1950. The motel covered a half city block in an L-shape. Built using stucco, the individual units looked like Spanish adobes, designed to evoke images of San Juan Capistrano, California, where the swallows depicted on the motel's sign returned to nest every March. The theme was fitting for the motel, where repeat business year after year was vitally important.

Capistrano Courts

The motor court consisted of six buildings, each containing two units. Fully covered carports were situated between the buildings and were shared by two of the units. In the late 1940s, the name was changed from "Courts" to "Motel" to give it the image of being more modern and up-to-date.

In 1954, the Capistrano Motel was purchased by Orville and Phyllis Mehaffey. They made sure the place had an outstanding reputation for cleanliness, knowing that this would go a long way in attracting motorists. Far ahead of their time, they also treated their guests to a continental breakfast. A children's playground was also added in the 1960s. Orville and Phyllis managed the motel until 1977, when it was sold to Harry Miller, who operated the place until 1977. The place was torn down in 1988 and a liquor store now stands on the half-block that was once filled by the Capistrano.

Home to one of the strangest motel "horror" stories on Route 66, **Baxter Modern Cabins** also greeted travelers in town. Built in the 1940s, this classic u-shaped motor court consisted of 12 guest rooms and a gas station that doubled as the court's office. Each of the gable-roofed units was connected by a covered carport that featured an unusual semi-circle façade.

Baxter Modern Cabins – home to a local "hotel horror" story

At some point during the time when Route 66 was bringing scores of travelers to town, Baxter Modern Cabins became the site of an often-told legend. The story claimed that the motor court became a favorite meeting place for an illicit affair that was being carried on by two married lovers. One evening, a faulty natural gas line filled their room with gas, and they never awoke from their blissful sleep. The next morning, they were found dead, together in bed, much to the dismay of their respective spouses.

Baxter Modern Cabins managed to hang on, becoming a little seedier every year, until 1965. A Walmart now stands on the former site of the motor court where travelers – and the occasional lovers – sought refuge. If you believe in ghosts, you have to wonder if the two lost souls who died in each other's arms, are now endlessly wandering the aisles of Walmart, wondering what happened to the motel that once rested there.

Ghosts of Baxter Springs

And the restless spirits of those two lovers may not be the only ones who wander through town.

The wild reputation of Baxter Springs has, not surprisingly, created a number of ghost stories in the small town. Each fall, the local historical society hosts an annual ghost tour in town, pointing out and visiting the homes and buildings where residents of the past have reportedly stayed behind.

Some of those ghost stories revolve around the site of Fort Blair, the Civil War post that saw violence and bloodshed in the fall of 1863 and then was abandoned after the war. Houses were built over the site of the fort as Baxter Springs began to grow in the late 1800s, and many years later, in the 1990s, the historical society began buying some of the old homes so that they could be preserved. During the negotiations, one elderly resident told the representative from the society that if they bought the house, the ghost came with it. When asked about it, the former owner responded that she and her daughter had often seen a dark-skinned man wearing a blue military uniform in the house. He had never caused any problems, but he had a tendency to show up – a lot.

Soon, the residents of other homes began telling their own ghost stories. They had also seen things, from dark presences to African-American soldiers in military uniforms. One of the real estate agents who was working on the sales even reported seeing a ghost herself while walking through one of the homes on the site of the old fort. She walked into an otherwise empty room and saw a dark-skinned soldier suddenly turn and dart out into the hallway. When she followed, she found no one was there.

It's very possible that this soldier might have been one of the men of the Kansas Colored Infantry, who had originally been stationed at the post. The unit was undoubtedly there during the attack by Quantrill and his raiders and perhaps the soldier (or soldiers?) that has been seen was one of the men killed during the attack.

His identity may never be known, but he is believed to still roam the area today. The houses on the site of the fort were eventually torn down and razed to create a historic site. Perhaps this soldier is just one of the many ghosts who still linger in Baxter Springs today.

Farewell Missouri and Kansas...

And with that, we leave the Show-Me State and the Sunflower State behind and motor on to the old Indian Territory of Oklahoma. Coming soon, more books in the "Weird Highway" series will take Route 66 readers on toward California. The books will include:

* **Oklahoma and Texas**
* **Arizona and New Mexico**
* **California**

Weird Highway: Illinois was released in Fall 2015.

Bibliography

Special thanks for this book goes to **Mark Moran** and **Mark Sceurman** of *Weird N.J.* and *Weird U.S.* fame! I was lucky enough to get to be part of their "weird empire" starting back in 2004 and lucky enough to get to do *Weird IL*, as well as help out on another state or two. I've learned a lot from them about what makes road tripping so much fun and how to find the truly "weird," whether at home or out on the open road. So, this book is definitely for them!

I'd also like to thank **Kathy Weiser** for her hard work and dedication with **Legends of America** over the years. She's a true aficionado of Route 66 and the American West and, while we have never met in person (although I hope to correct that one day), I have known and been inspired by her for at least a decade. We'd hoped to get to pull off some sort of project like this together one day, but could never work it out to make it happen. But thanks for everything, Kathy!

And thanks to radio legend **Steve Dahl** (and sons **Patrick, Matt,** and **Mike**) for their live broadcasts from Route 66 in the 1990s. The daily shows were hilarious and fun, and while they never made me want to pack up kids in an RV and travel from California to Chicago, they certainly inspired me to take the trip again!

Anderson, Warren H. – *Vanishing Roadside America*; 1981
Antonson, Rick – *Route 66 Still Kicks*; 2012
Baeder, John – *Gas, Food, and Lodging*; 1982
Butler, John L. – *First Highways of America*; 1994
Clark, Marian – *The Route 66 Cookbook*; 1993
Crump, Spencer – *Route 66: America's First Main Street*; 1994
Hinckley, Jim – *Ghost Towns of Route 66*; 2011
--------------- - *Illustrated Route 66 Historical Atlas*; 2014
--------------- - *Route 66 Encyclopedia*; 2012
--------------- - *Travel Route 66;* 2014
Knowles, Drew – *Route 66 Adventure Handbook*; 2006
Krim, Arthur – *Route 55: Iconography of the American Highway;* 2005
Livingston-Martin, Lisa – *Missouri's Wicked Route 66;* 2013
Margolies, John – *Home Away from Home: Motels in America*; 1995
Olsen, Russell A. – *Route 66: Lost and Found*; 2011
Patton, Phil – *Open Road: A Celebration of the American Highway*; 1986

Repp, Thomas Arthur – *Empires of Amusement*; 1999
Ross, Jim, with art by Jerry McLanahan – *Route 66: The Map Series*; 1990
Scott, Quinta – *Along Route 66*; 2000
Snyder, Tom – *The Route 66 Traveler's Companion*; 1990
Taylor, Troy – *Mysterious Illinois*; 2006
--------------- - *Weird Illinois*; 2005
Tremear, Janice – *Missouri's Haunted Route 66;* 2010
Voyageur Press – *Greetings from Route 66*; 2010
------------------ - *Route 66 Treasures*; 2013
Wallis, Michael – *Route 66: The Mother Road*; 1990
Weiser, Kathy – *Legends of America*; current
Witzel, Michael – *The American Gas Station*; 1992
------------------ - *Gas Station Memories;* 1994
------------------ - *Route 66 Remembered*; 2003
Witzel, Michael Karl and Gyvel Young Witzel – *Legendary Route 66*; 2007
Wood, Anthony and Jenny L. Wood – *Motel America*; 2004
Wood, Larry – *Wicked Joplin;* 2011

Special Thanks to:

April Slaughter: Cover Design & Artwork
Lois Taylor: Editing & Proofreading
Lisa Taylor Horton & Lux
Haven & Helayna Taylor
Orrin Taylor
Rene Kruse
Rachael Horath
Elyse & Thomas Reihner
Bethany Horath
John Winterbauer
Kaylan Schardan
Staff & Crew from American Hauntings
Mary DeLong

Drive Safely on U.S. 66 in Missouri!

www.ingramcontent.com/pod-product-compliance
Lightning Source LLC
Chambersburg PA
CBHW070141100426
42743CB00013B/2791